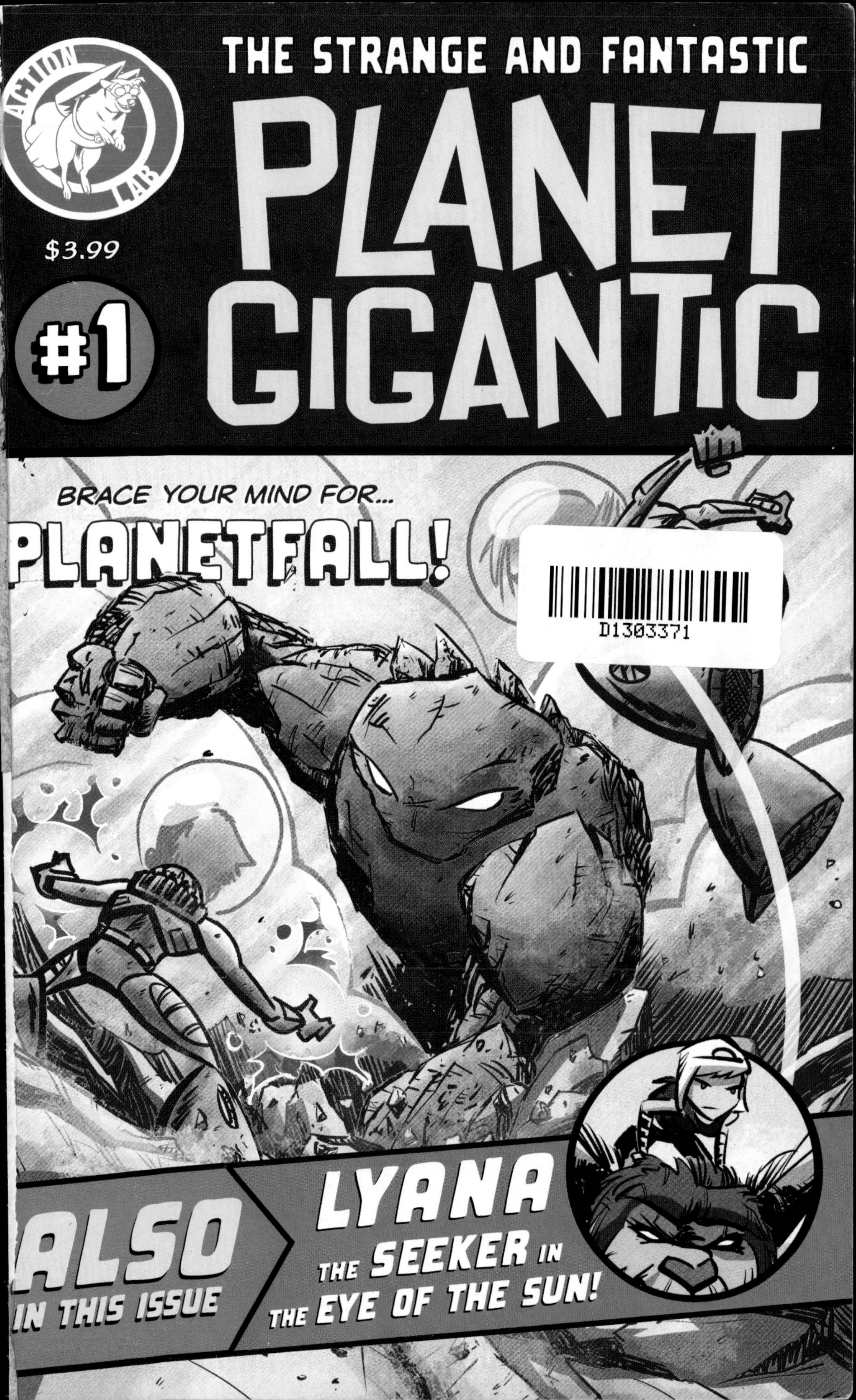
ACTION LAB
$3.99
#1
THE STRANGE AND FANTASTIC
PLANET GIGANTIC
BRACE YOUR MIND FOR...
PLANETFALL!
ALSO IN THIS ISSUE
LYANA THE SEEKER IN THE EYE OF THE SUN!

PLANET GIGANTIC

"Planetfall!" and "The Eye of the Sun"
story and letters by ERIC GRISSOM
art and cover by DAVID HALVORSON

fonts by COMICRAFT
planetgigantic.com

Bryan Seaton: Publisher
Kevin Freeman: President
Editor In Chief: Shawn Gabborin
Creative Director: Dave Dwonch
Co-Directors of Marketing: Jamal Igle & Kelly Dale
Social Media Director: Jim Dietz
Education Outreach Director: Jeremy Whitley
Associate Editors: Chad Cicconi & Colleen Boyd

PLANET GIGANTIC #1, October 2014. Copyright Eric Grissom and David Halvorson, 2014. Published by Action Lab Comics.
All rights reserved. All characters are fictional. Any likeness to anyone living or dead is purely coincidental. No part of this
publication may be reproduced or transmitted without permission, except for small excerpts for review purposes. Printed in
Canada. First Printing.

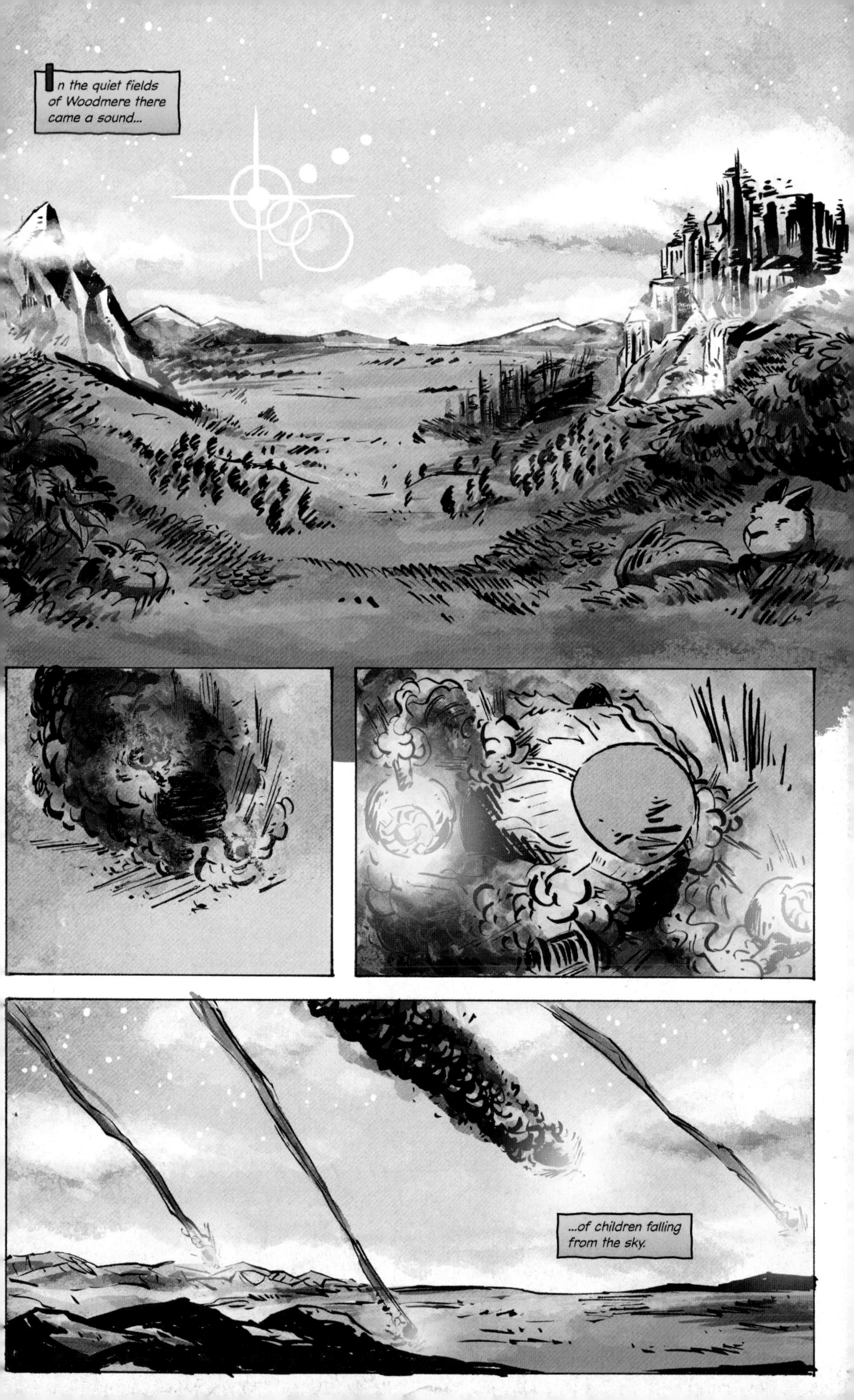
In the quiet fields of Woodmere there came a sound...
...of children falling from the sky.

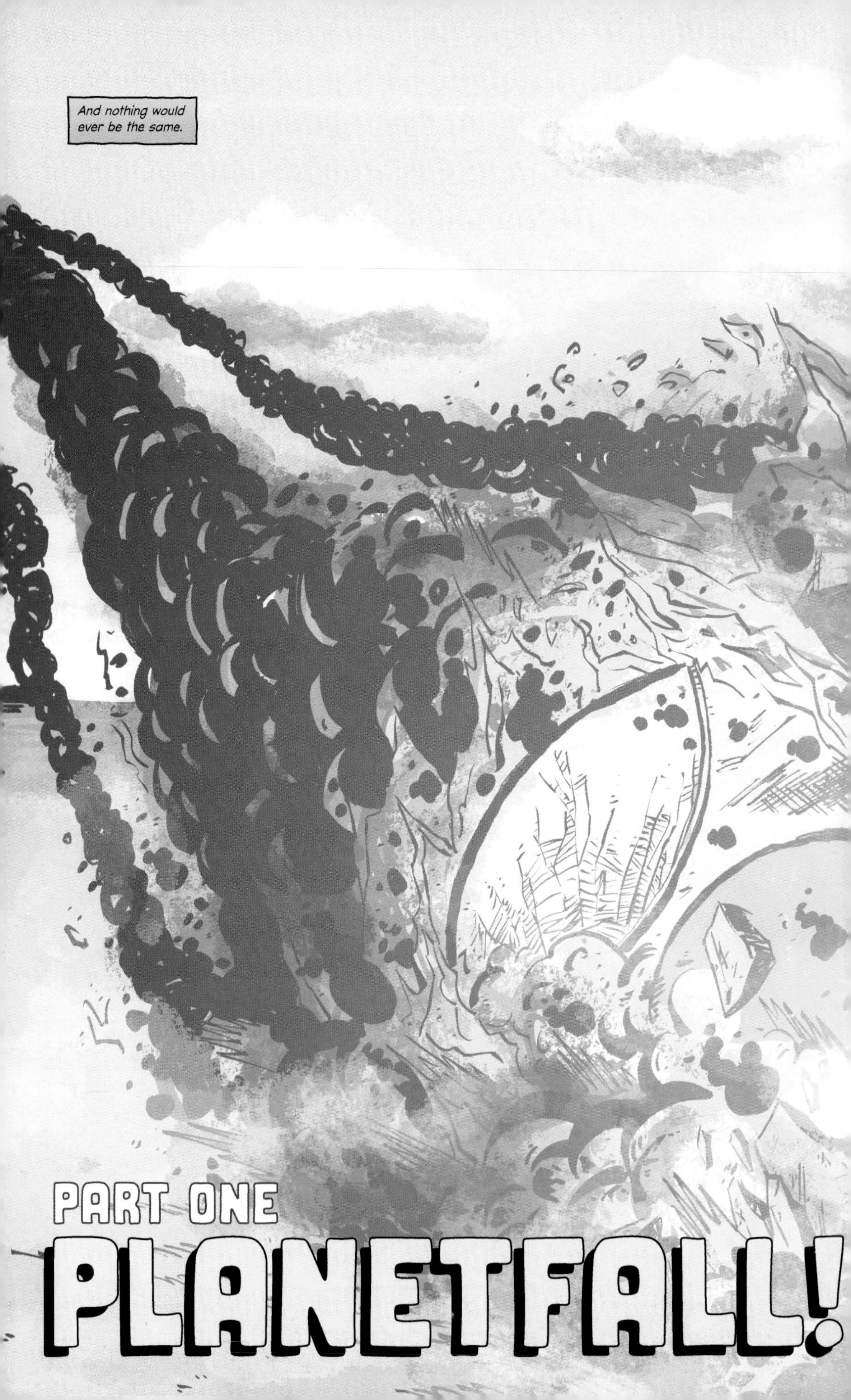
And nothing would ever be the same.
PART ONE
PLANETFALL!

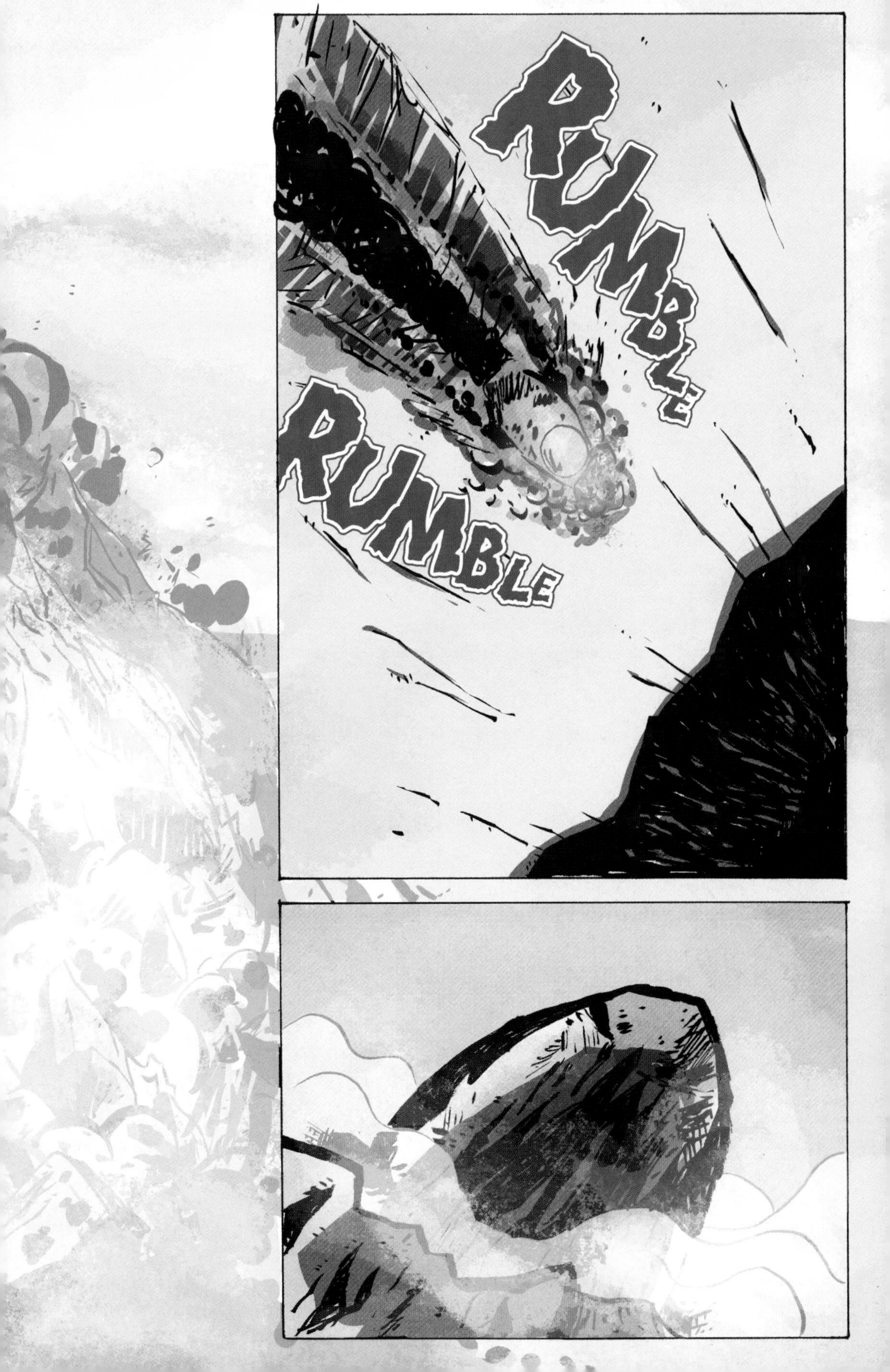
RUMBLE
RUMBLE

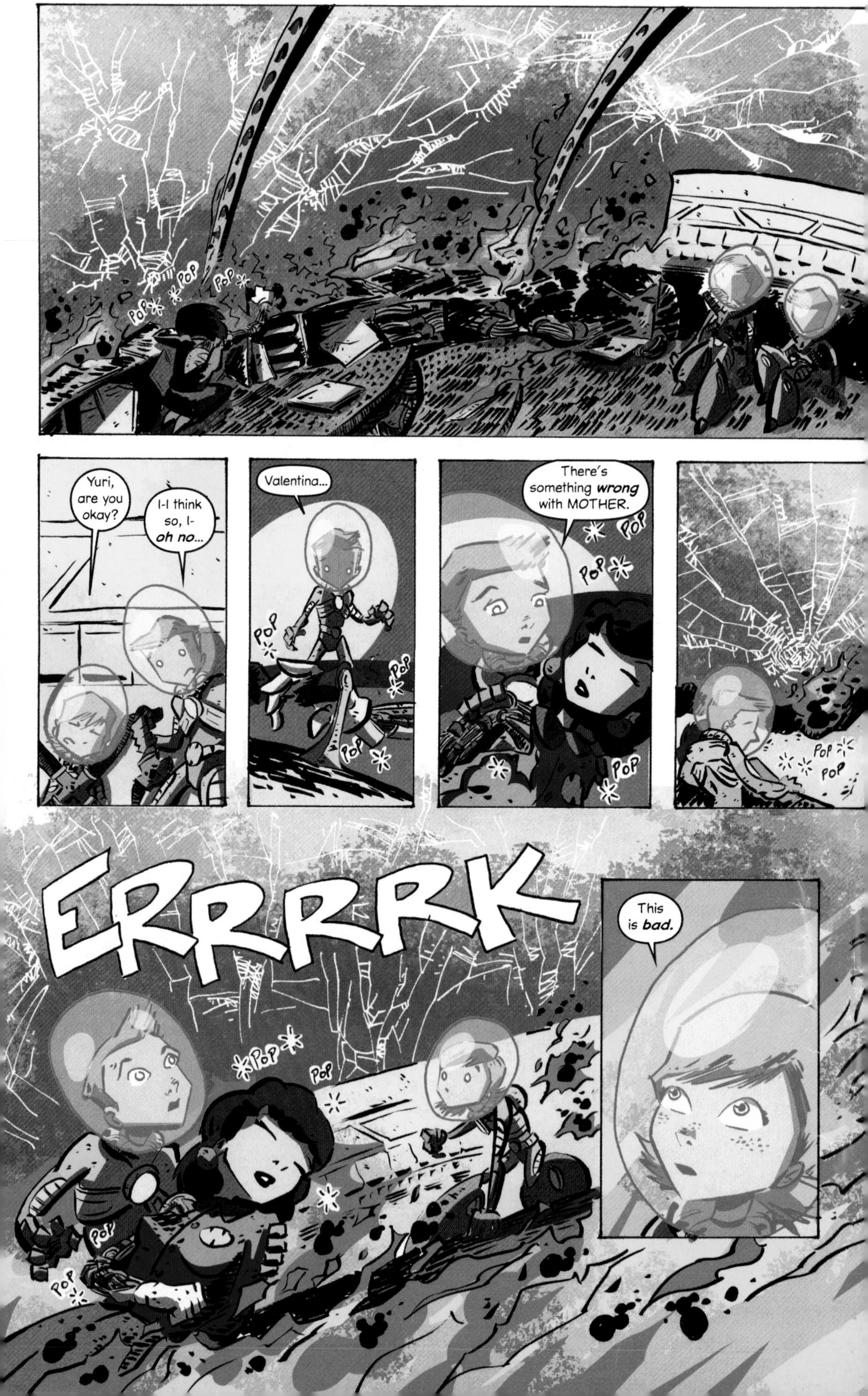
POP
POP
POP
POP
Yuri, are you okay?
I-I think so, I- oh no...
Valentina...
POP
POP
POP
There's something wrong with MOTHER.
POP
POP
POP
POP
POP
ERRRRK
POP
POP
This is bad.
POP
POP

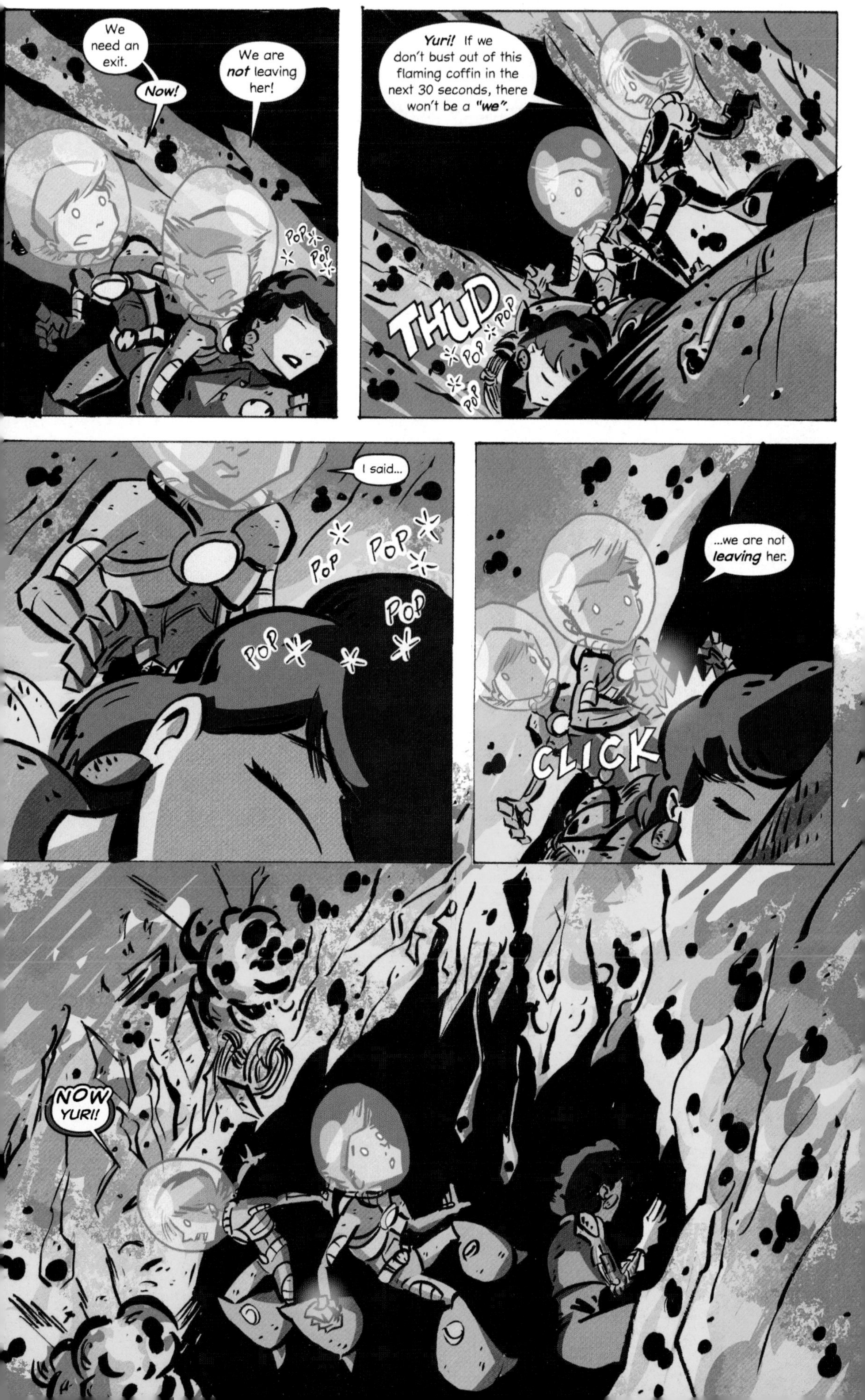

We need an exit.
Now!
We are not leaving her!
POP POP
Yuri! If we don't bust out of this flaming coffin in the next 30 seconds, there won't be a "we".
THUD
POP POP POP POP
I said...
POP POP POP POP
...we are not leaving her.
CLICK
NOW YURI!!

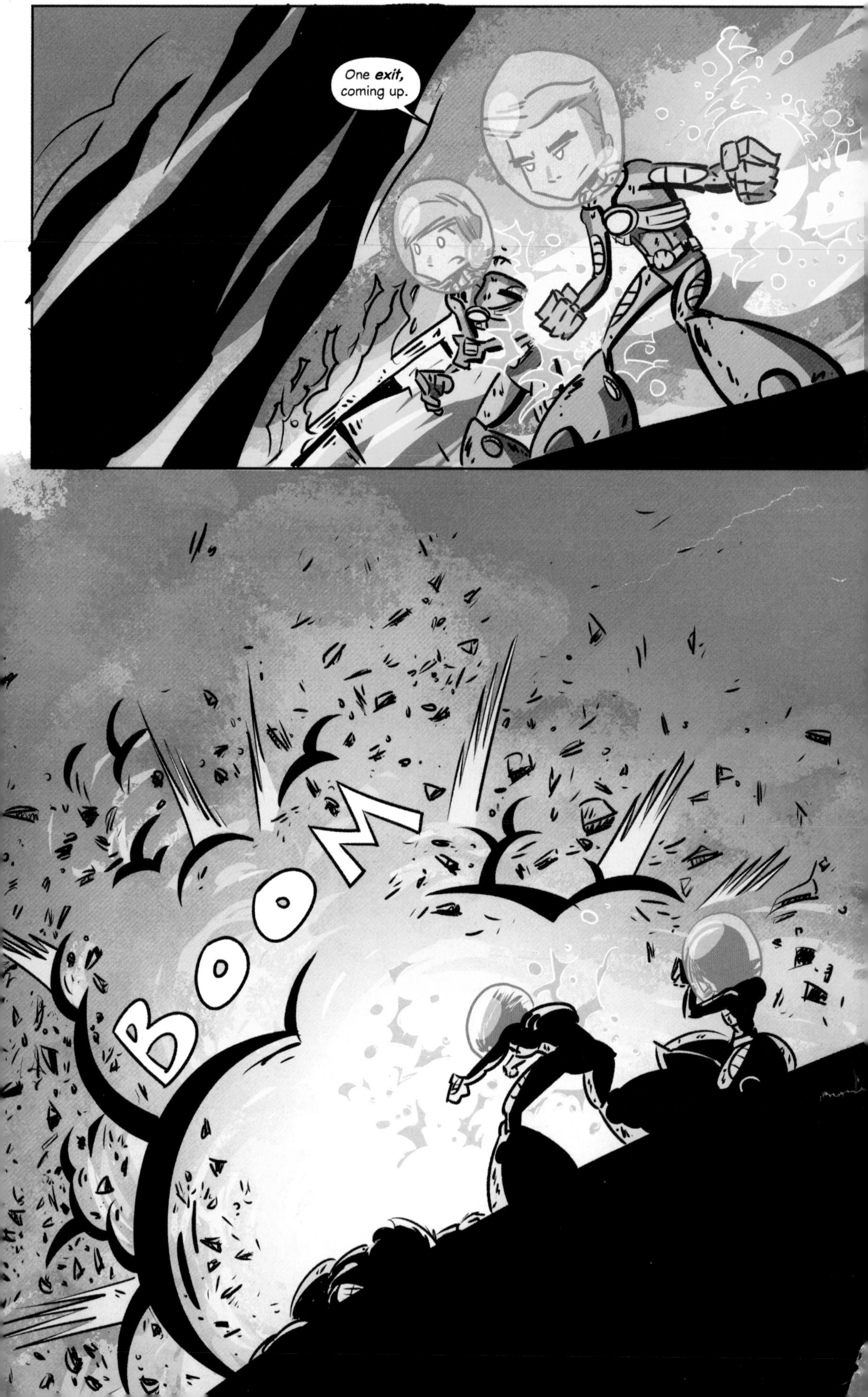
One **exit,** coming up.
BOOM

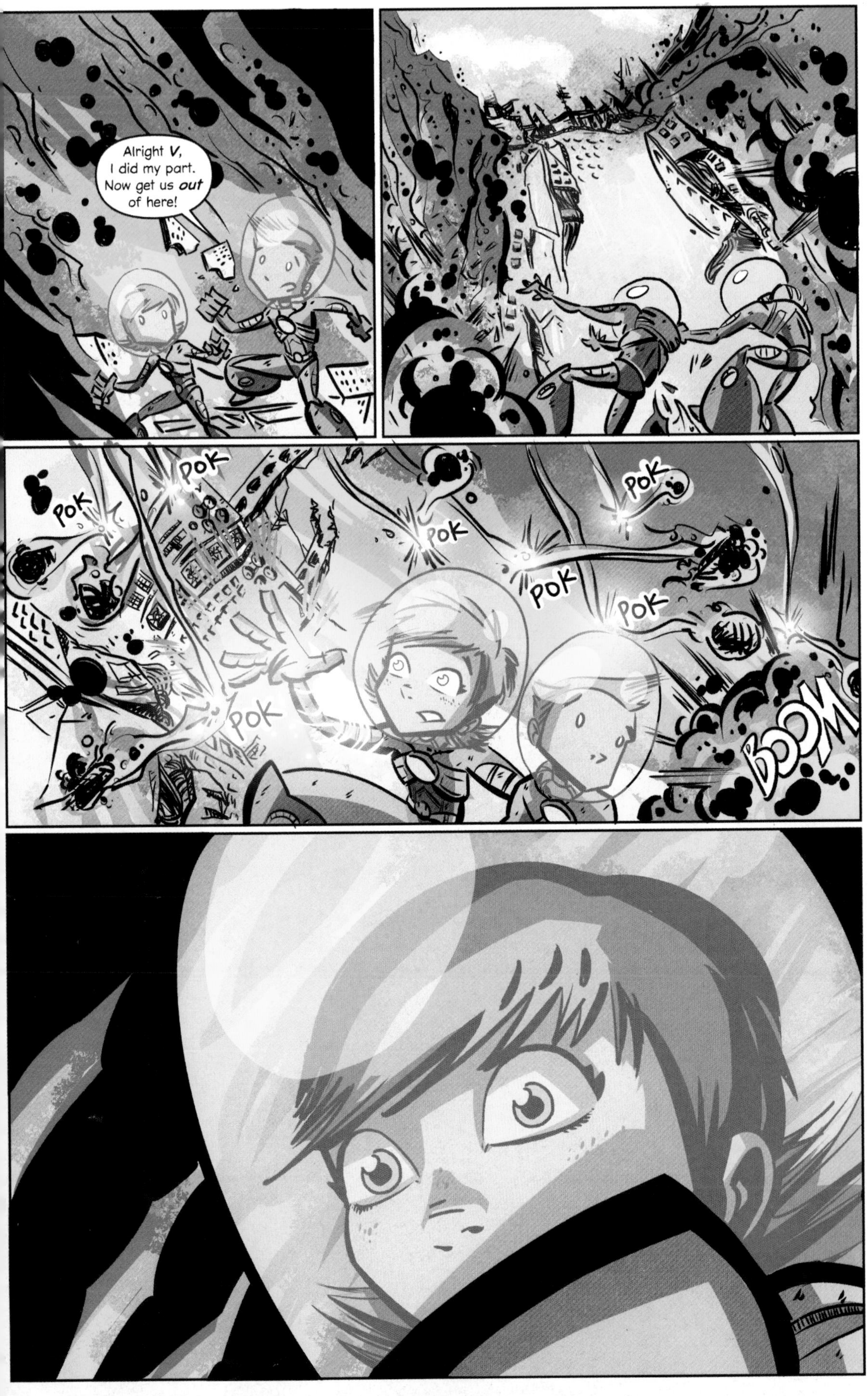
Alright V,
I did my part.
Now get us out
of here!
POK
POK
POK
POK
POK
POK
POK
POK
BOOM

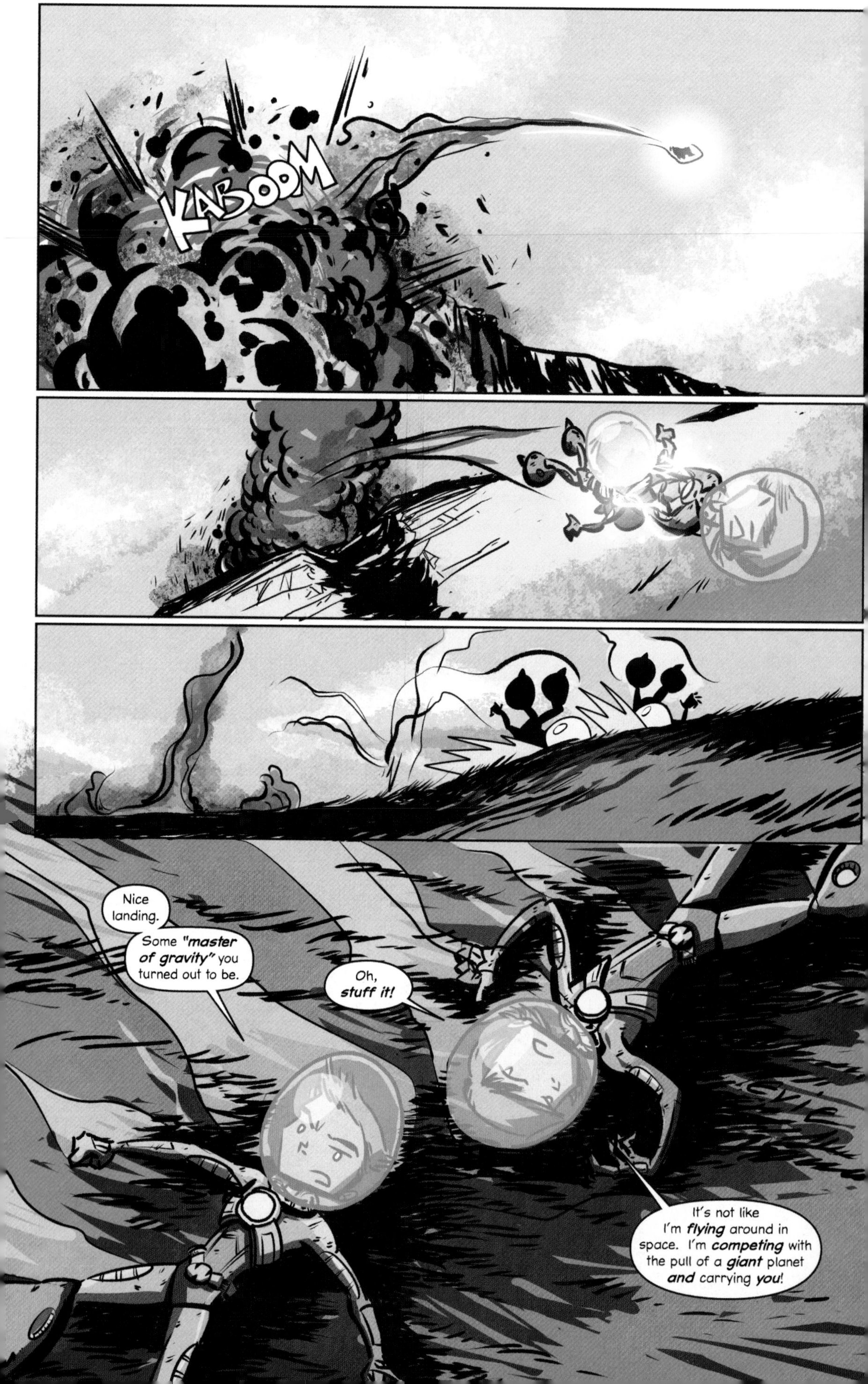
KABOOM
Nice landing.
Some "master of gravity" you turned out to be.
Oh, stuff it!
It's not like I'm flying around in space. I'm competing with the pull of a giant planet and carrying you!

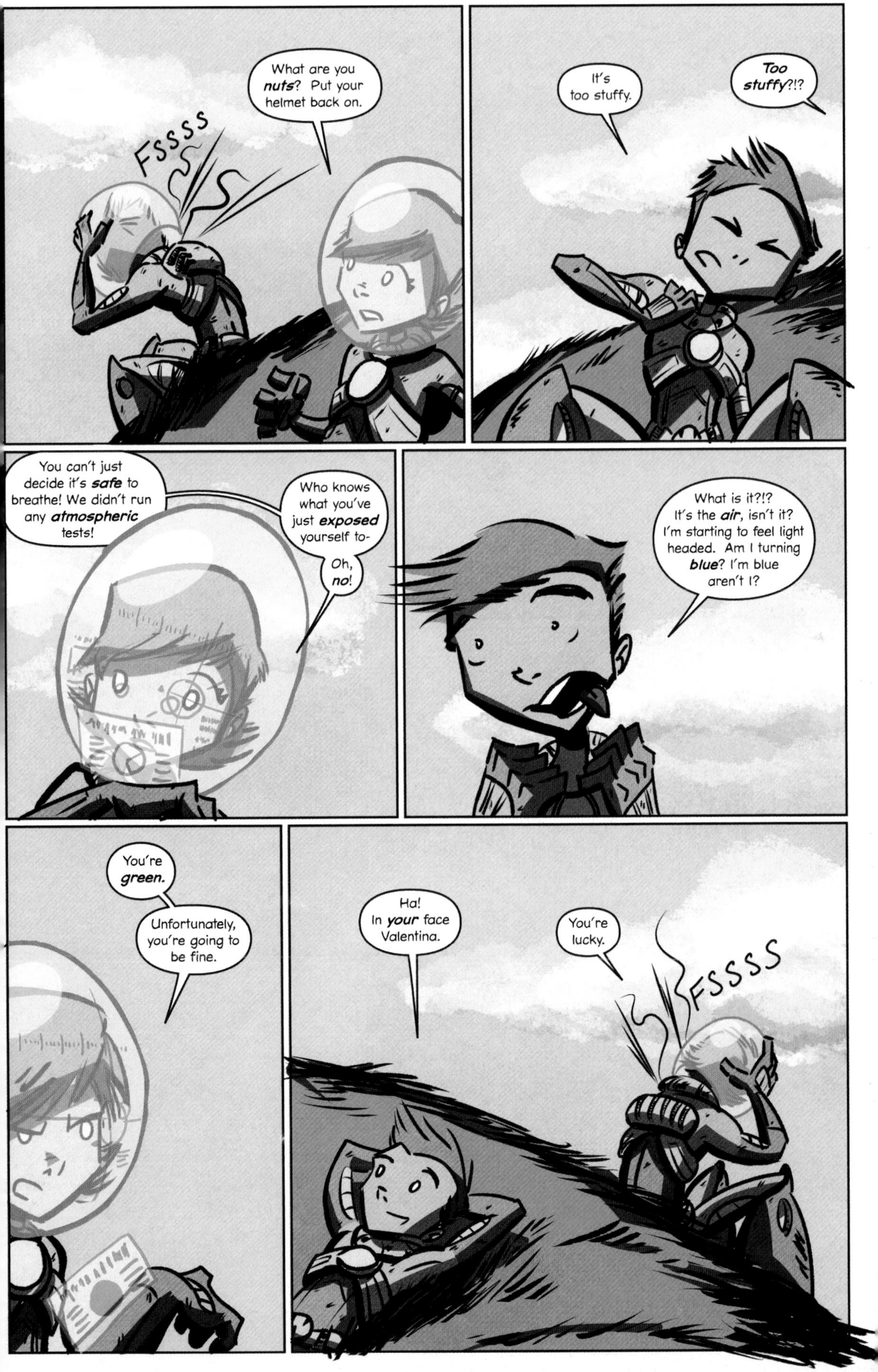
What are you *nuts*? Put your helmet back on.
FSSSS
It's too stuffy.
Too stuffy?!?
You can't just decide it's *safe* to breathe! We didn't run any *atmospheric* tests!
Who knows what you've just *exposed* yourself to-
Oh, *no*!
What is it?!? It's the *air*, isn't it? I'm starting to feel light headed. Am I turning *blue*? I'm blue aren't I?
You're *green.*
Unfortunately, you're going to be fine.
Ha! In *your* face Valentina.
You're lucky.
FSSSS

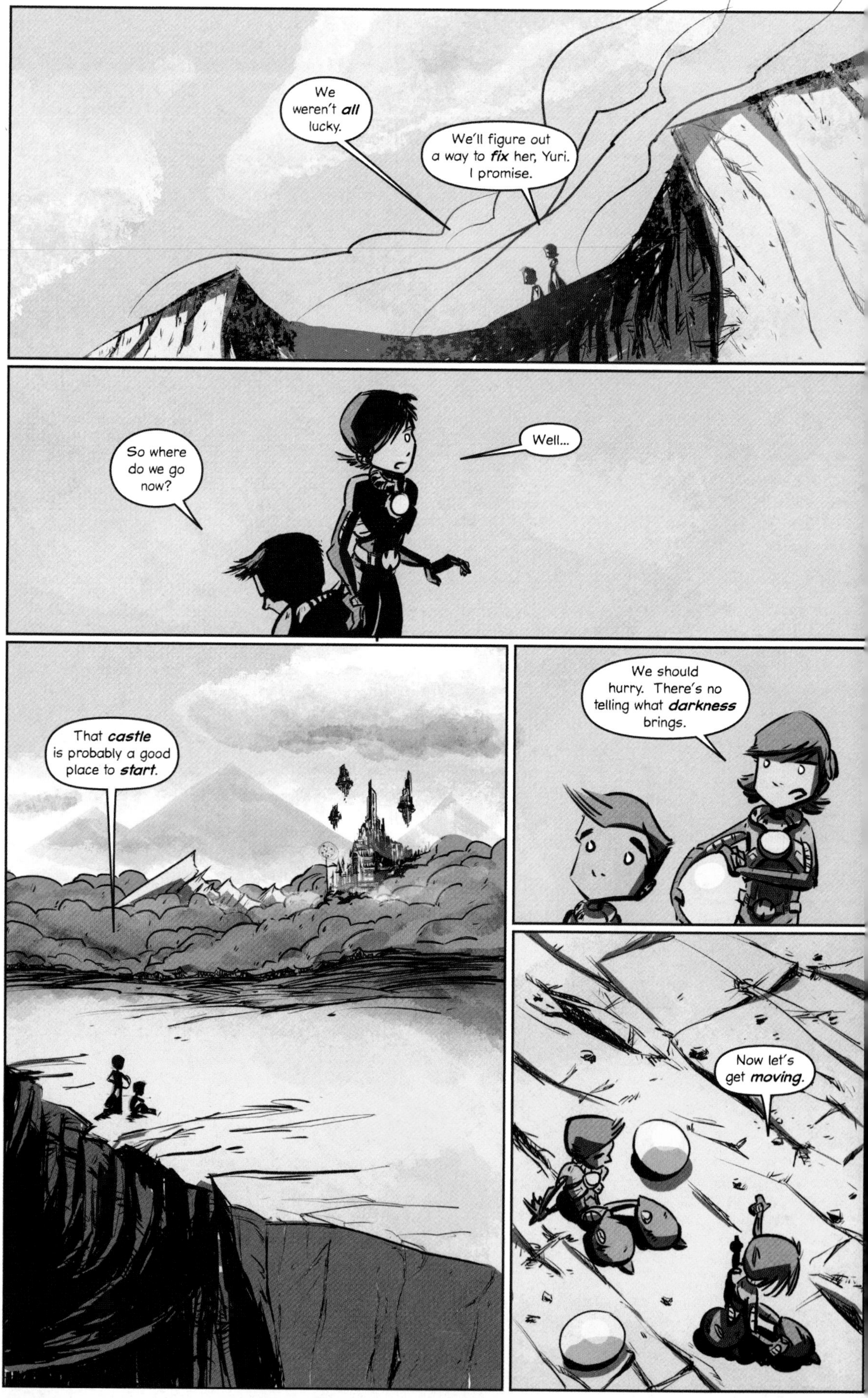
We weren't *all* lucky.
We'll figure out a way to *fix* her, Yuri. I promise.
So where do we go now?
Well...
That *castle* is probably a good place to *start*.
We should hurry. There's no telling what *darkness* brings.
Now let's get *moving*.

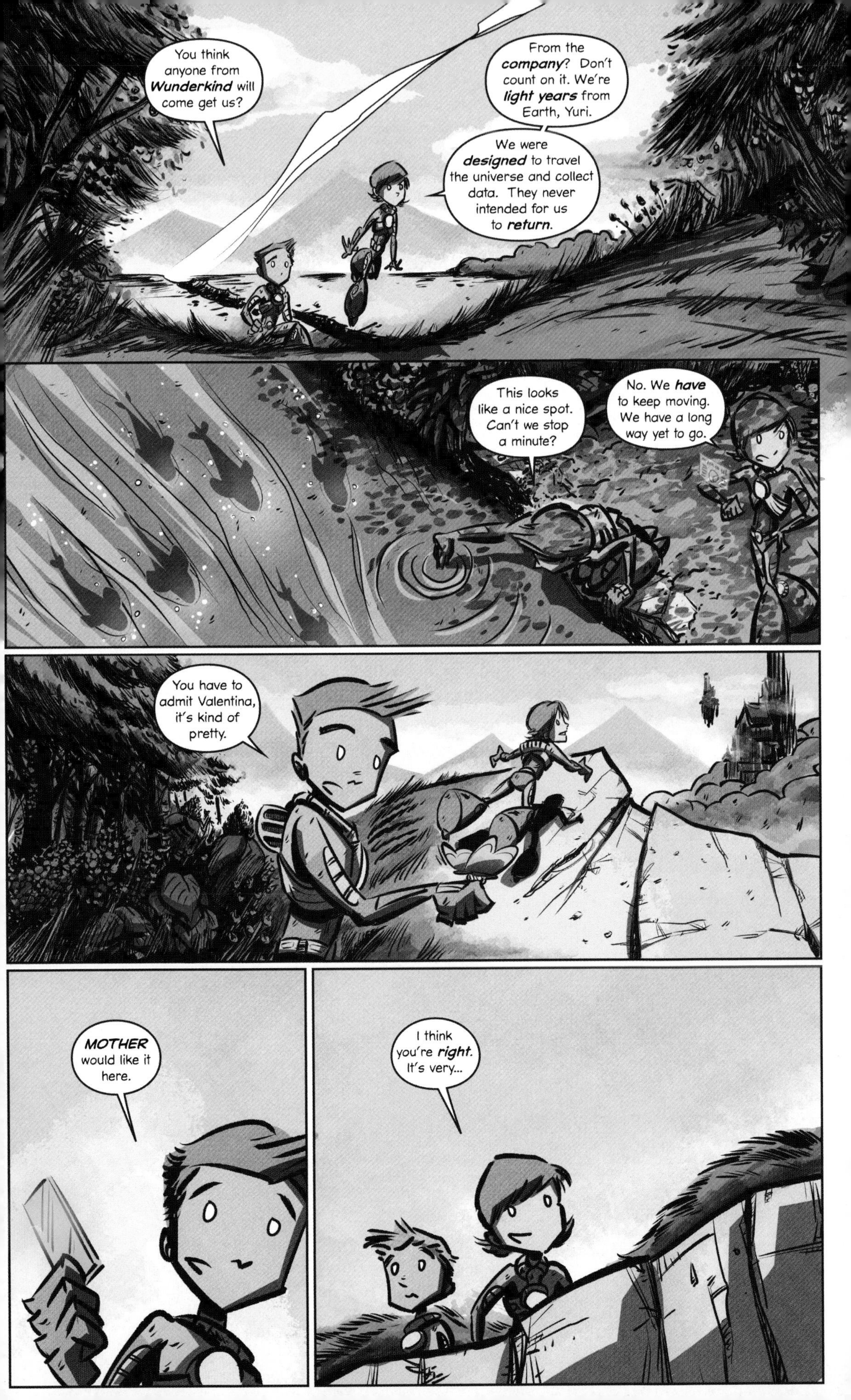
You think anyone from Wunderkind will come get us?
From the company? Don't count on it. We're light years from Earth, Yuri.
We were designed to travel the universe and collect data. They never intended for us to return.
This looks like a nice spot. Can't we stop a minute?
No. We have to keep moving. We have a long way yet to go.
You have to admit Valentina, it's kind of pretty.
MOTHER would like it here.
I think you're right. It's very...

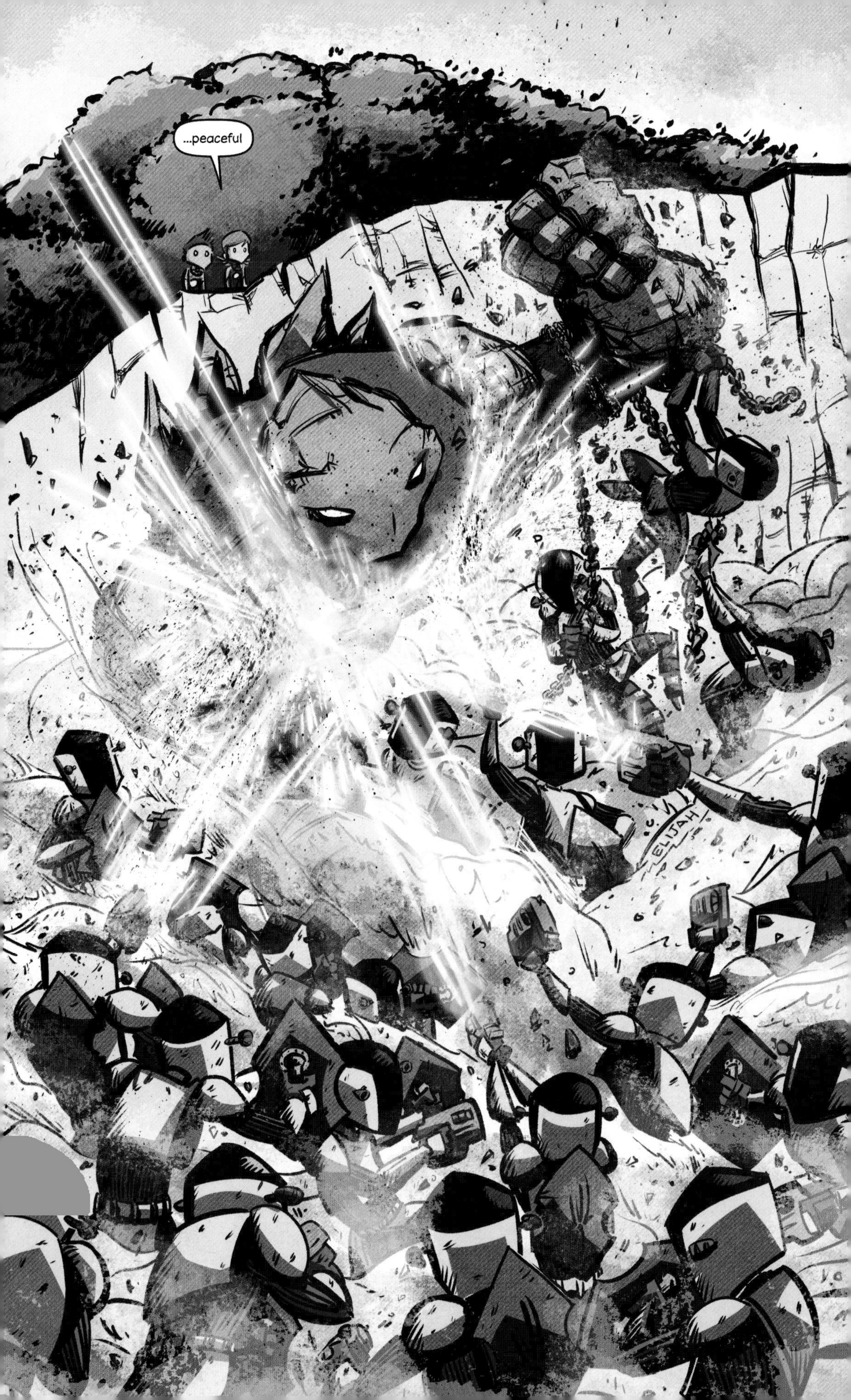
...peaceful
ELIJAH

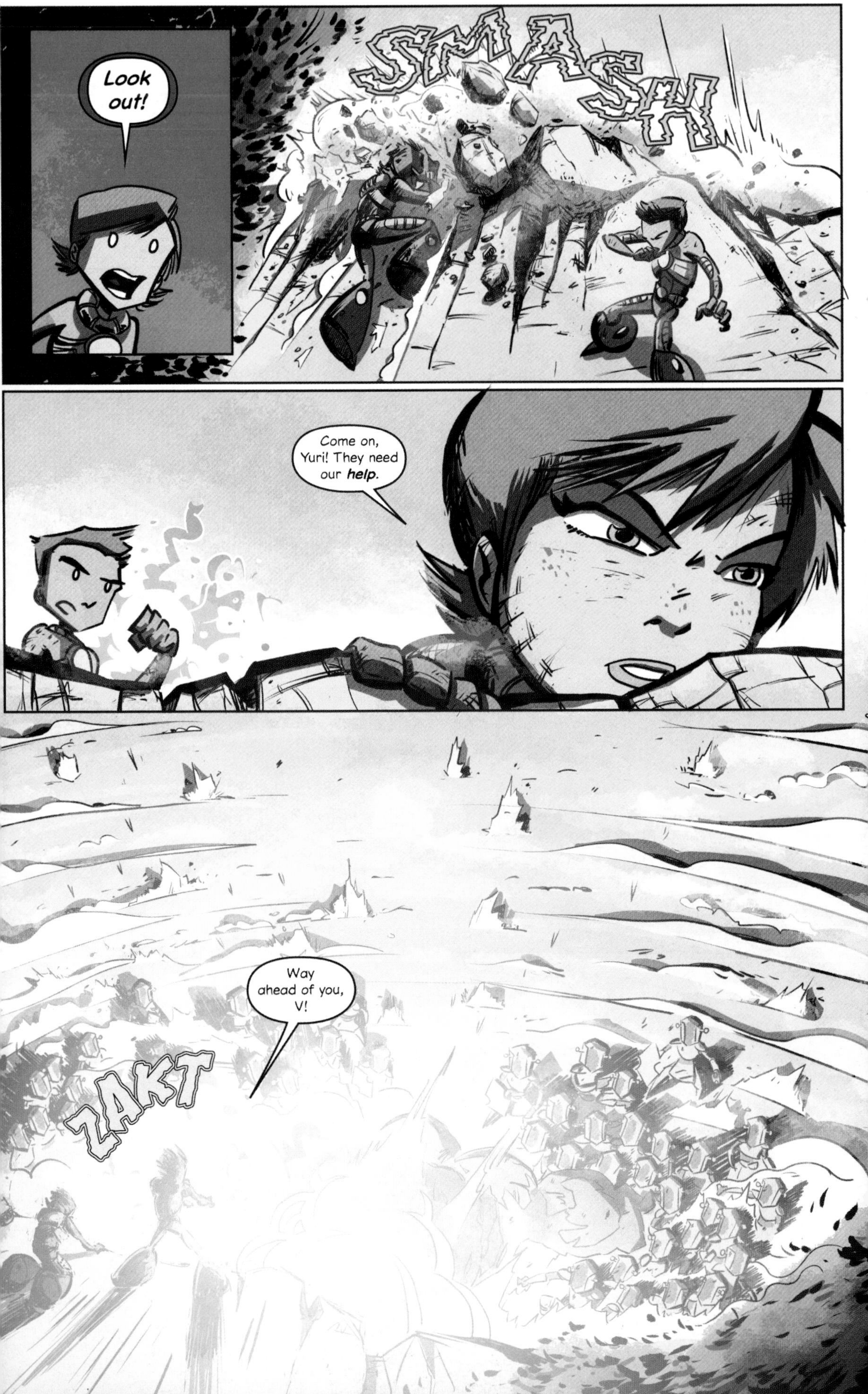
Look out!
SMASH
Come on, Yuri! They need our **help**.
Way ahead of you, V!
ZAKT

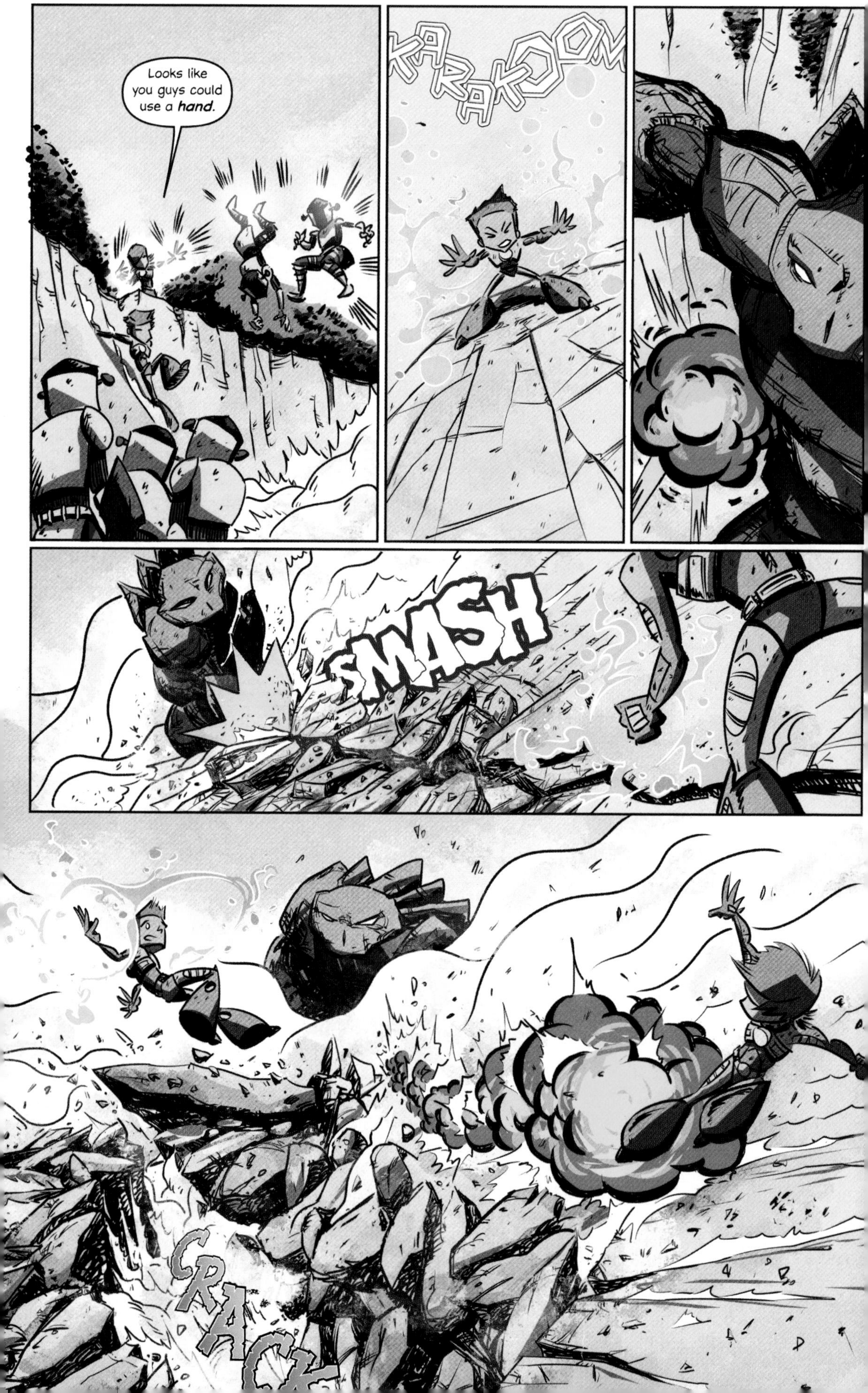
Looks like you guys could use a *hand*.
KARAKOOM
SMASH
CRACK

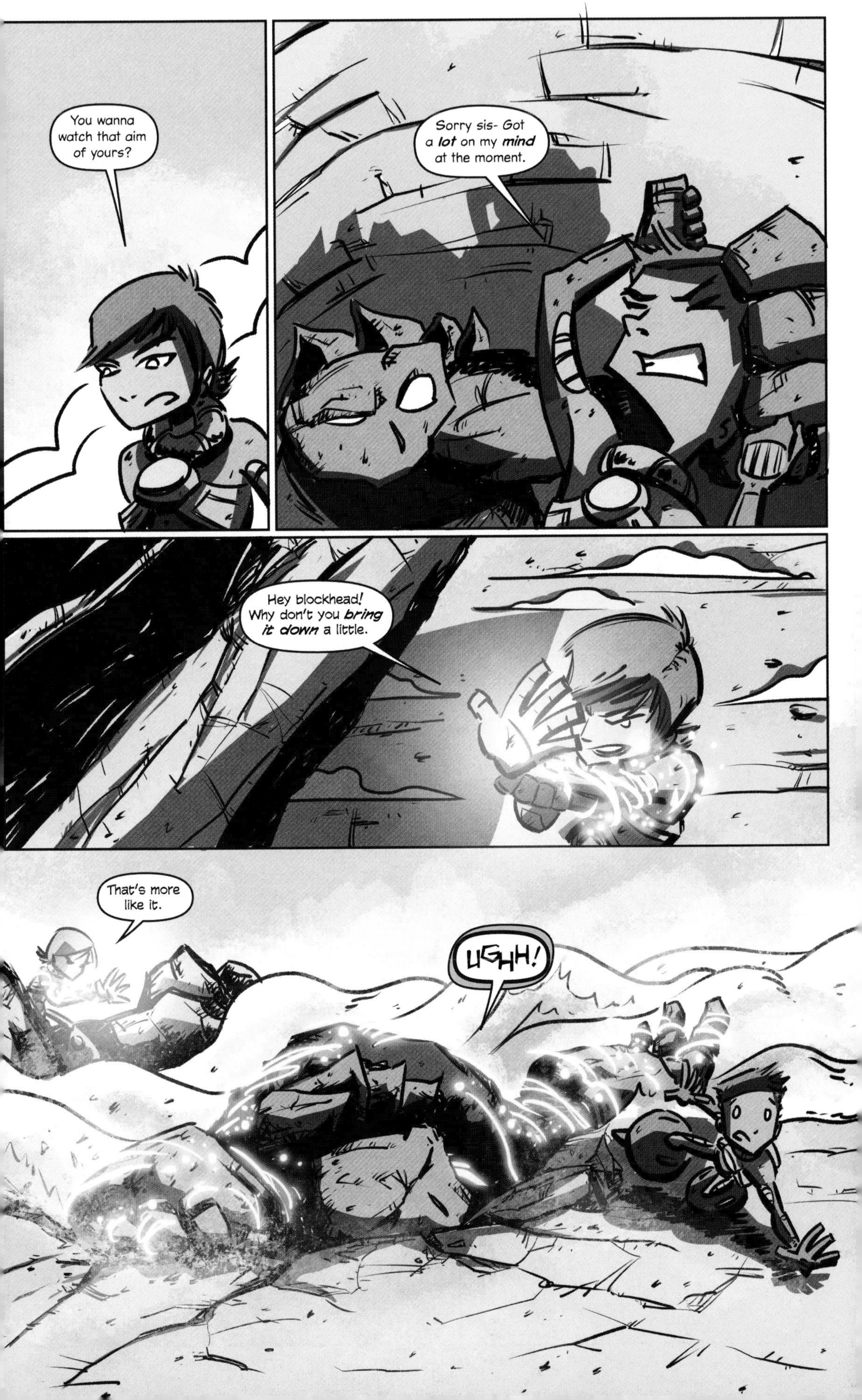
You wanna watch that aim of yours?
Sorry sis- Got a ***lot*** on my ***mind*** at the moment.
Hey blockhead! Why don't you ***bring it down*** a little.
That's more like it.
UGHH!

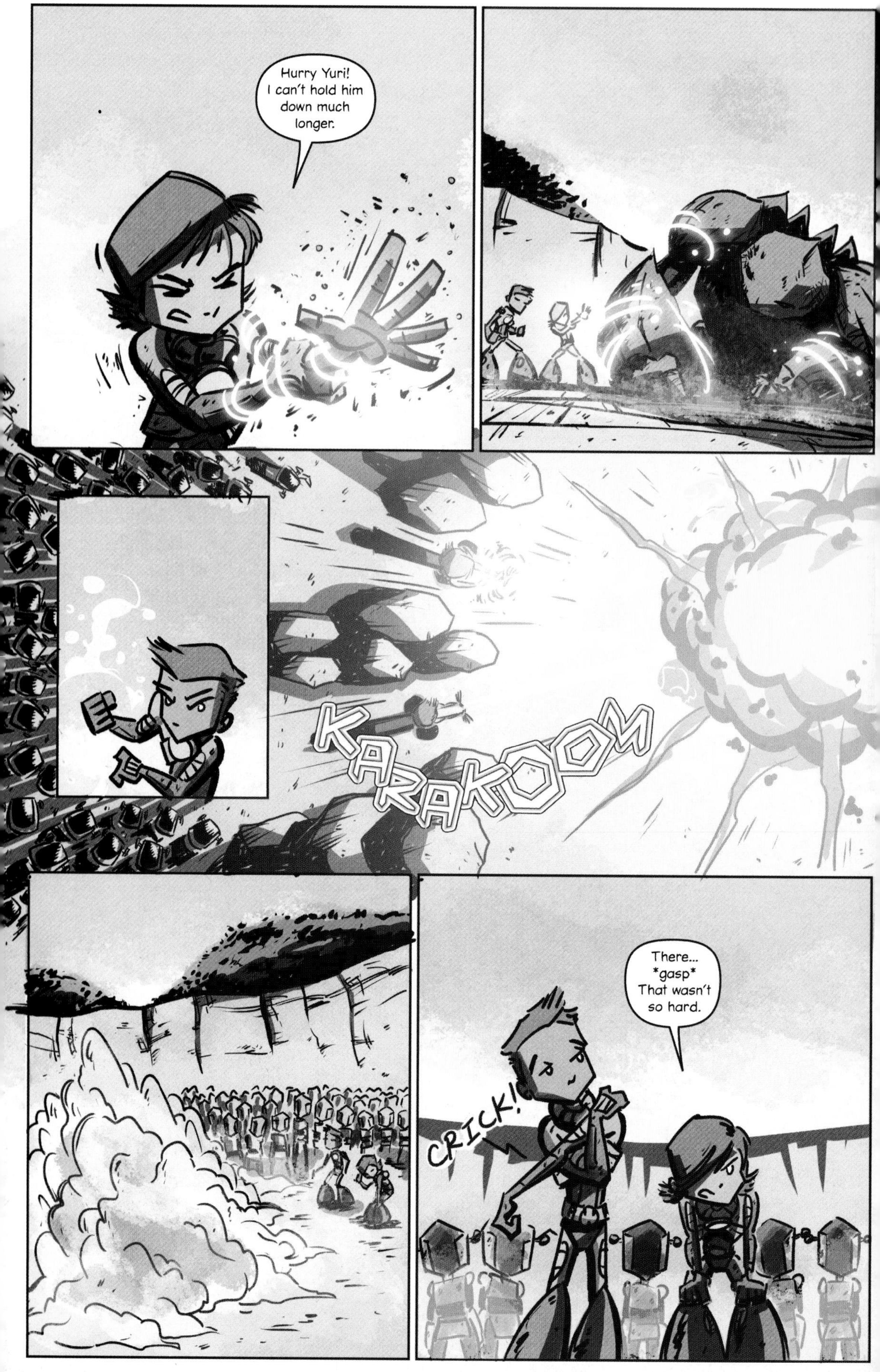
Hurry Yuri! I can't hold him down much longer.
KARAKOOM
There... *gasp* That wasn't so hard.
CRICK!

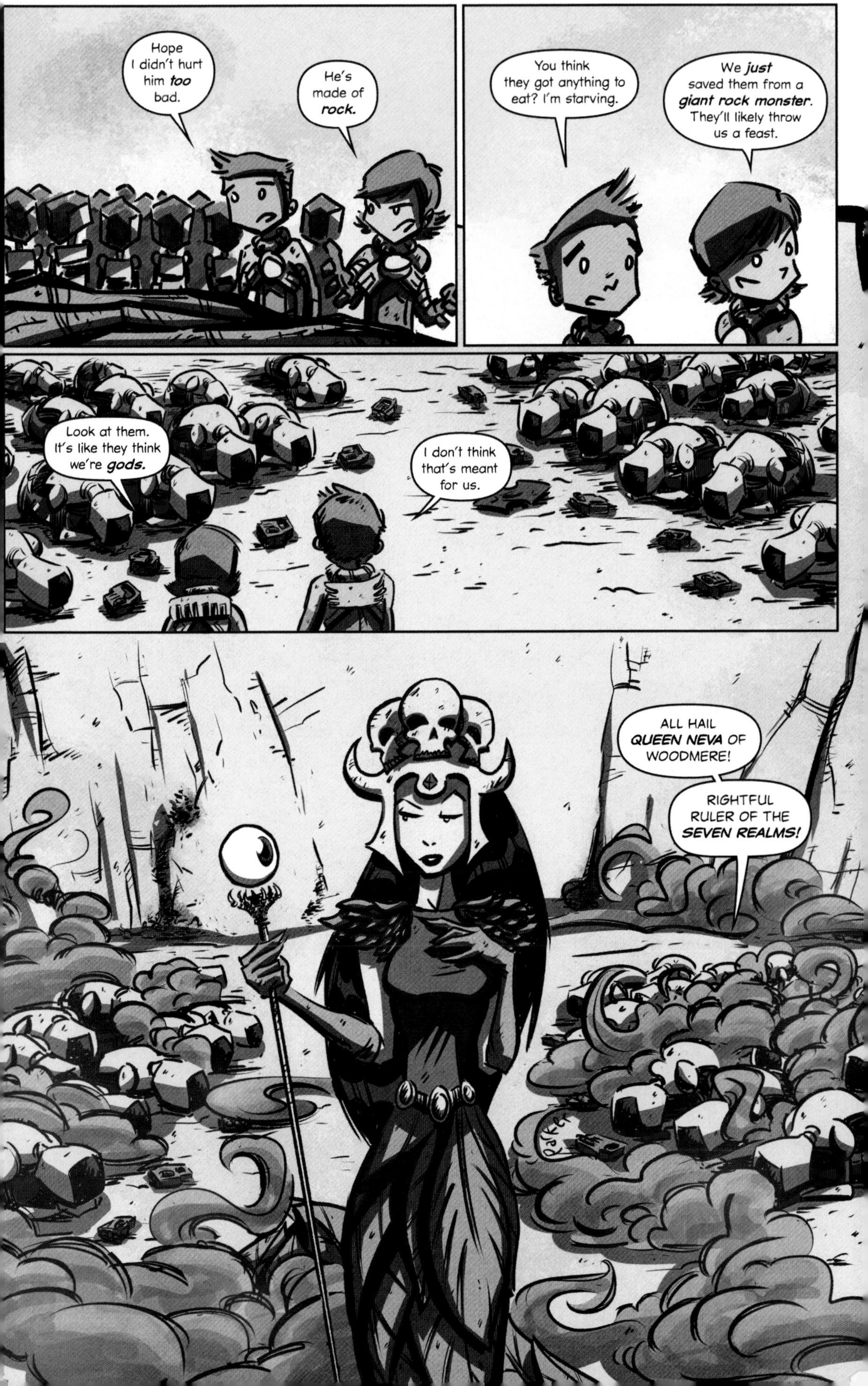
Hope I didn't hurt him *too* bad.
He's made of ***rock.***
You think they got anything to eat? I'm starving.
We ***just*** saved them from a ***giant rock monster.*** They'll likely throw us a feast.
Look at them. It's like they think we're ***gods.***
I don't think that's meant for us.
ALL HAIL ***QUEEN NEVA*** OF WOODMERE!
RIGHTFUL RULER OF THE ***SEVEN REALMS!***

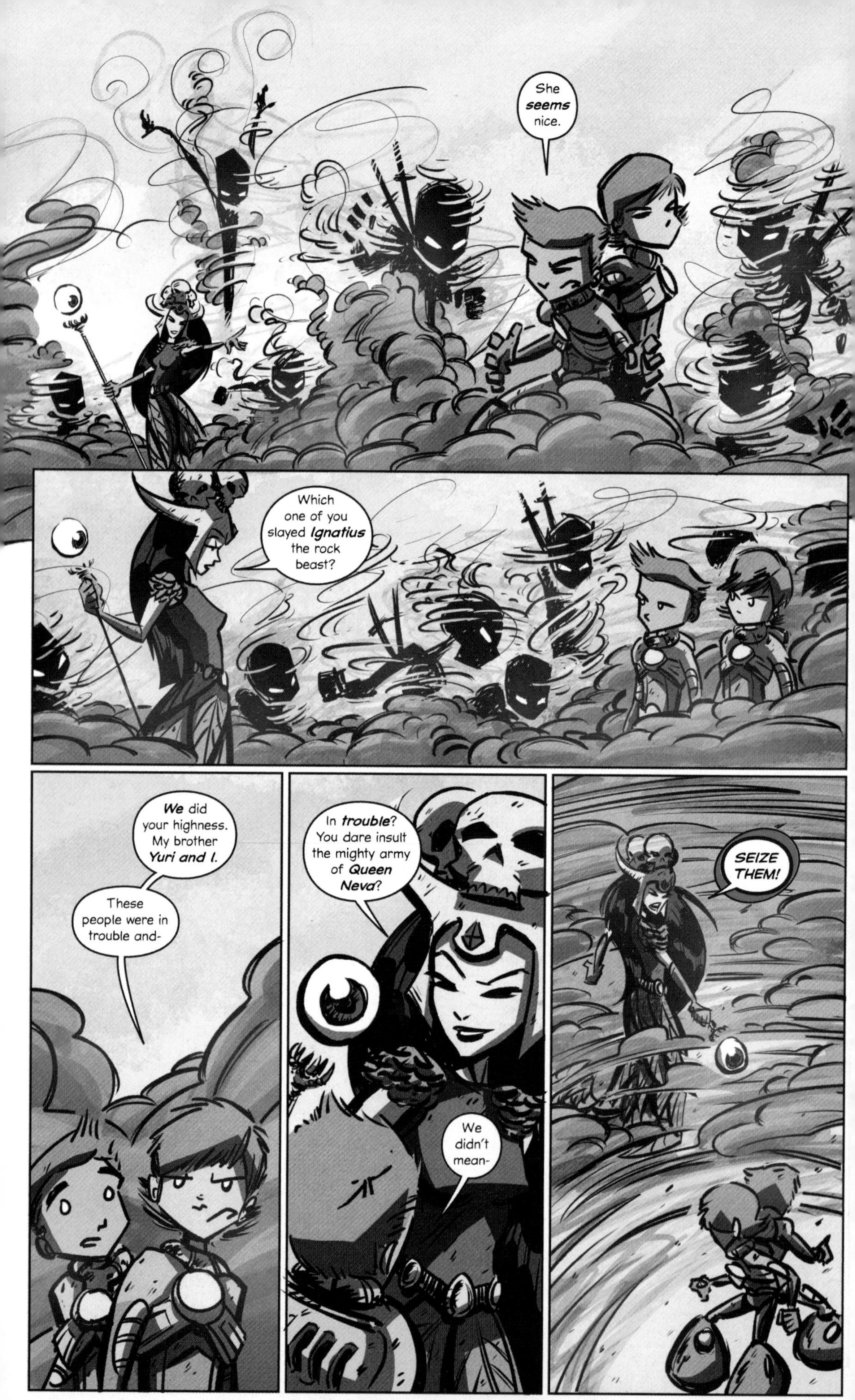
She seems nice.
Which one of you slayed Ignatius the rock beast?
We did your highness. My brother Yuri and I.
These people were in trouble and-
In trouble? You dare insult the mighty army of Queen Neva?
We didn't mean-
SEIZE THEM!

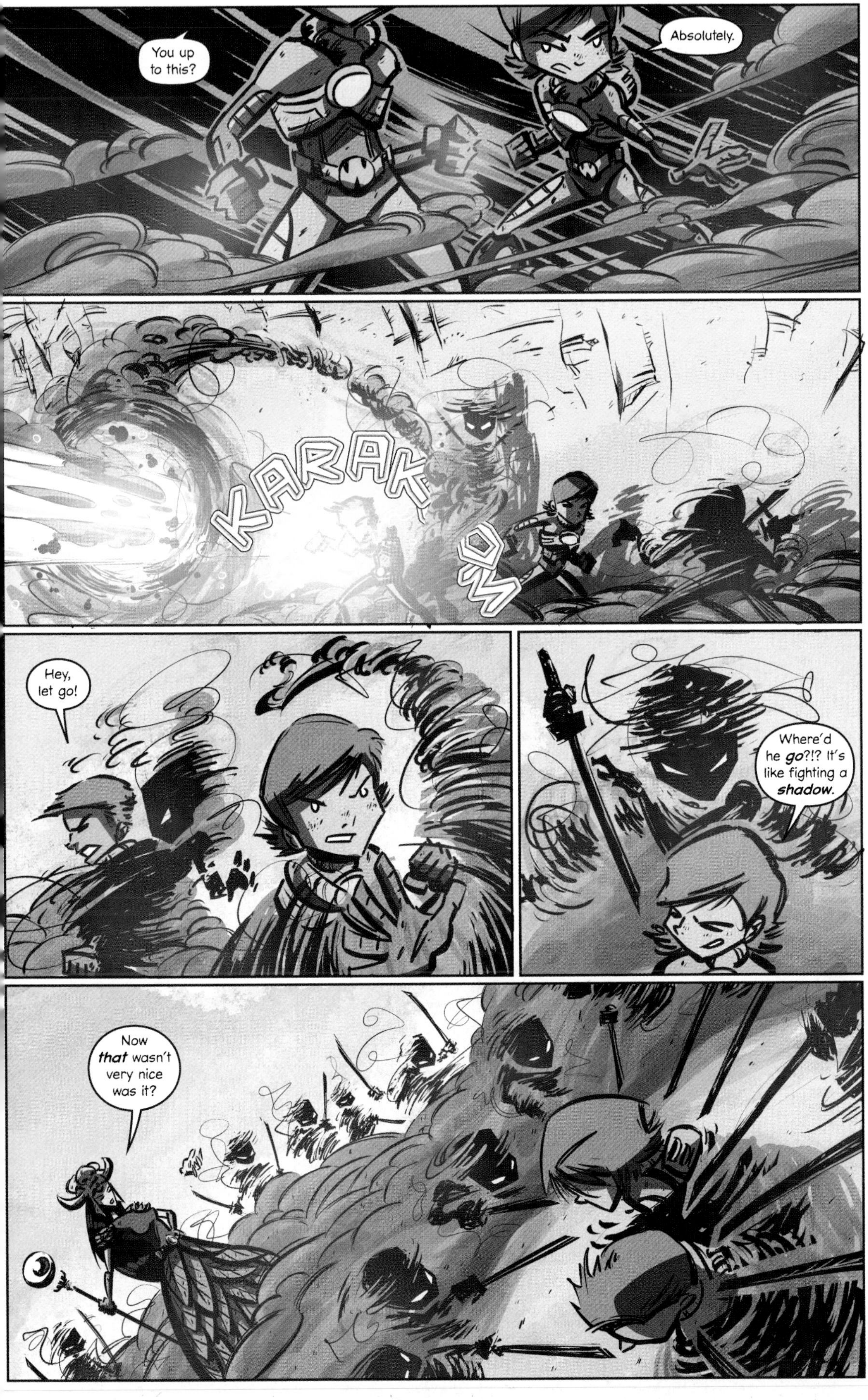
You up to this?
Absolutely.
KARAKOOM
Hey, let go!
Where'd he *go*?!? It's like fighting a ***shadow***.
Now ***that*** wasn't very nice was it?

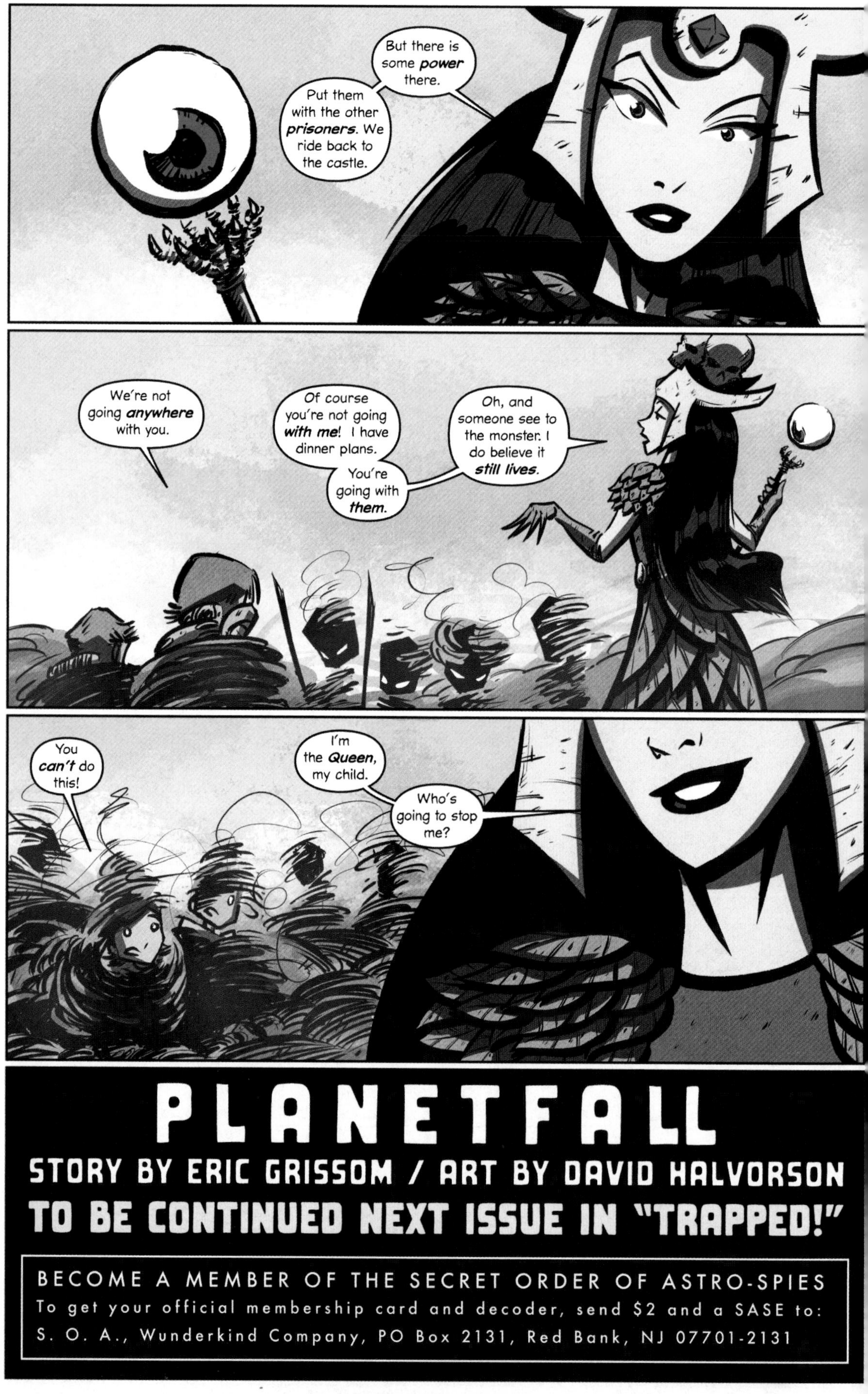
But there is some *power* there.
Put them with the other *prisoners*. We ride back to the castle.
We're not going *anywhere* with you.
Of course you're not going *with me*! I have dinner plans.
You're going with *them*.
Oh, and someone see to the monster. I do believe it *still lives*.
You *can't* do this!
I'm the *Queen*, my child.
Who's going to stop me?

PLANETFALL

STORY BY ERIC GRISSOM / ART BY DAVID HALVORSON

TO BE CONTINUED NEXT ISSUE IN "TRAPPED!"

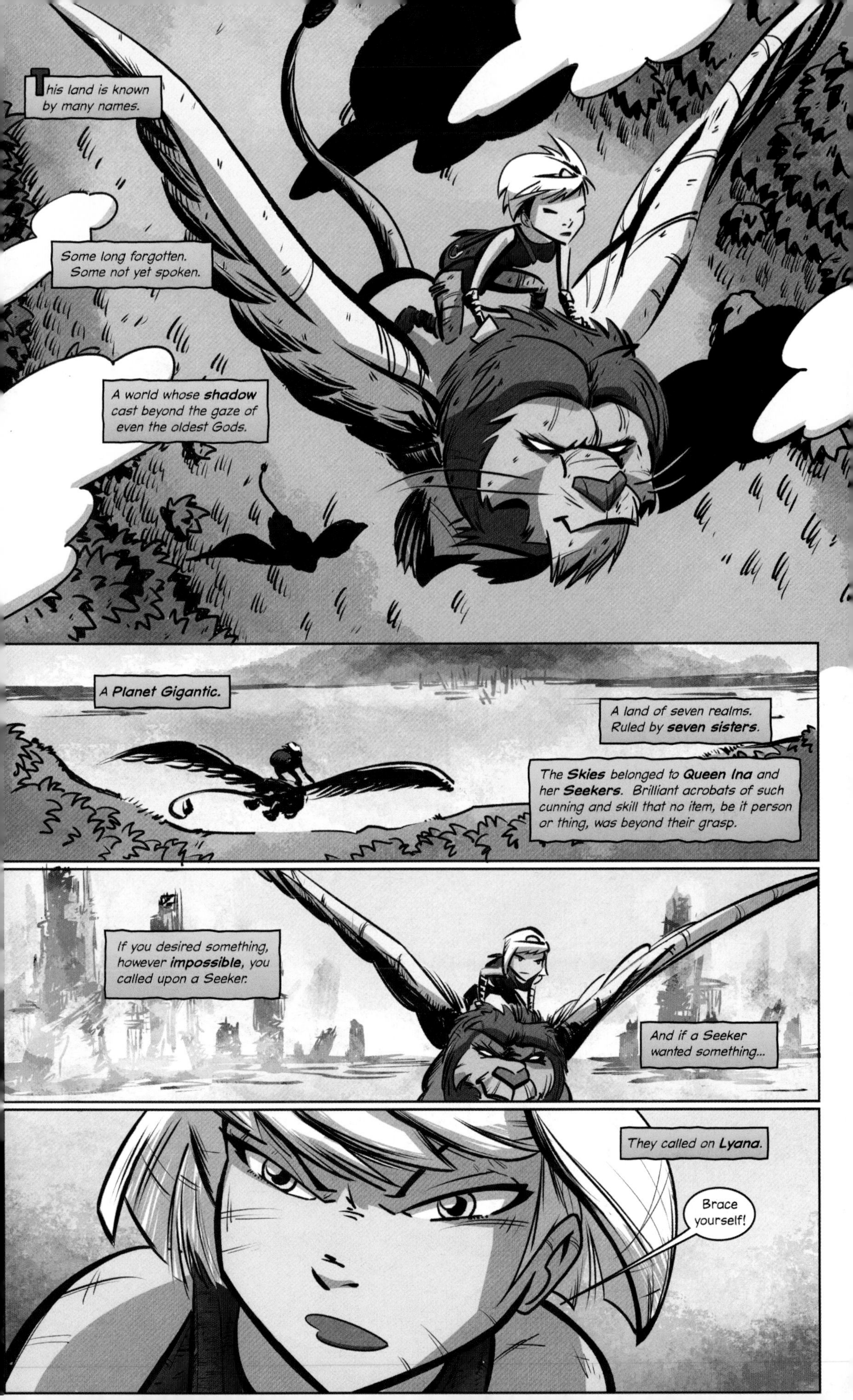
This land is known by many names.
Some long forgotten. Some not yet spoken.
A world whose shadow cast beyond the gaze of even the oldest Gods.
A Planet Gigantic.
A land of seven realms. Ruled by seven sisters.
The Skies belonged to Queen Ina and her Seekers. Brilliant acrobats of such cunning and skill that no item, be it person or thing, was beyond their grasp.
If you desired something, however impossible, you called upon a Seeker.
And if a Seeker wanted something...
They called on Lyana.
Brace yourself!

THE EYE OF THE SUN
A TALE FROM THE PLANET GIGANTIC

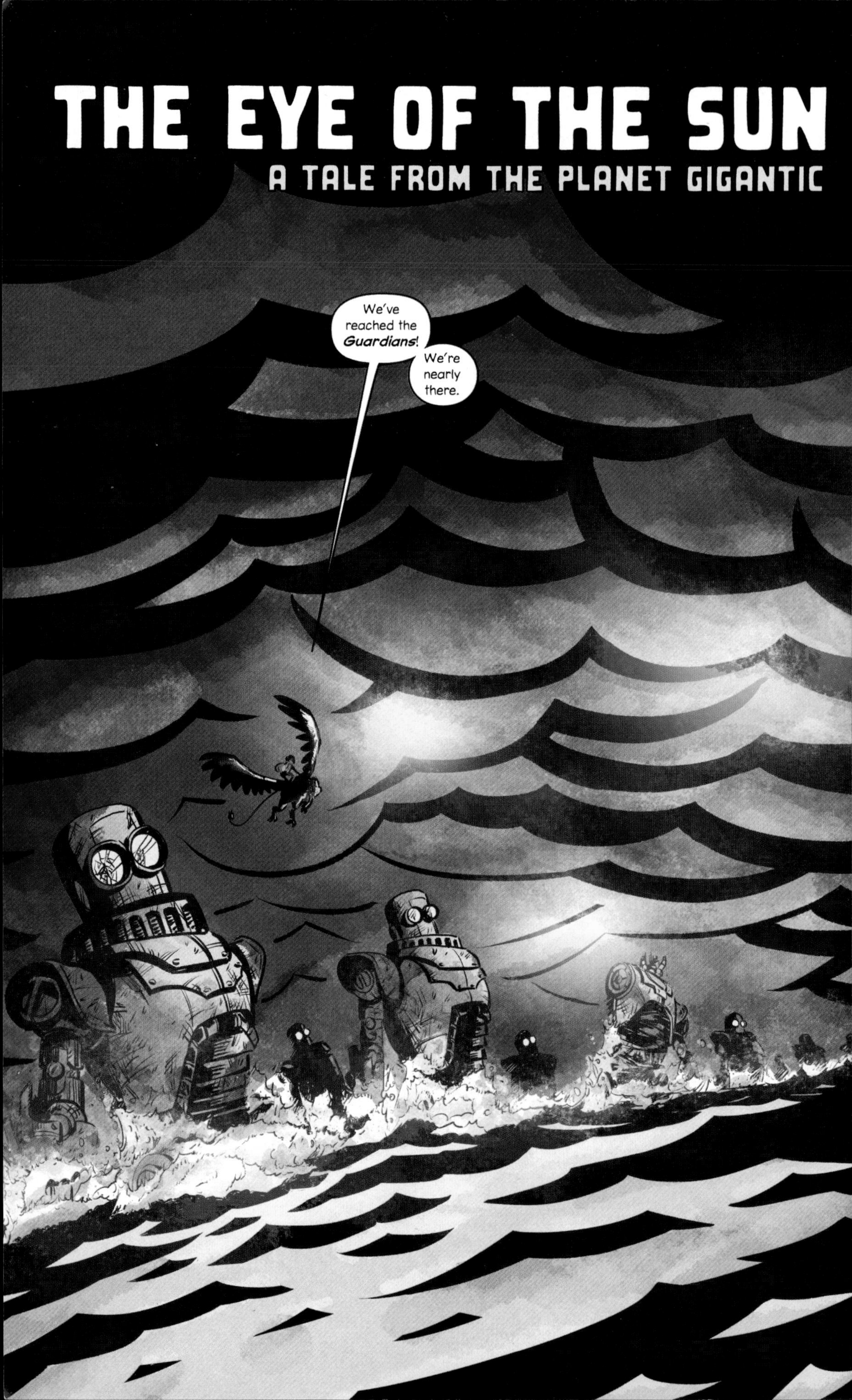
We've reached the *Guardians*!
We're nearly there.

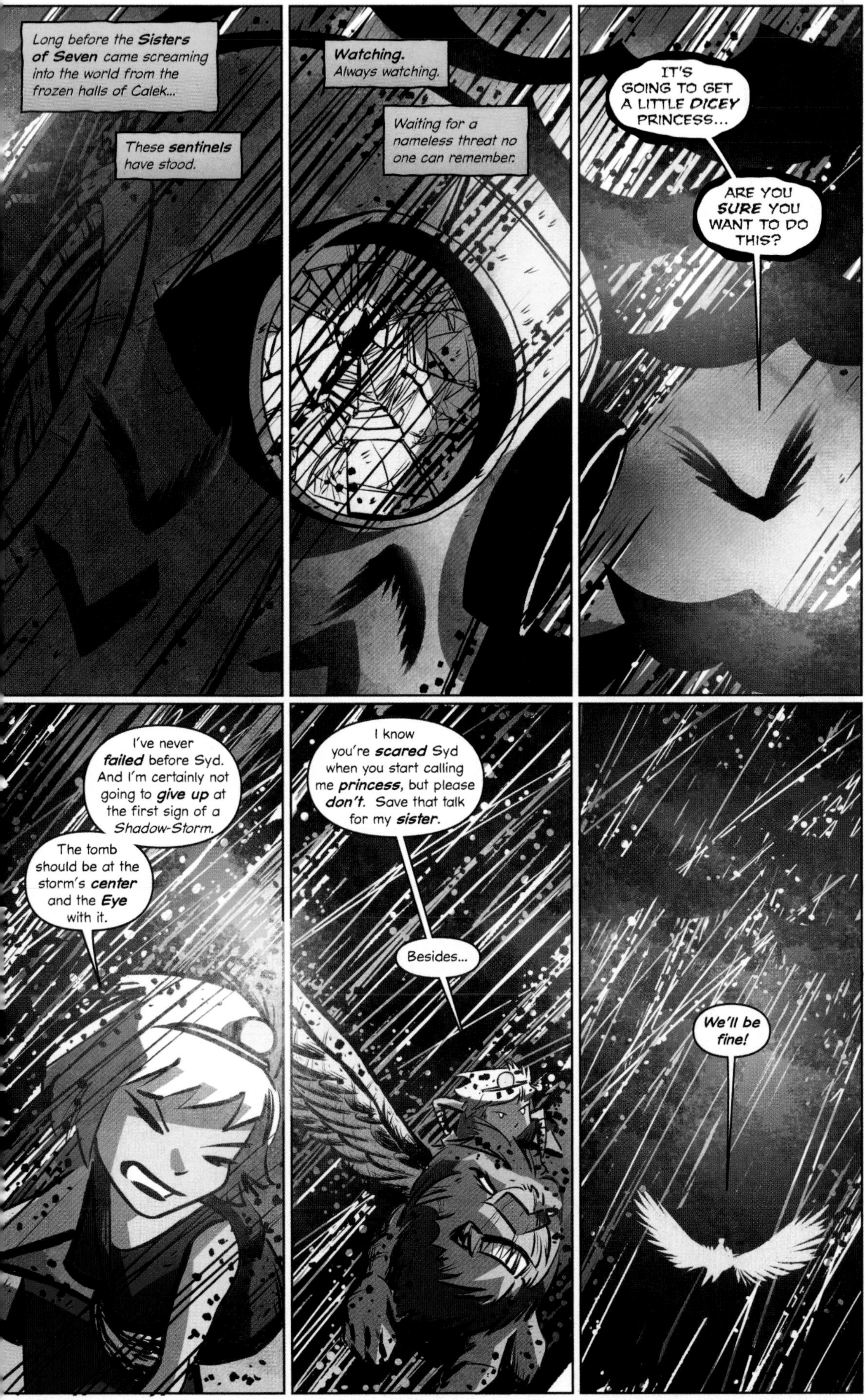
Long before the **Sisters of Seven** came screaming into the world from the frozen halls of Calek...
These **sentinels** have stood.
Watching. Always watching.
Waiting for a nameless threat no one can remember.
IT'S GOING TO GET A LITTLE *DICEY* PRINCESS...
ARE YOU *SURE* YOU WANT TO DO THIS?
I've never **failed** before Syd. And I'm certainly not going to **give up** at the first sign of a Shadow-Storm.
The tomb should be at the storm's **center** and the **Eye** with it.
I know you're **scared** Syd when you start calling me **princess**, but please **don't**. Save that talk for my **sister**.
Besides...
We'll be fine!

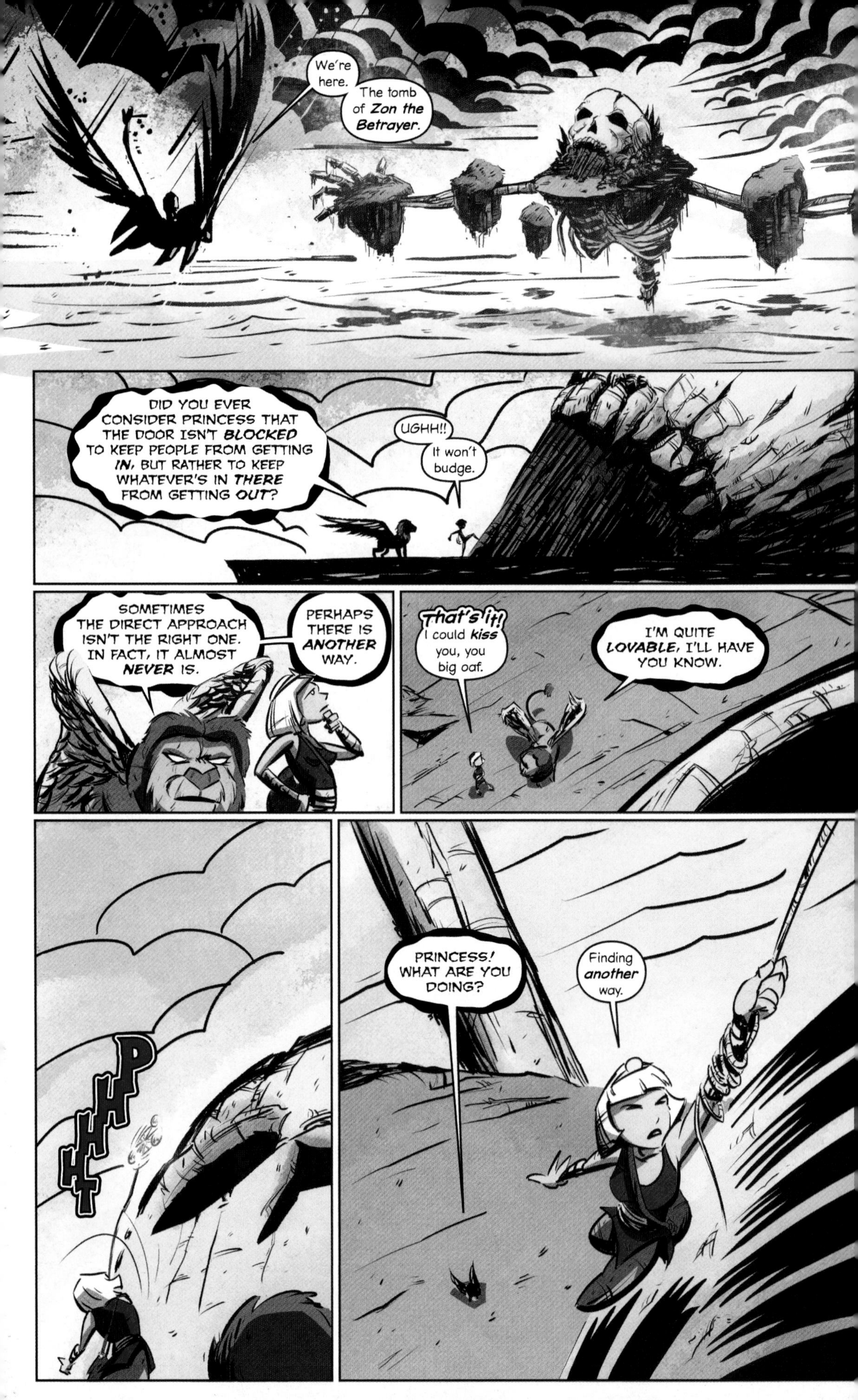
We're here.
The tomb of *Zon the Betrayer*.
DID YOU EVER CONSIDER PRINCESS THAT THE DOOR ISN'T *BLOCKED* TO KEEP PEOPLE FROM GETTING *IN*, BUT RATHER TO KEEP WHATEVER'S IN *THERE* FROM GETTING *OUT*?
UGHH!!
It won't budge.
SOMETIMES THE DIRECT APPROACH ISN'T THE RIGHT ONE. IN FACT, IT ALMOST *NEVER* IS.
PERHAPS THERE IS *ANOTHER* WAY.
That's it! I could *kiss* you, you big oaf.
I'M QUITE *LOVABLE*, I'LL HAVE YOU KNOW.
THHHP
PRINCESS! WHAT ARE YOU DOING?
Finding *another* way.

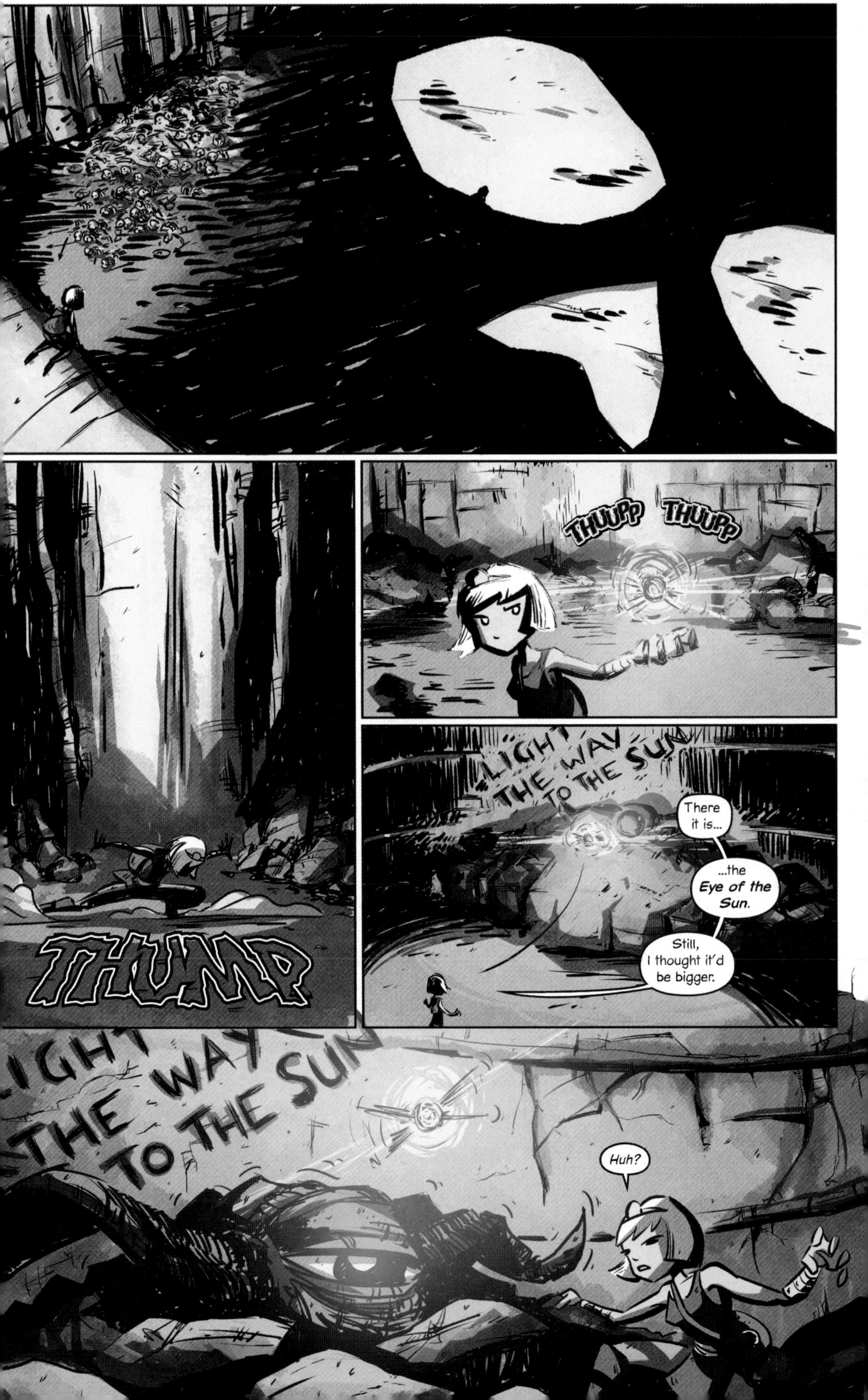
THUMP
THUUPP THUUPP
LIGHT THE WAY TO THE SUN
There it is...
...the *Eye of the Sun*.
Still, I thought it'd be bigger.
LIGHT THE WAY TO THE SUN
Huh?

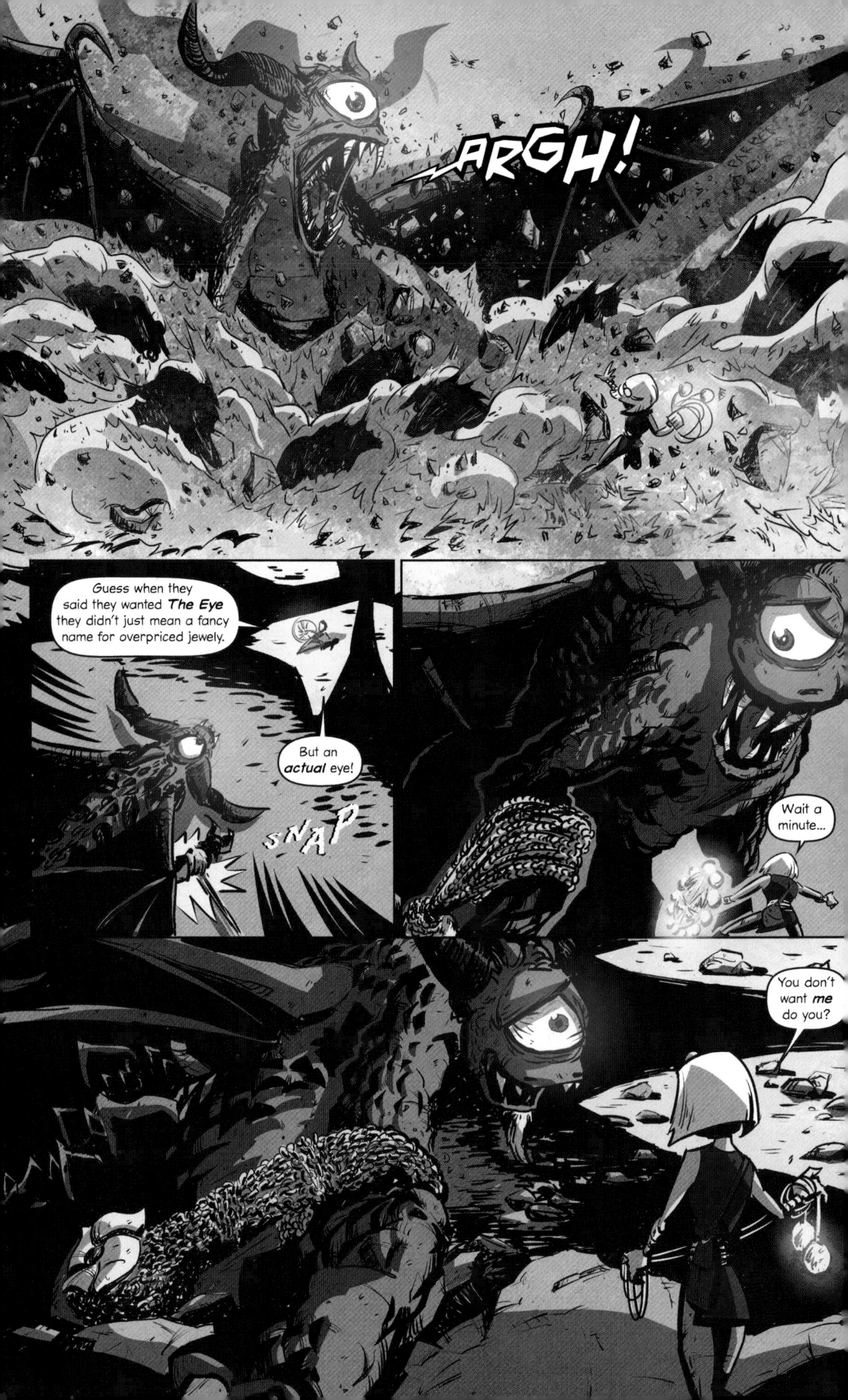
ARGH!
Guess when they said they wanted The Eye they didn't just mean a fancy name for overpriced jewely.
But an actual eye!
SNAP
Wait a minute...
You don't want me do you?

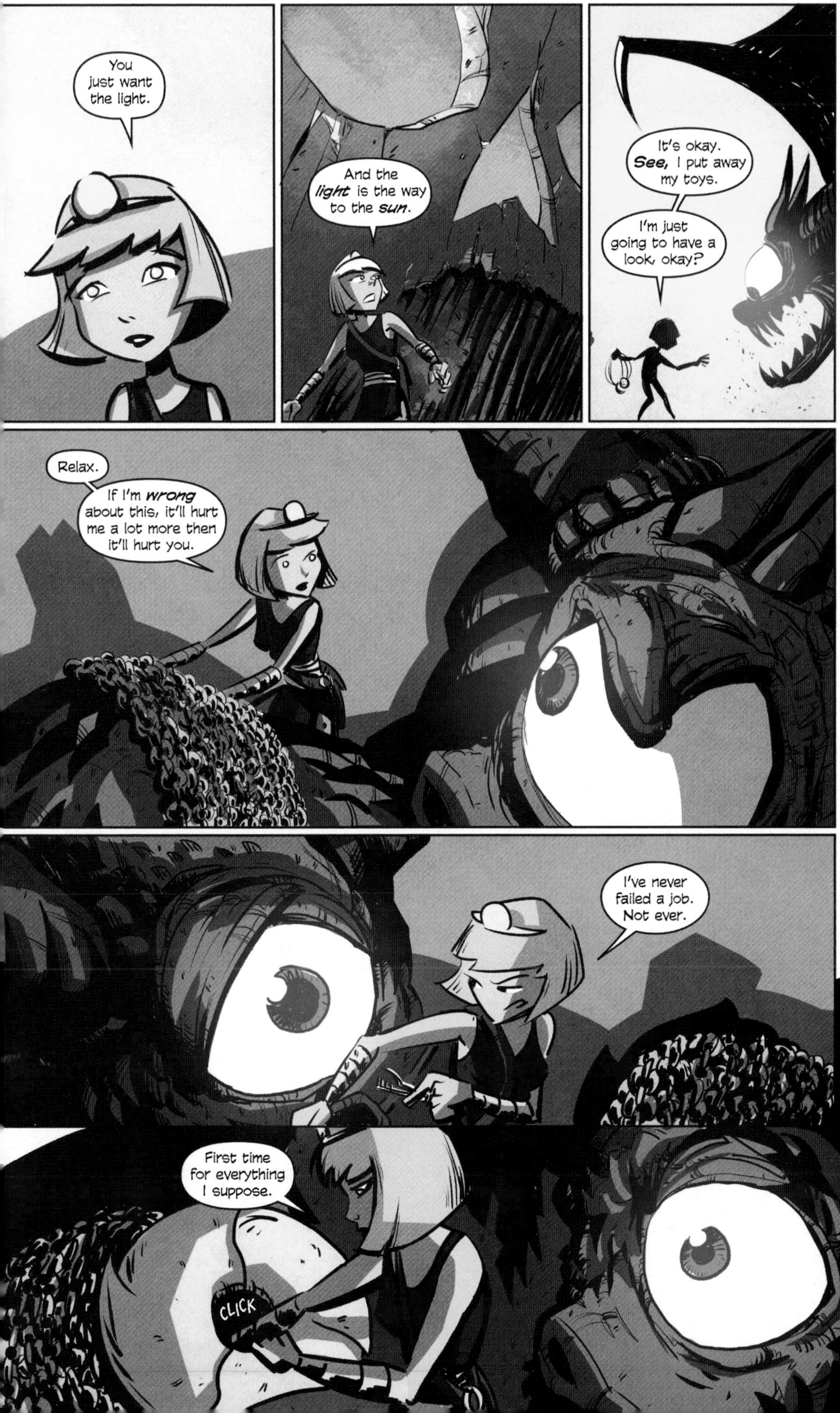
You just want the light.
And the *light* is the way to the *sun*.
It's okay. **See,** I put away my toys.
I'm just going to have a look, okay?
Relax.
If I'm ***wrong*** about this, it'll hurt me a lot more then it'll hurt you.
I've never failed a job. Not ever.
First time for everything I suppose.
CLICK

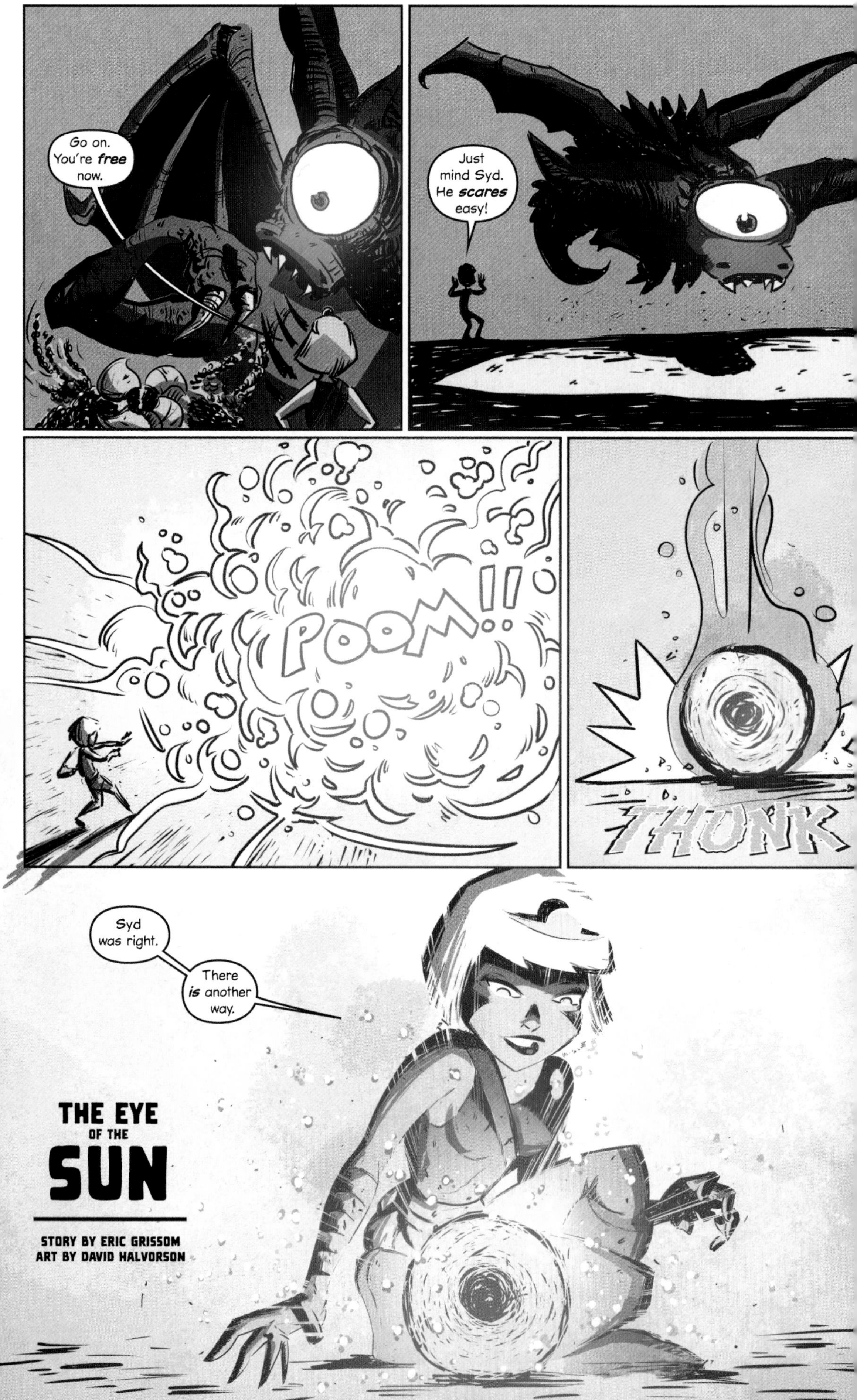
Go on. You're **free** now.
Just mind Syd. He **scares** easy!
POOM!!
THUNK
Syd was right.
There **is** another way.
THE EYE OF THE SUN
STORY BY ERIC GRISSOM
ART BY DAVID HALVORSON

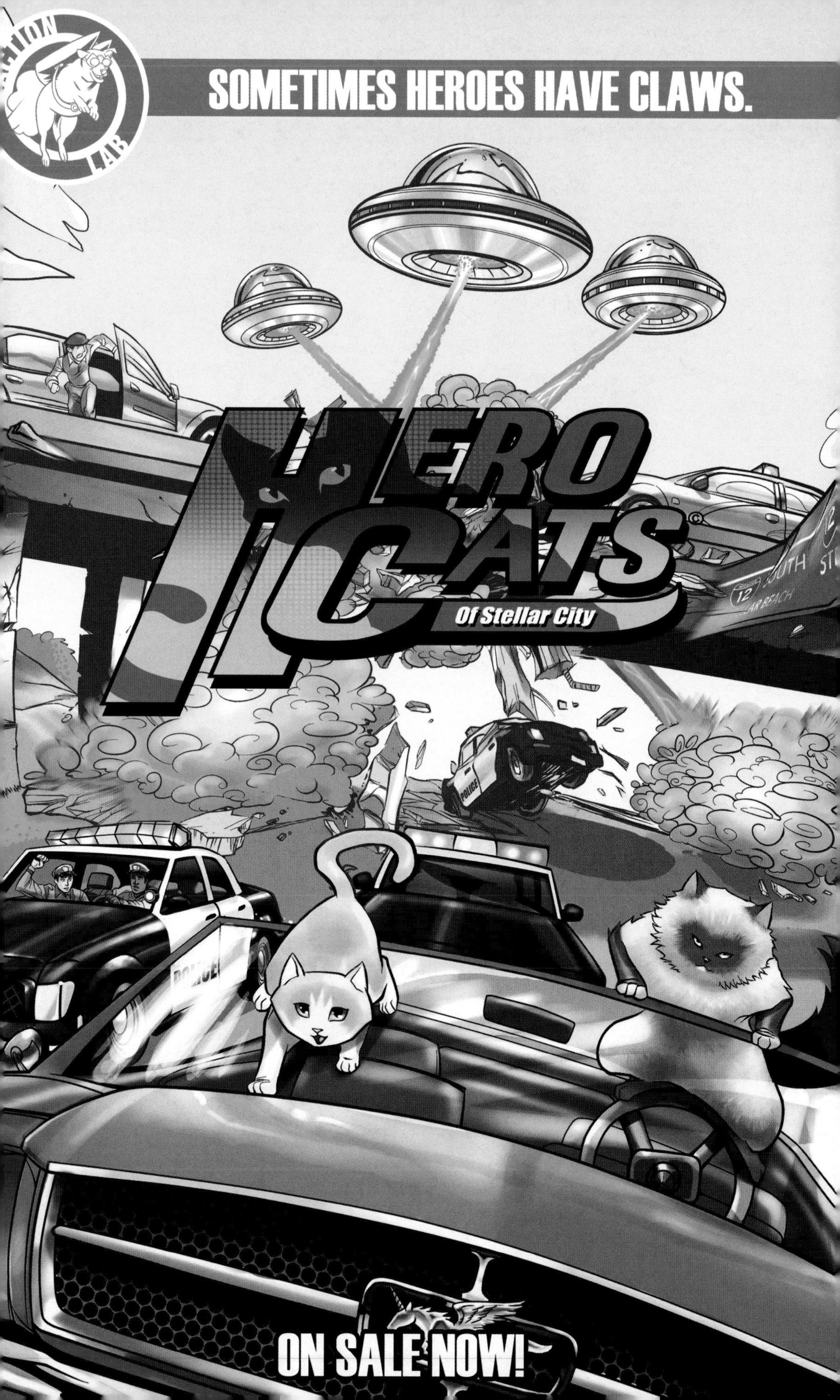

ACTION LAB
SOMETIMES HEROES HAVE CLAWS.
HERO CATS
Of Stellar City
12 SOUTH
POLICE
ON SALE NOW!

READ MORE NOW

Planet Gigantic - Action Lab
www.actionlabcomics.com

00111

7 00465 77246 6

ACTIONLABCOMICS.COM

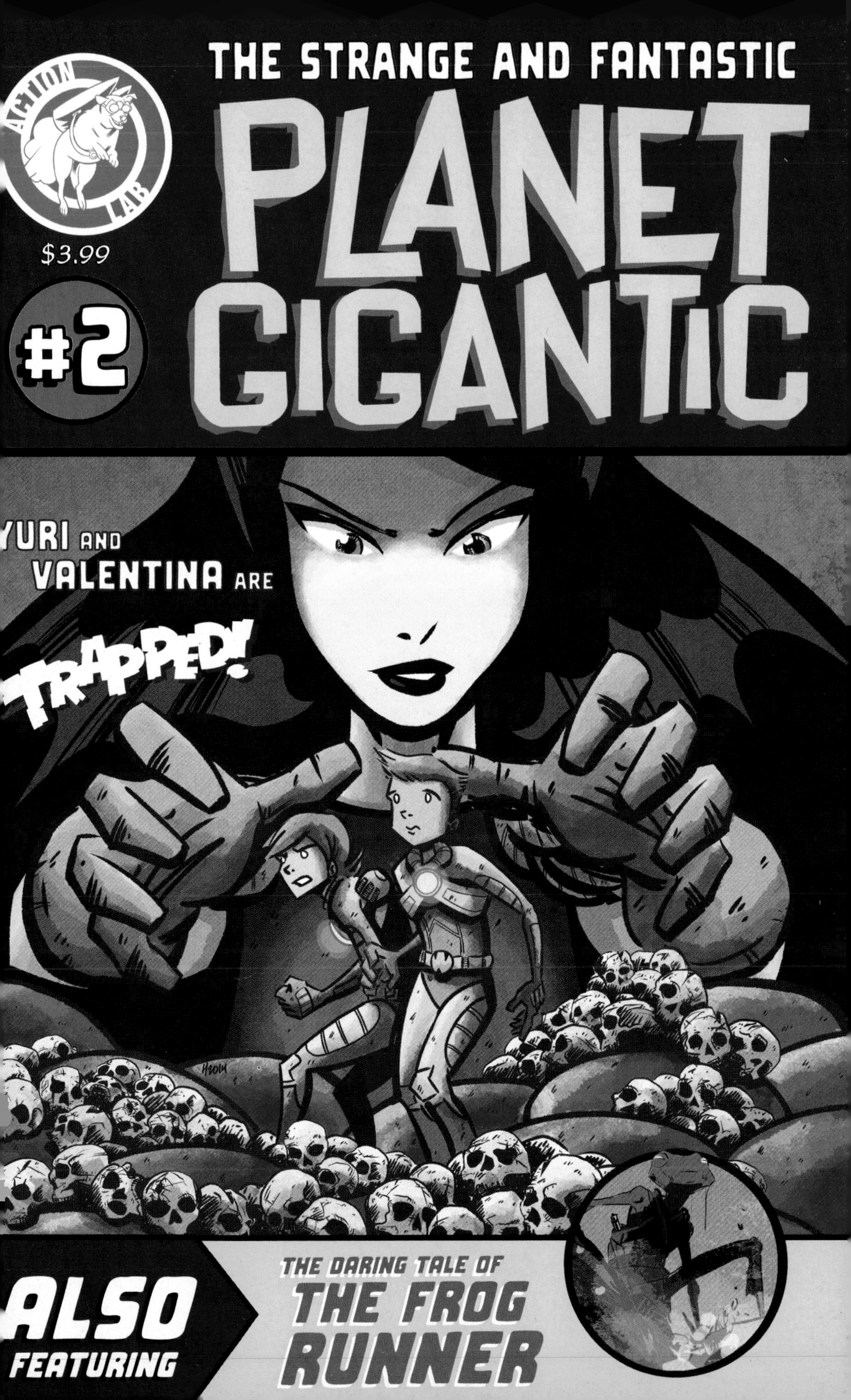
THE STRANGE AND FANTASTIC
PLANET GIGANTIC
ACTION LAB
$3.99
#2
YURI AND VALENTINA ARE
TRAPPED!
ALSO FEATURING
THE DARING TALE OF
THE FROG RUNNER

PLANET GIGANTIC

"Trapped!"
story and letters by ERIC GRISSOM
art and cover by DAVID HALVORSON

"The Frog Runner"
story and letters by ERIC GRISSOM
art by WILL PERKINS
colors by DAVID HALVORSON

Astro-Spies ad designed by DAVID HALVORSON

fonts by COMICRAFT
planetgigantic.com

publisher BRYAN SEATON
president KEVIN FREEMAN
editor-in-chief SHAWN GABBORIN
creative director DAVE DWONCH
co-directors of marketing JAMAL IGLE & KELLY DALE
social media director JIM DIETZ
education outreach director JEREMY WHITLEY
associate editors CHAD CICCONI & COLLEEN BOYD

PLANET GIGANTIC #1, November 2014. Published by Action Lab Entertainment. Planet Gigantic, its logos and all related cah-racters are TM and   2014 Eric Grissom and David Halvorson. All rights reserved. The characters and events presented are purely fictional. Any similarities to events or persons living or dead is purely cuincidental. No portion of this publication may be reproduced without the written consent from Action Lab Entertainment, Eric Grissom or David Halvorson. Printed in Canada. First Printing. For more information visit planetgigantic.com or actionlab.com

Valentina...
Valentina... wake up.
We're *moving* again.
Great, so where are we now?

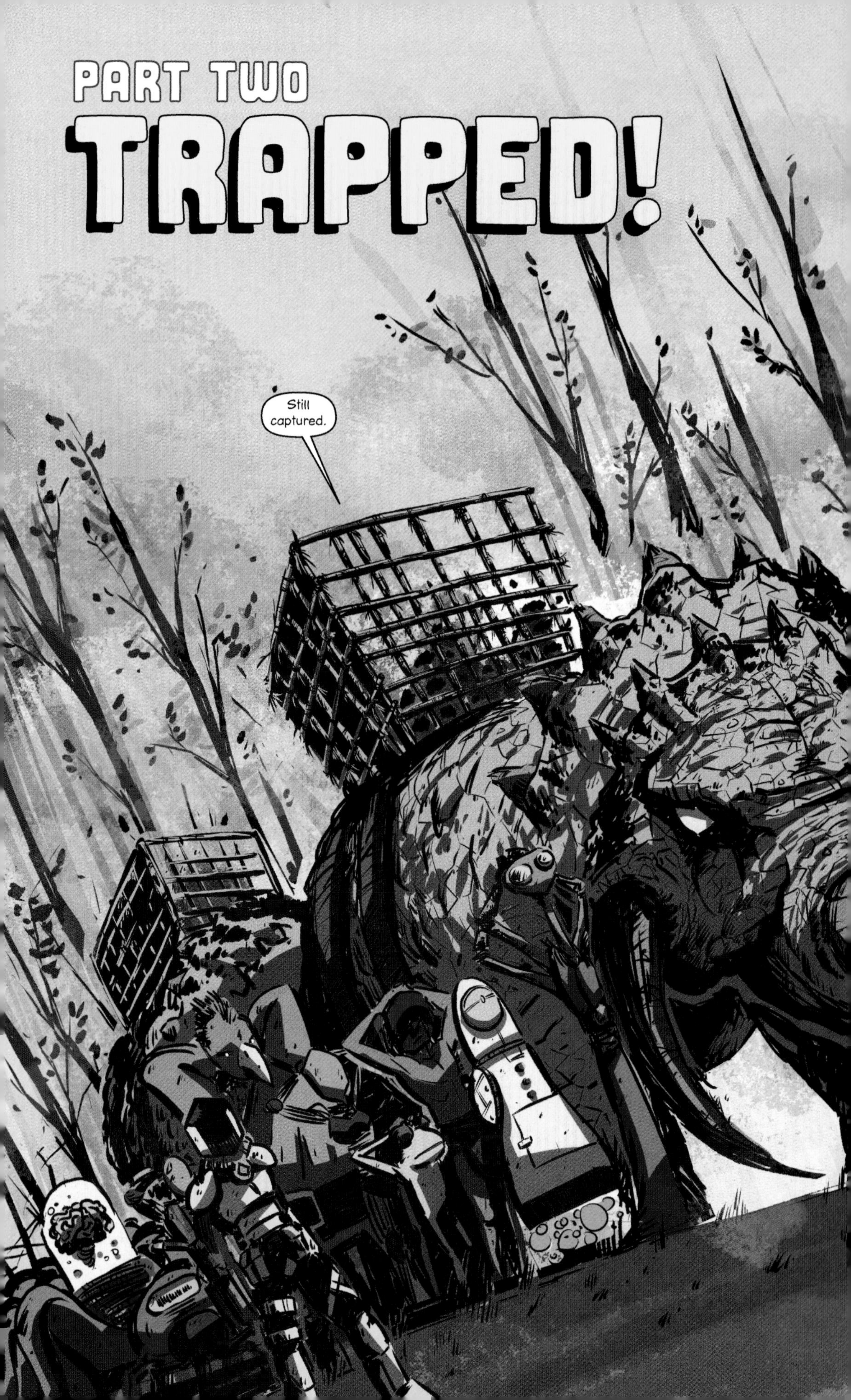
PART TWO
TRAPPED!
Still captured.

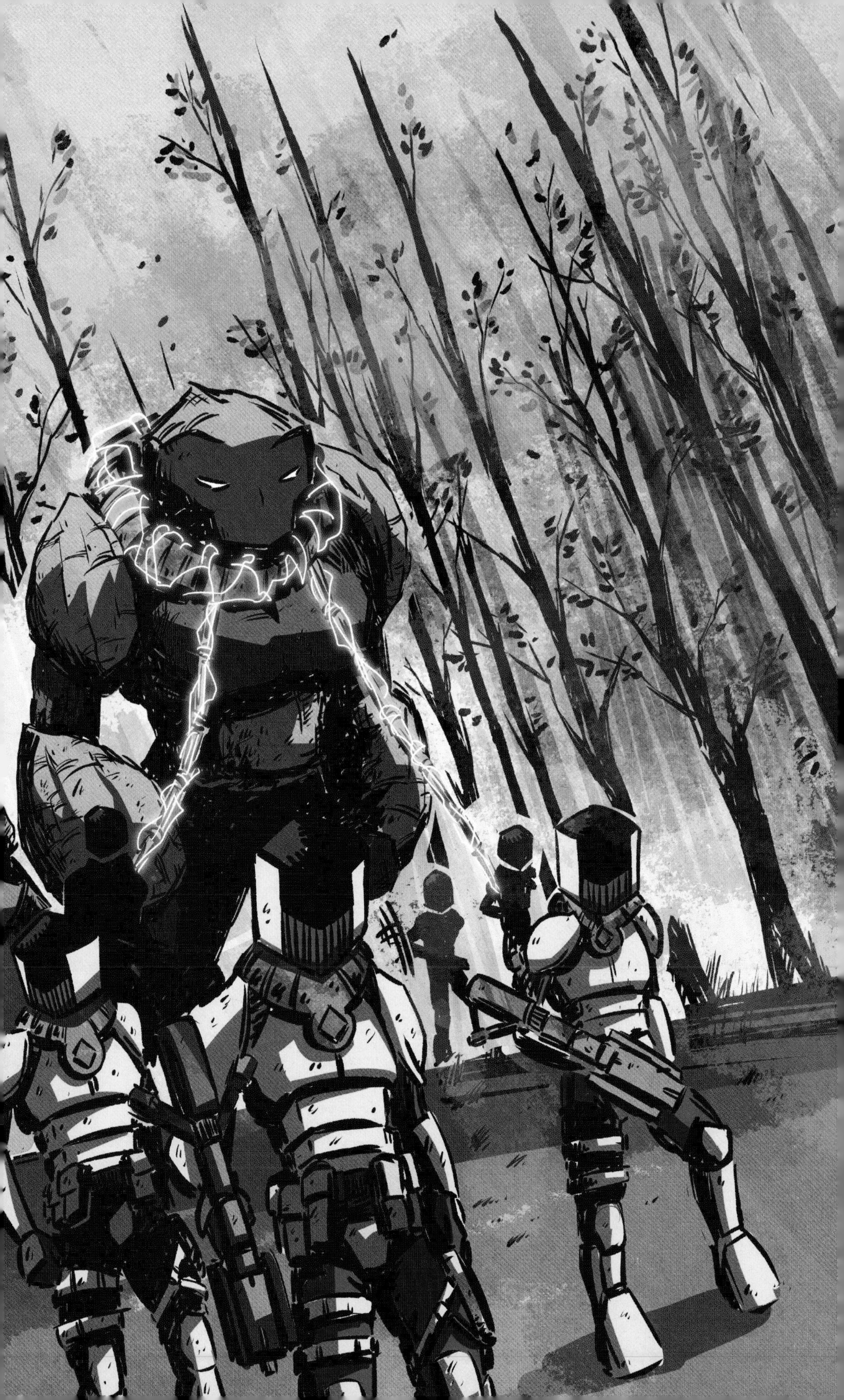

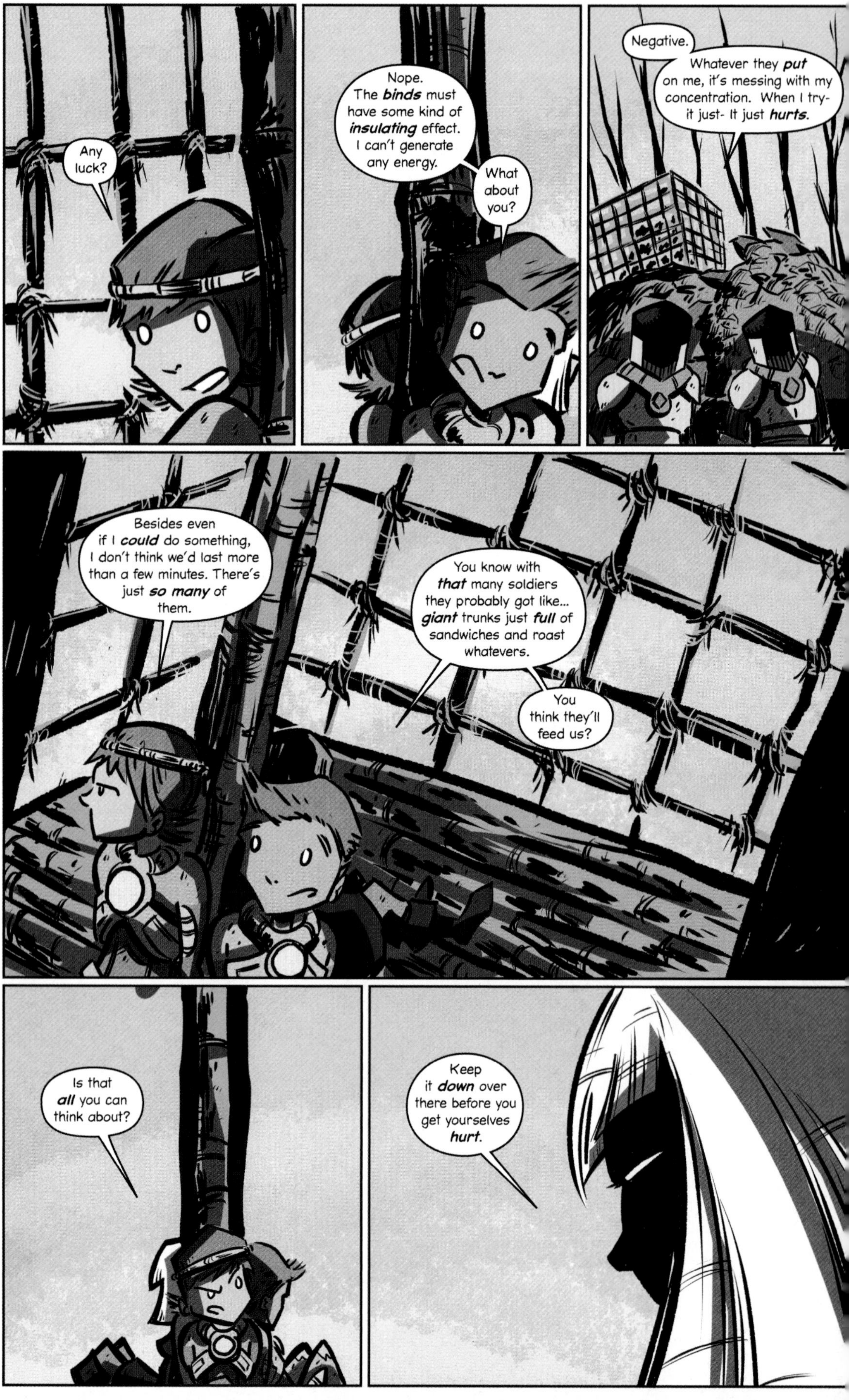
Any luck?
Nope. The binds must have some kind of insulating effect. I can't generate any energy.
What about you?
Negative.
Whatever they put on me, it's messing with my concentration. When I try- it just- It just hurts.
Besides even if I could do something, I don't think we'd last more than a few minutes. There's just so many of them.
You know with that many soldiers they probably got like... giant trunks just full of sandwiches and roast whatevers.
You think they'll feed us?
Is that all you can think about?
Keep it down over there before you get yourselves hurt.

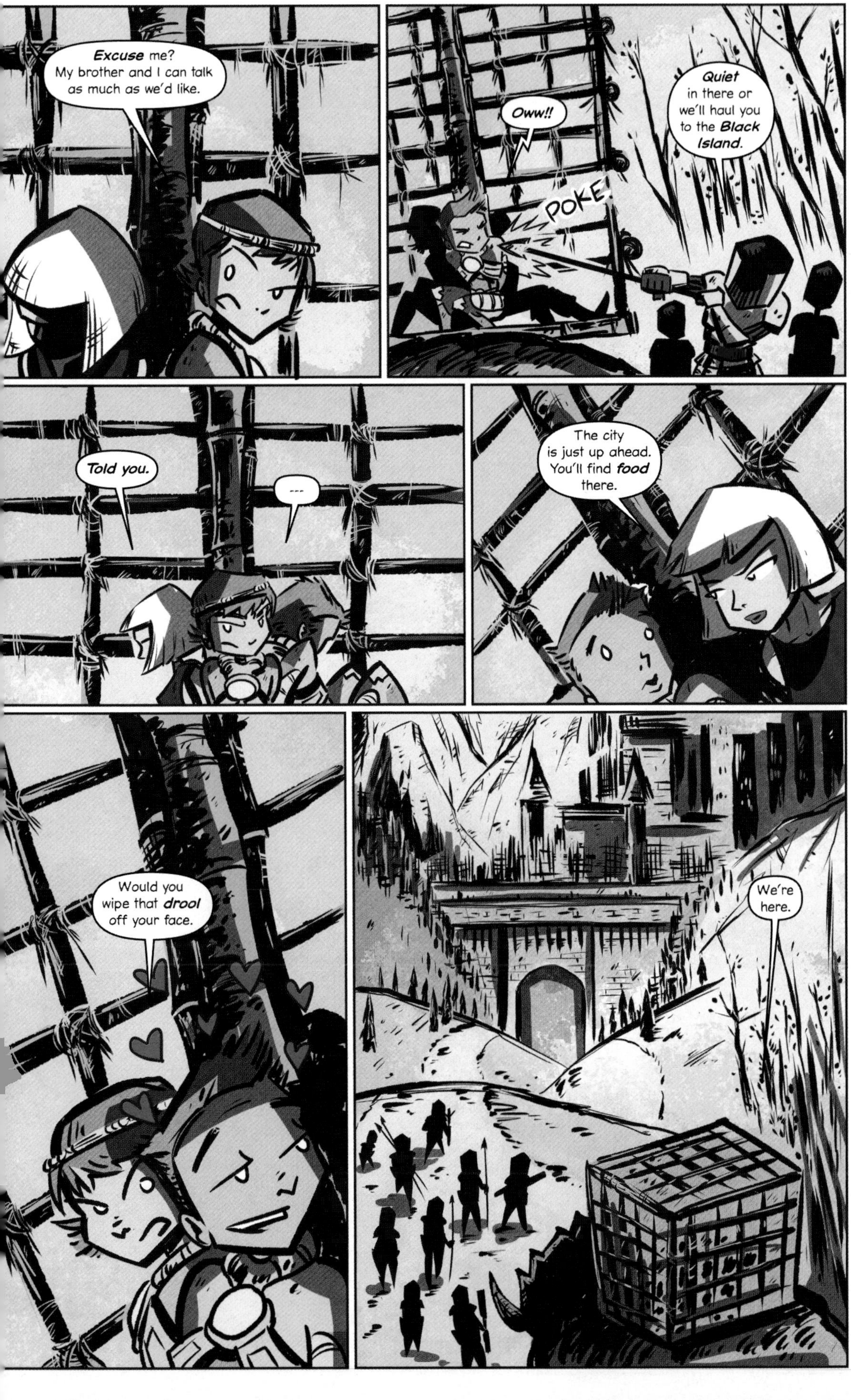

Excuse me? My brother and I can talk as much as we'd like.
Oww!!
Quiet in there or we'll haul you to the Black Island.
POKE
Told you.

The city is just up ahead. You'll find food there.
Would you wipe that drool off your face.
We're here.

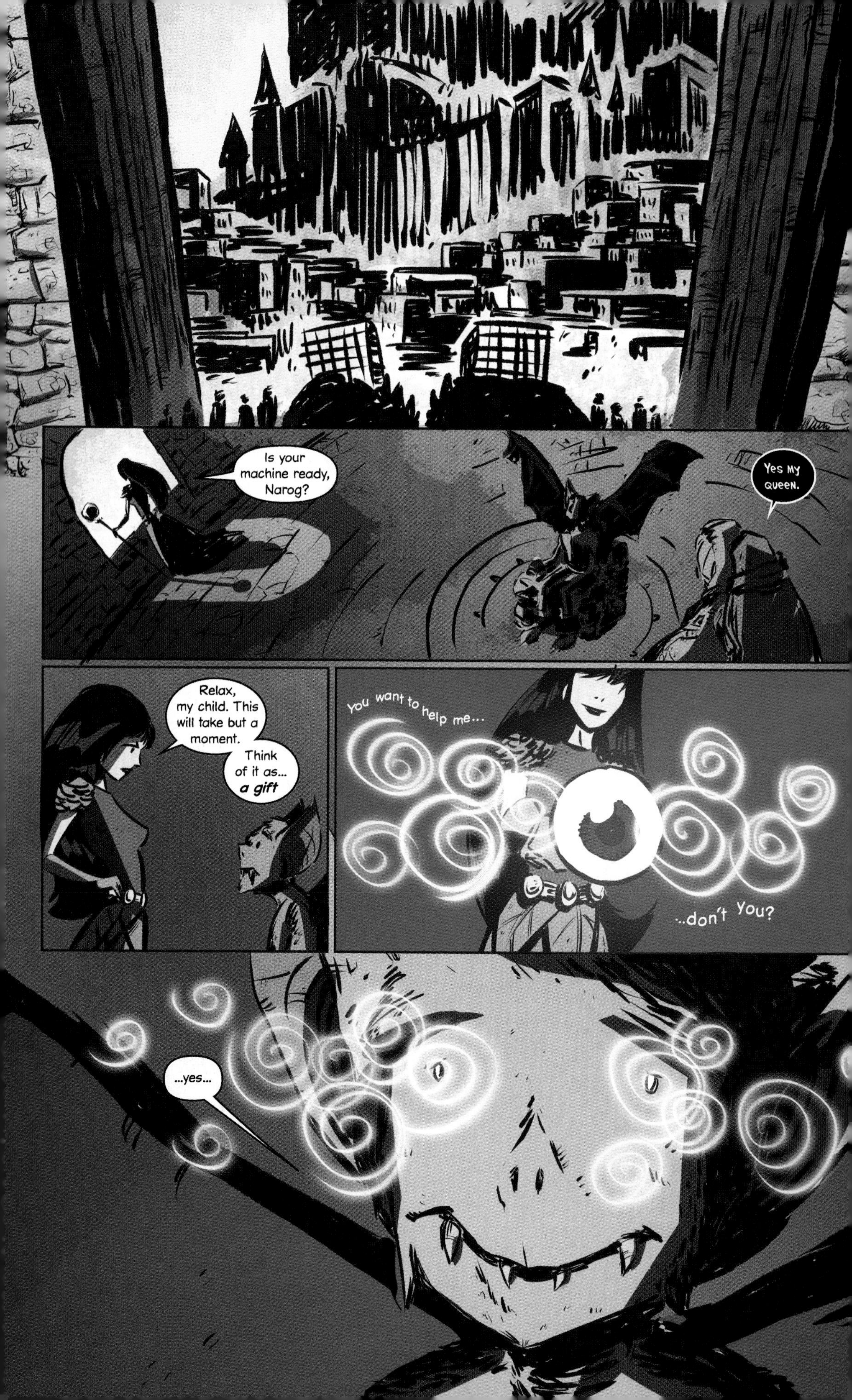
Is your machine ready, Narog?
Yes my queen.
Relax, my child. This will take but a moment.
Think of it as... *a gift*
You want to help me...
...don't you?
...yes...

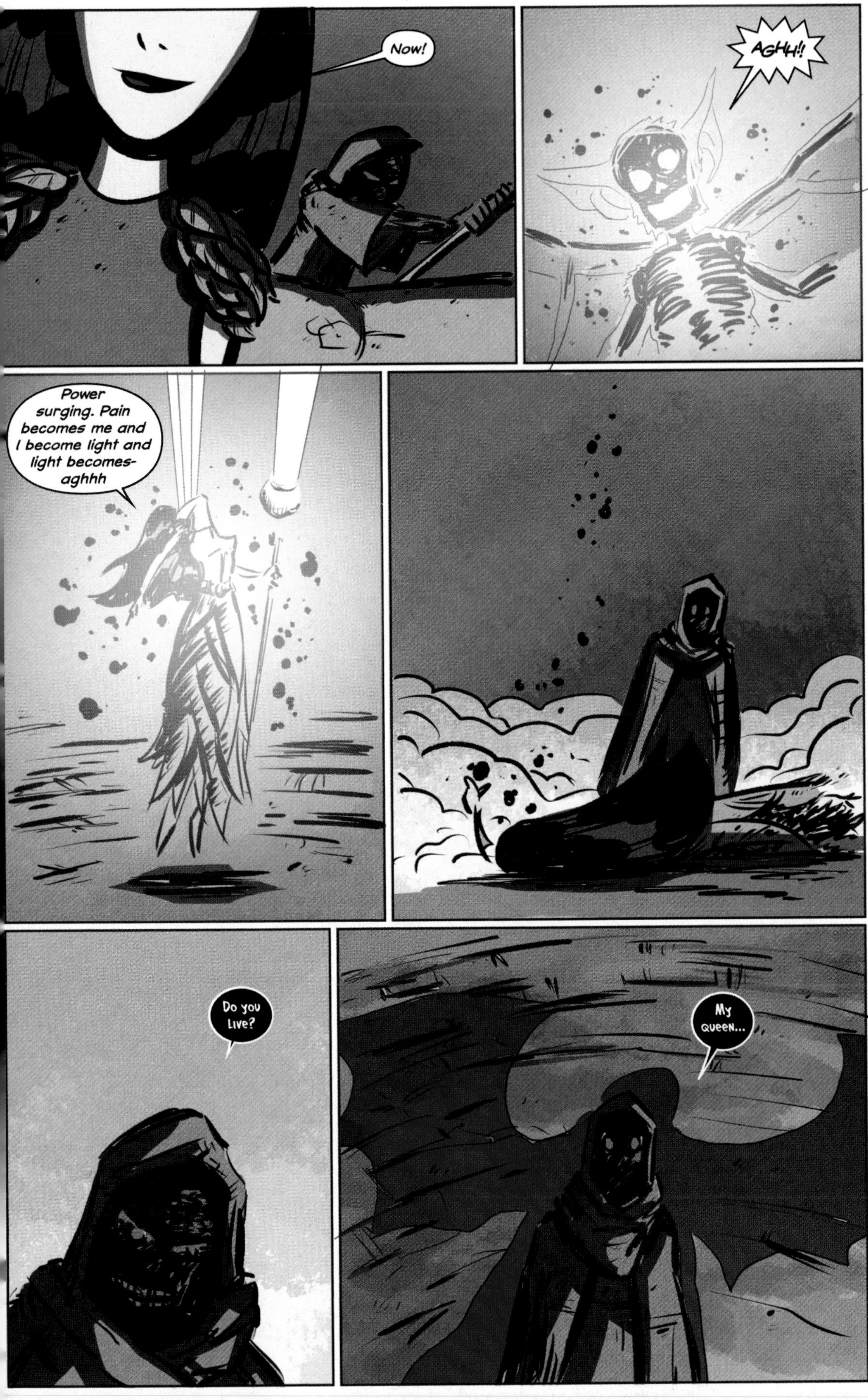
Now!
AGHH!!
Power surging. Pain becomes me and I become light and light becomes-aghhh
Do you live?
My queen...

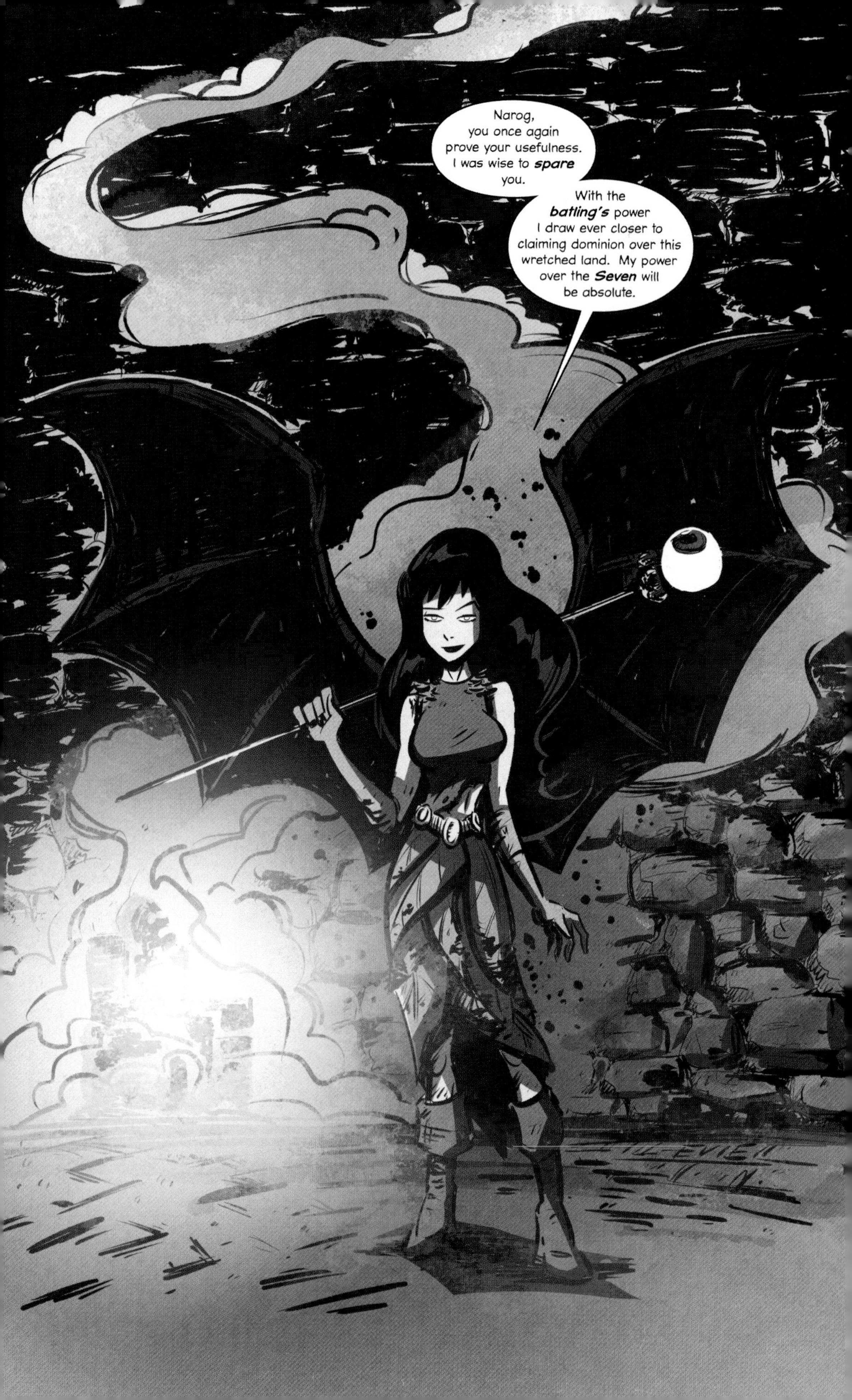

Narog, you once again prove your usefulness. I was wise to ***spare*** you.
With the ***batling's*** power I draw ever closer to claiming dominion over this wretched land. My power over the ***Seven*** will be absolute.

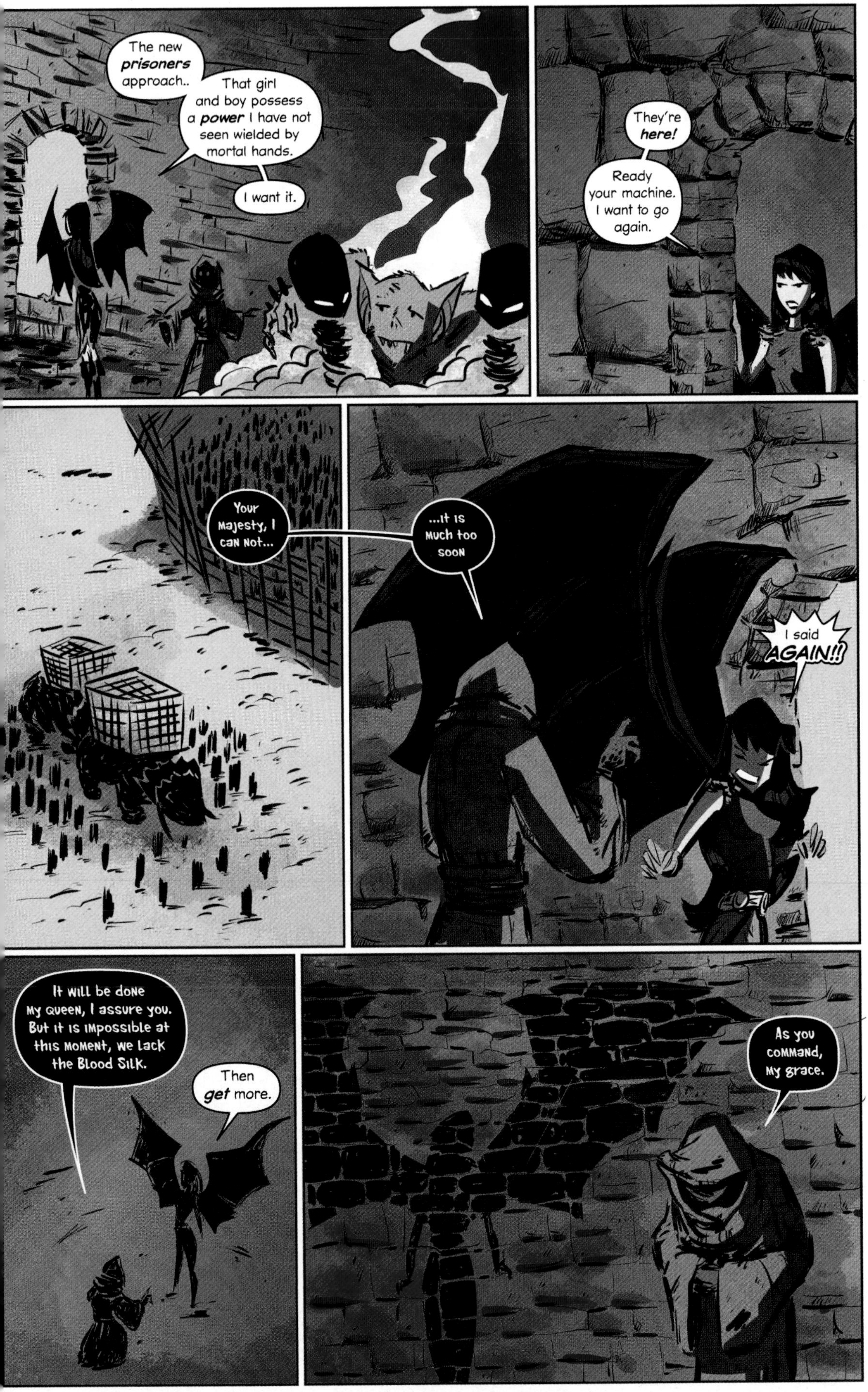
The new *prisoners* approach..
That girl and boy possess a *power* I have not seen wielded by mortal hands.
I want it.
They're *here!*
Ready your machine. I want to go again.
Your Majesty, I can not...
...it is much too soon
I said AGAIN!!
It will be done my queen, I assure you. But it is impossible at this moment, we lack the Blood Silk.
Then *get* more.
As you command, my grace.

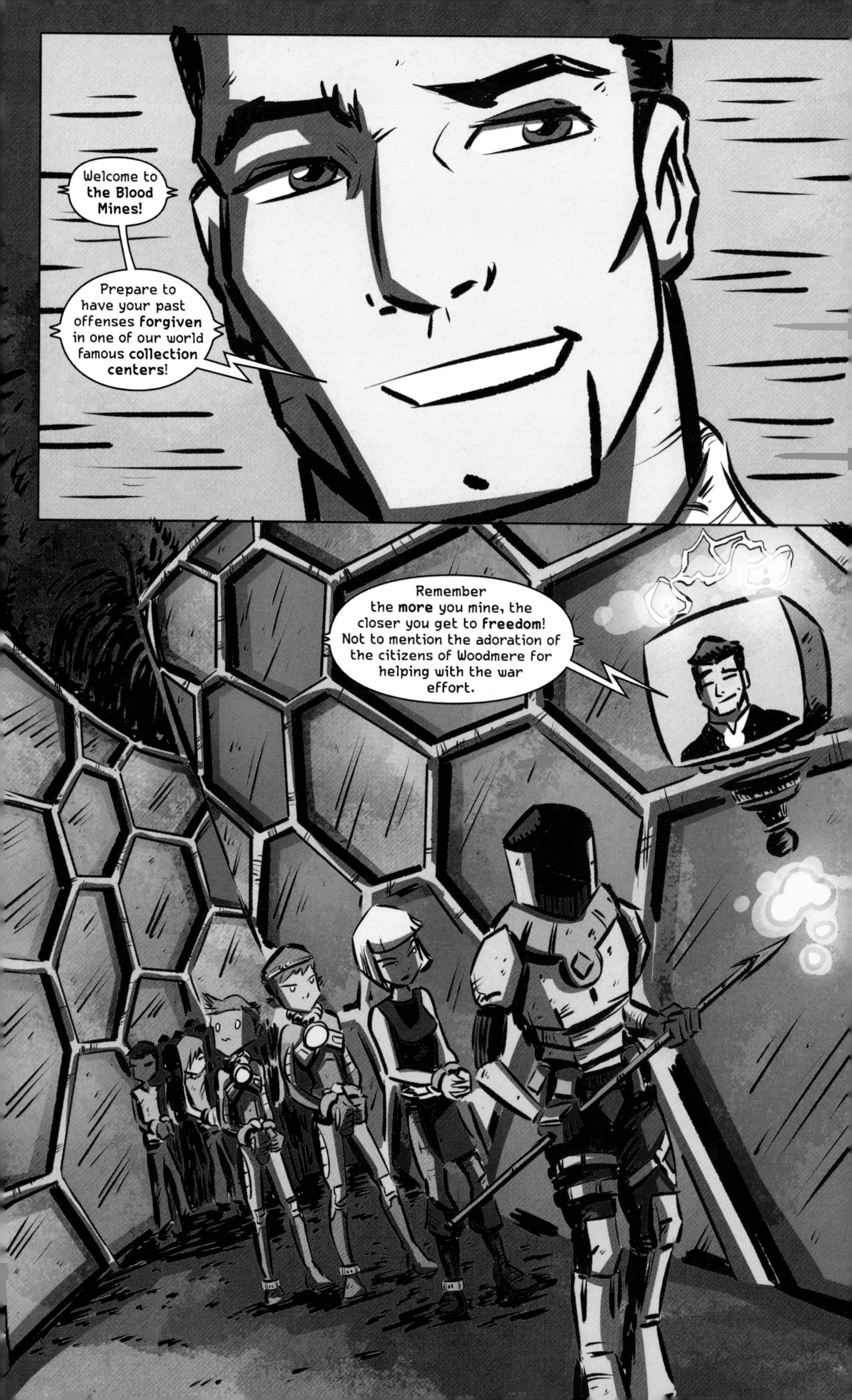
Welcome to the Blood Mines!
Prepare to have your past offenses forgiven in one of our world famous collection centers!
Remember the more you mine, the closer you get to freedom! Not to mention the adoration of the citizens of Woodmere for helping with the war effort.

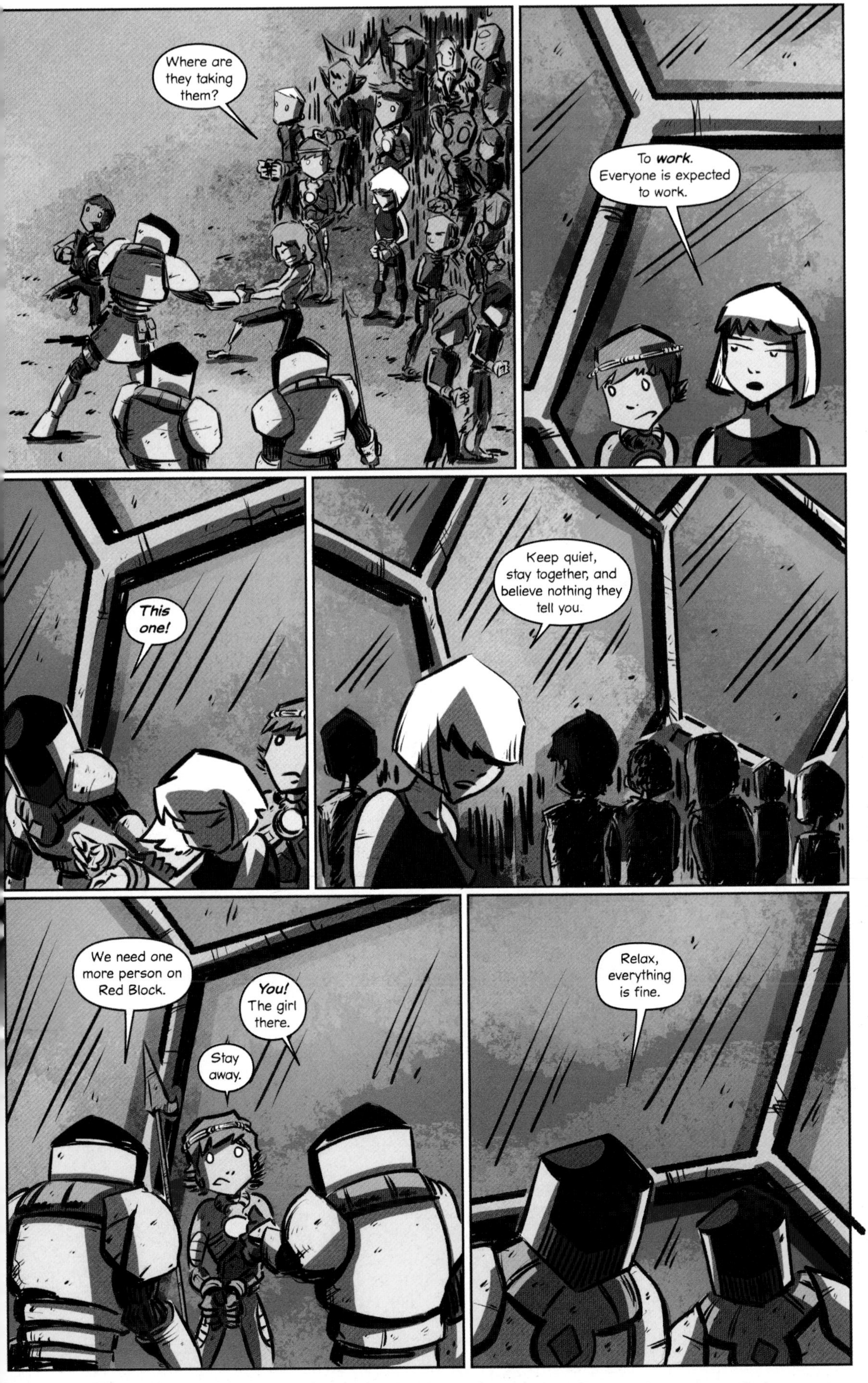
Where are they taking them?
To work. Everyone is expected to work.
This one!
Keep quiet, stay together, and believe nothing they tell you.
We need one more person on Red Block.
You! The girl there.
Stay away.
Relax, everything is fine.

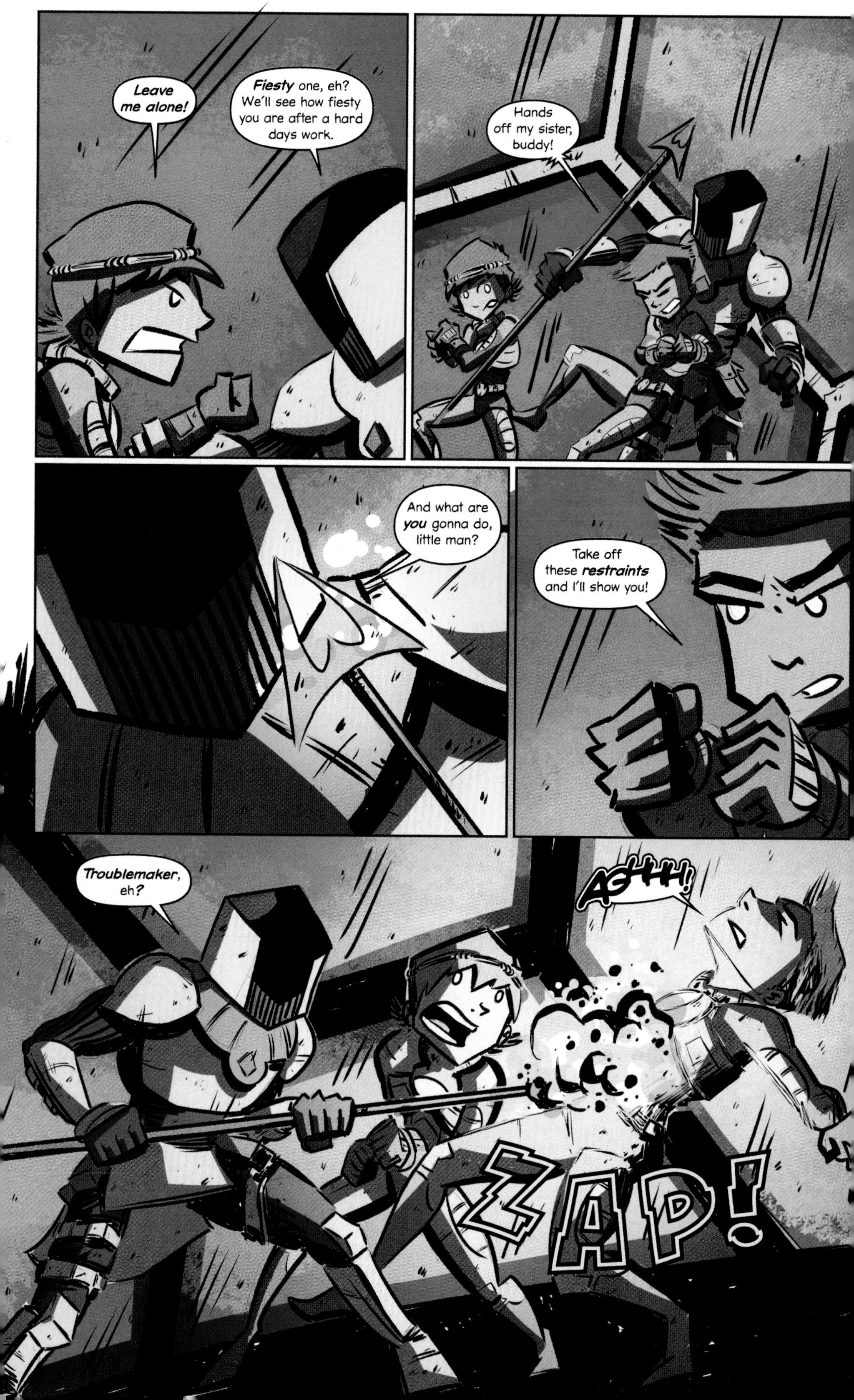
Leave me alone!
Fiesty one, eh? We'll see how fiesty you are after a hard days work.
Hands off my sister, buddy!
And what are you gonna do, little man?
Take off these restraints and I'll show you!
Troublemaker, eh?
AGHHH!
ZAP!

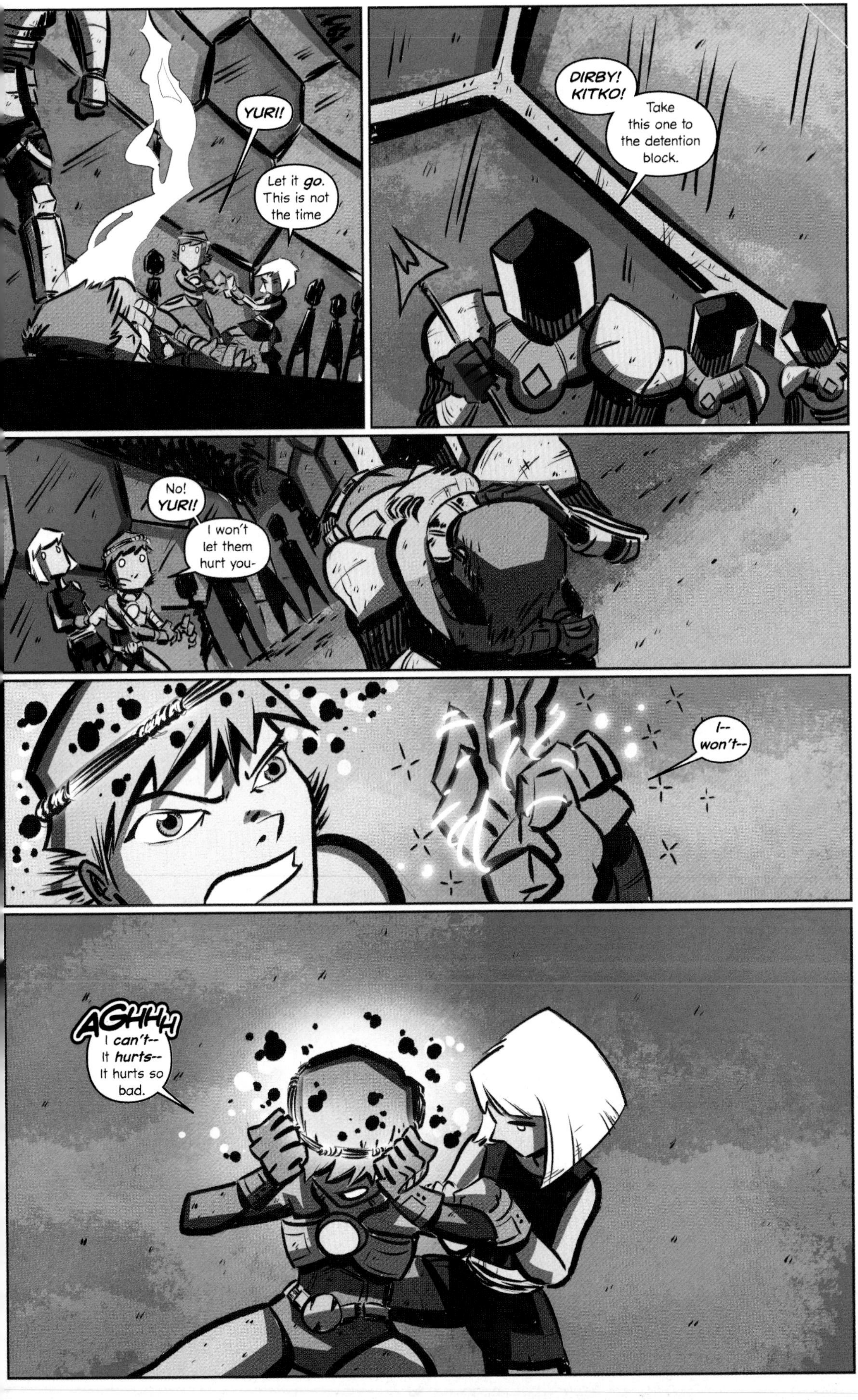

YURI!
Let it go. This is not the time
DIRBY! KITKO!
Take this one to the detention block.
No! YURI!
I won't let them hurt you-
I-- won't--
AGHHH
I can't-- It hurts-- It hurts so bad.

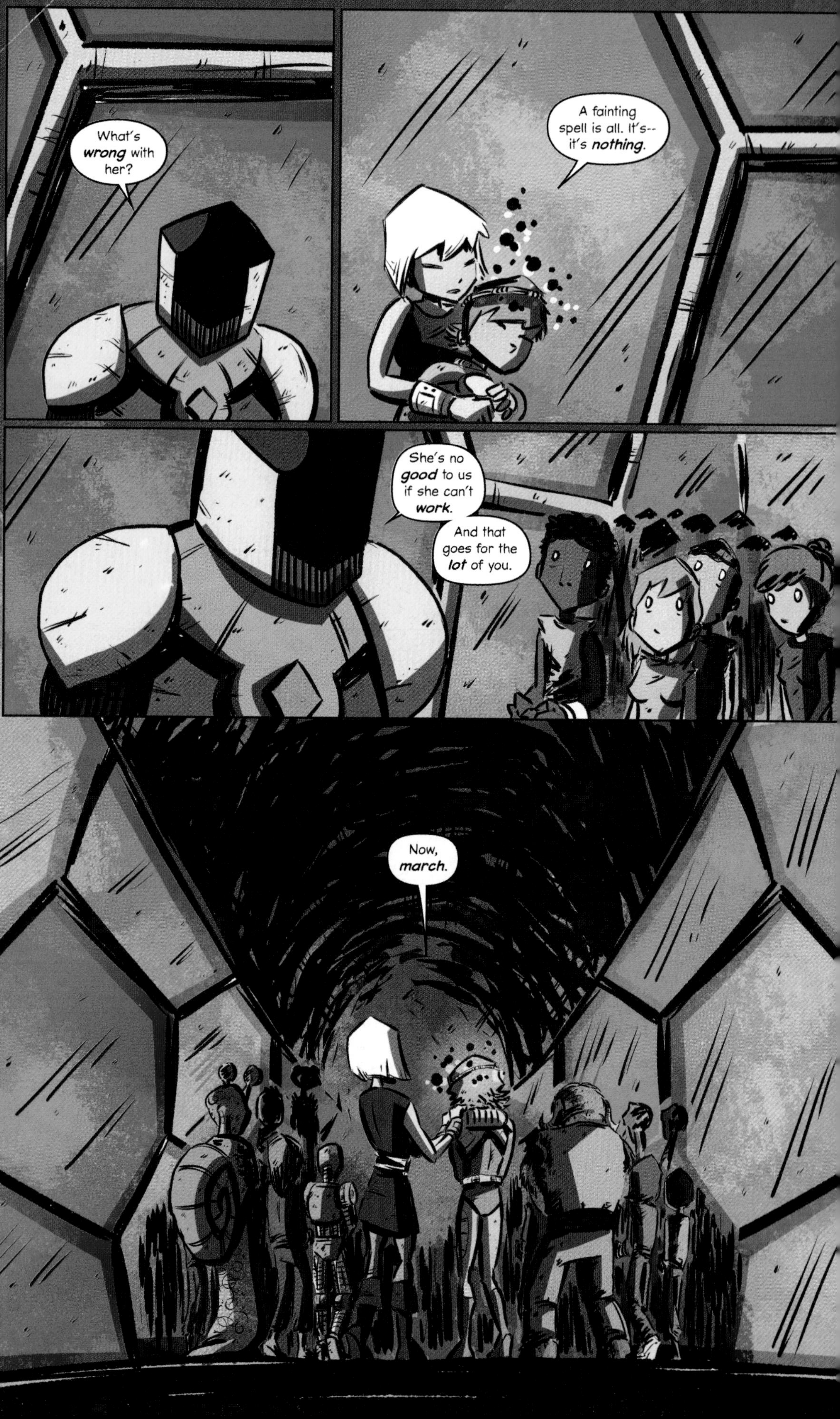
What's *wrong* with her?
A fainting spell is all. It's-- it's *nothing*.
She's no *good* to us if she can't *work*.
And that goes for the *lot* of you.
Now, *march*.

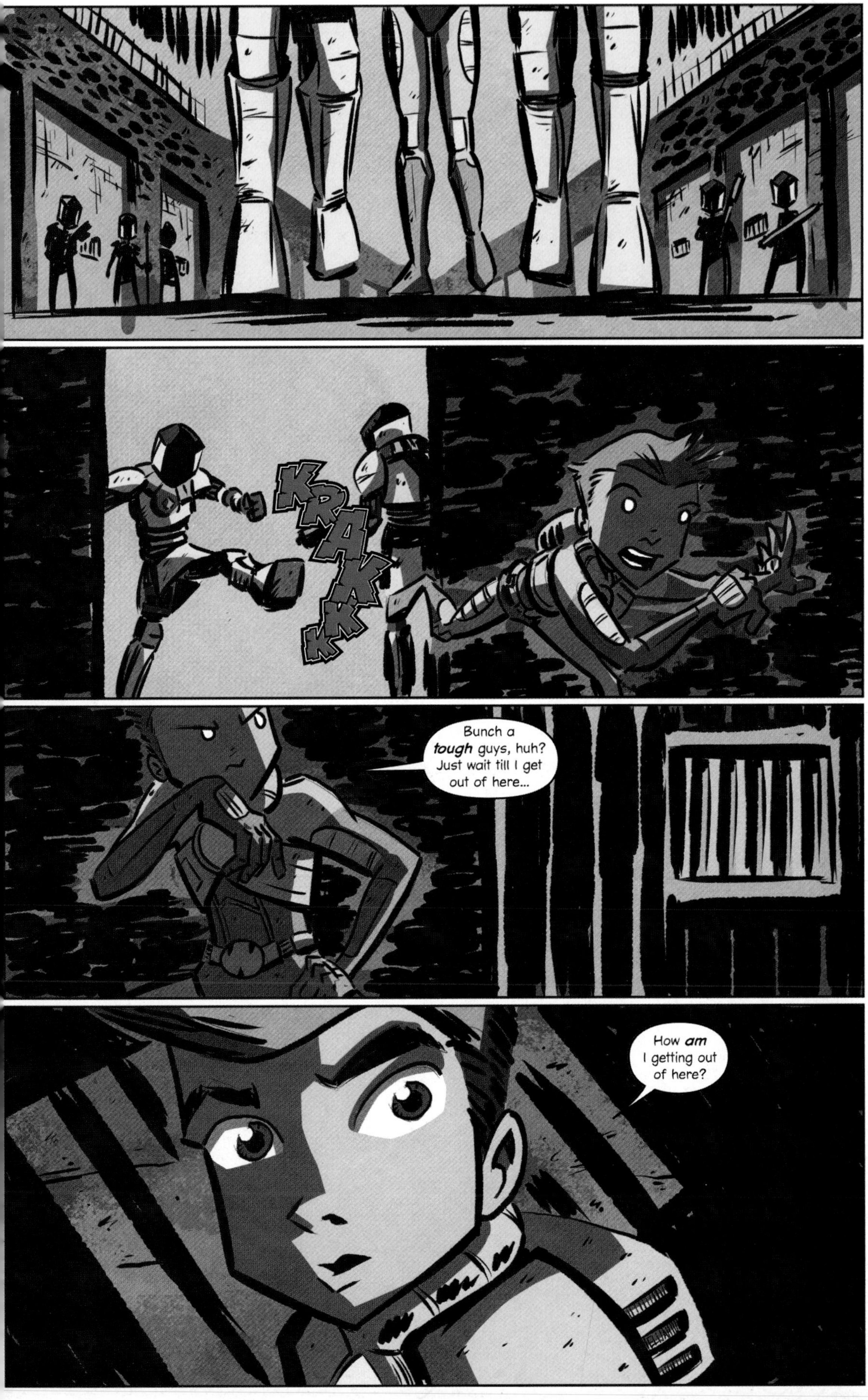
KRAKAKK
Bunch a tough guys, huh? Just wait till I get out of here...
How am I getting out of here?

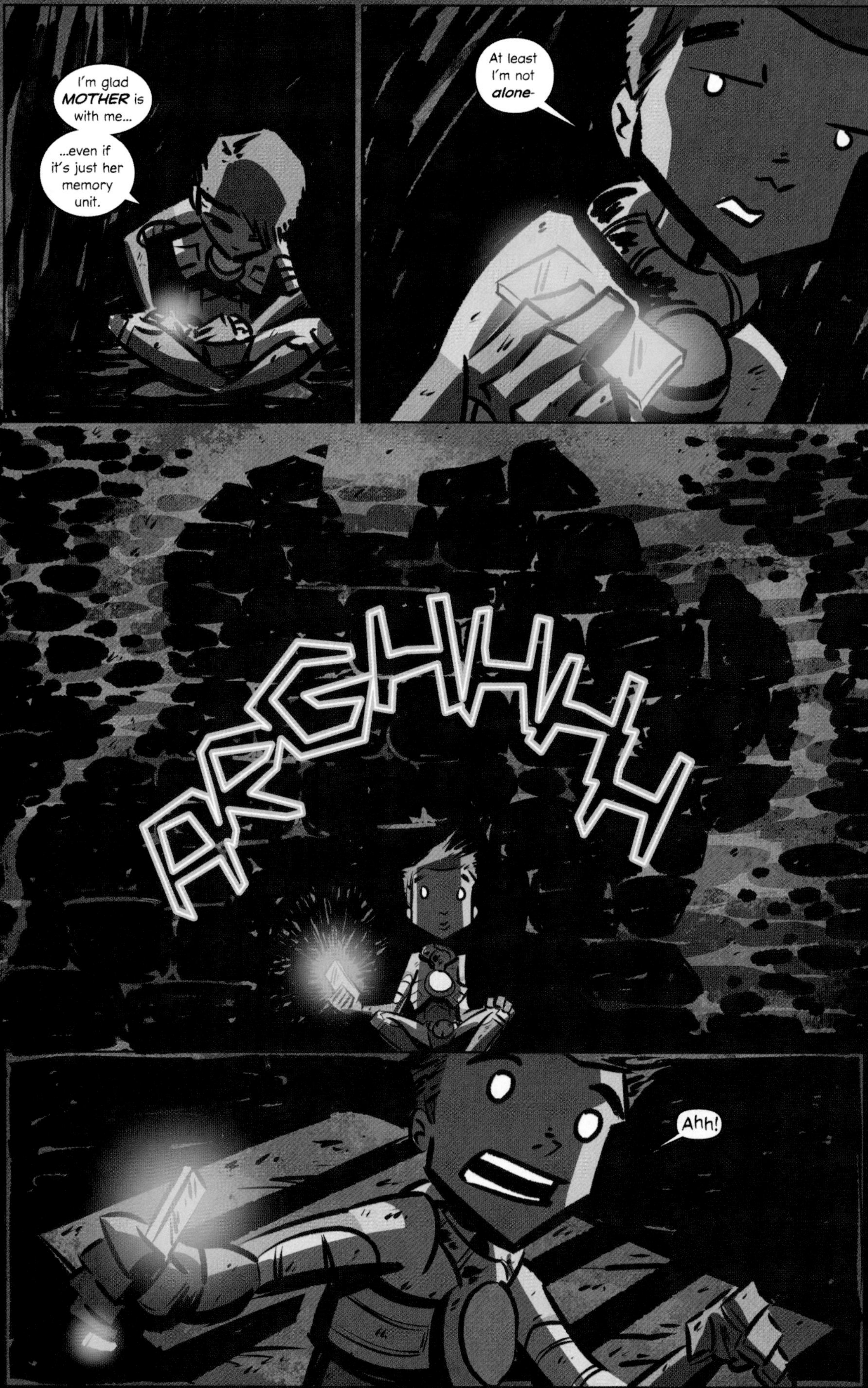

I'm glad ***MOTHER*** is with me...
...even if it's just her memory unit.
At least I'm not ***alone-***
ARGHHHH
Ahh!

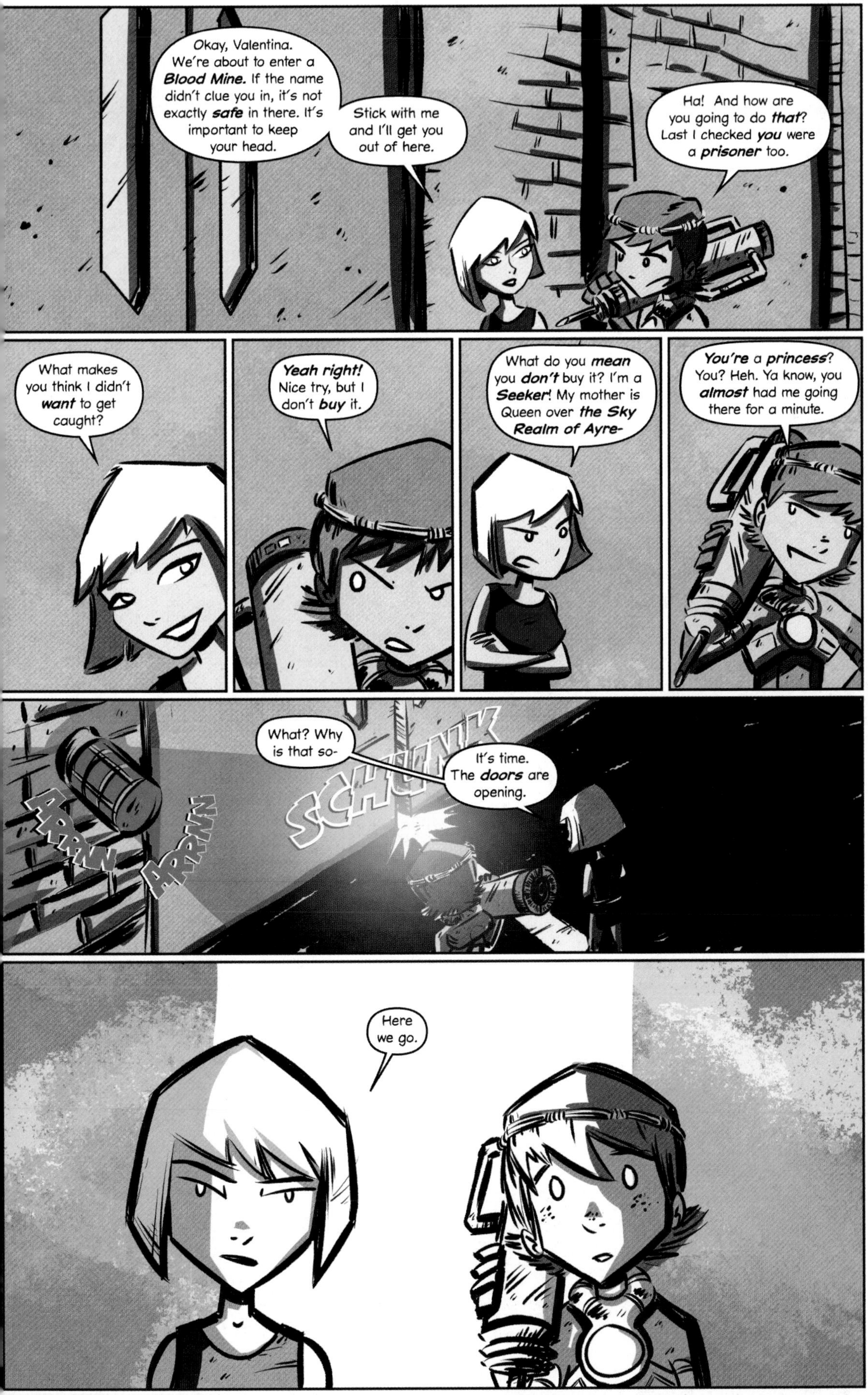
Okay, Valentina. We're about to enter a Blood Mine. If the name didn't clue you in, it's not exactly safe in there. It's important to keep your head.
Stick with me and I'll get you out of here.
Ha! And how are you going to do that? Last I checked you were a prisoner too.
What makes you think I didn't want to get caught?
Yeah right! Nice try, but I don't buy it.
What do you mean you don't buy it? I'm a Seeker! My mother is Queen over the Sky Realm of Ayre-
You're a princess? You? Heh. Ya know, you almost had me going there for a minute.
ARRNN
ARRNN
SCHUNK
What? Why is that so-
It's time. The doors are opening.
Here we go.

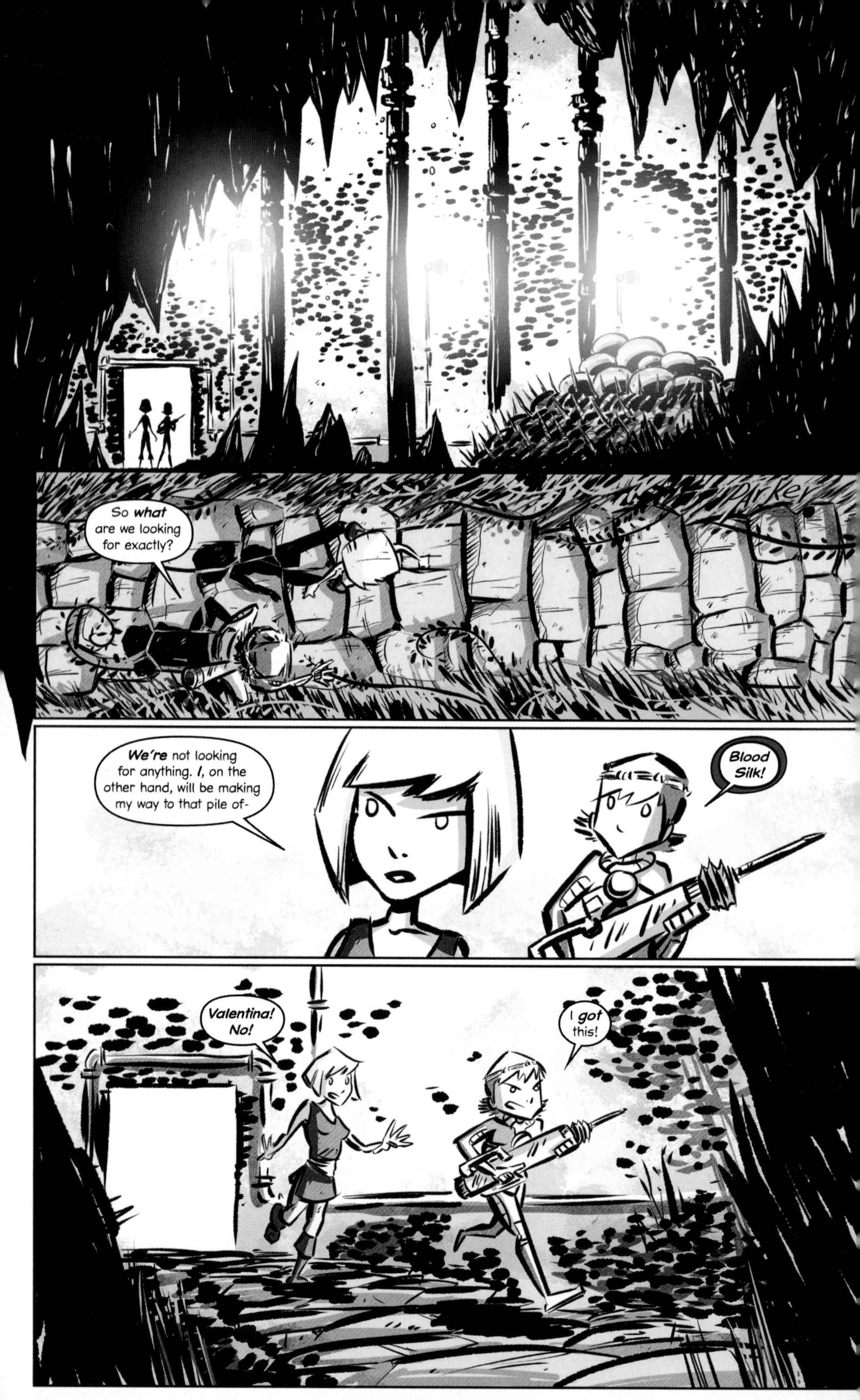
So *what* are we looking for exactly?
We're not looking for anything. *I*, on the other hand, will be making my way to that pile of-
Blood Silk!
Valentina! No!
I *got* this!

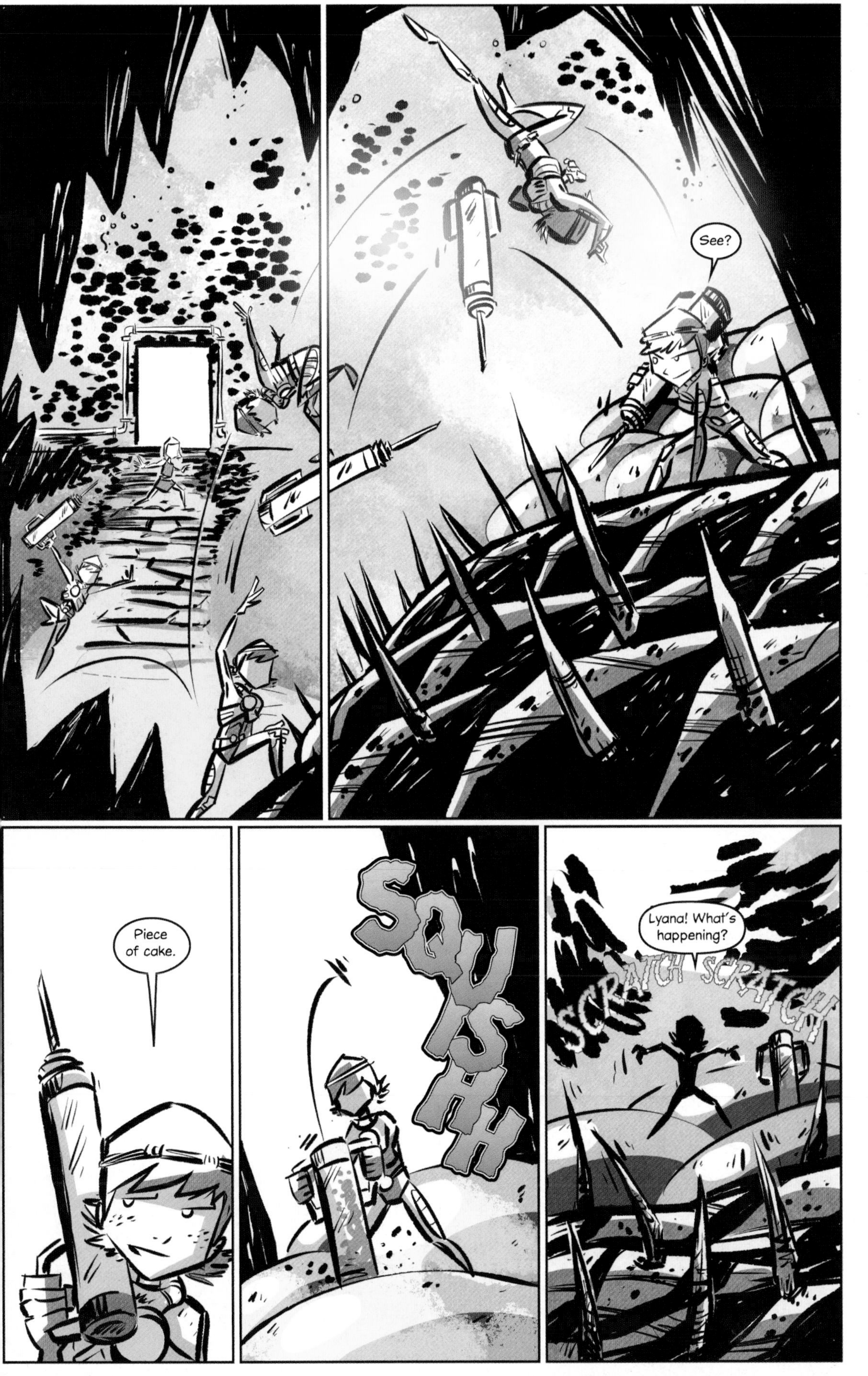
See?
Piece of cake.
SQUISHH
Lyana! What's happening?
SCRATCH SCRATCH SCRATCH

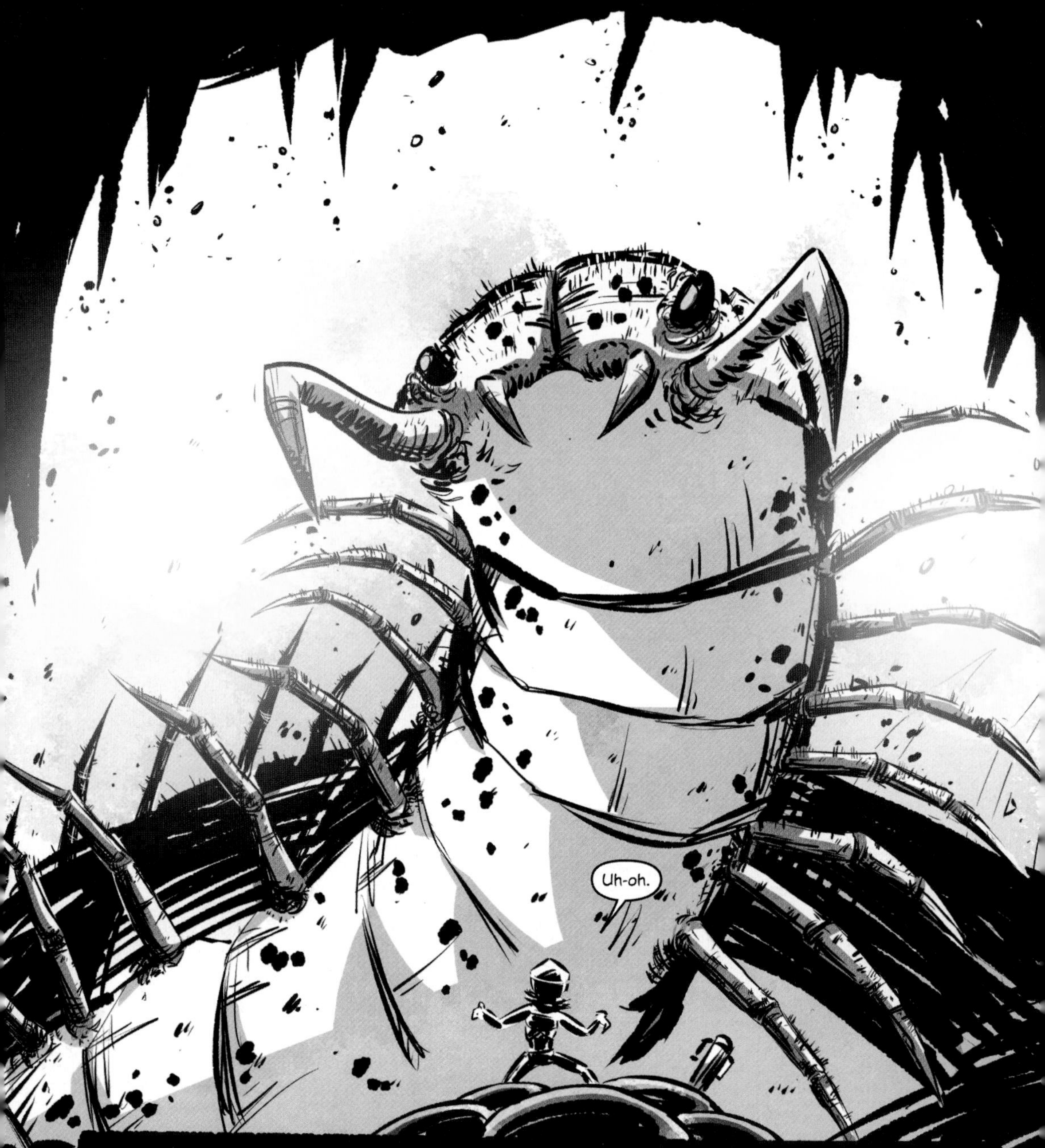
Uh-oh.

TRAPPED!

STORY BY ERIC GRISSOM / ART BY DAVID HALVORSON

TO BE CONTINUED NEXT ISSUE IN
"DEATH WITH A HUNDRED LEGS!"

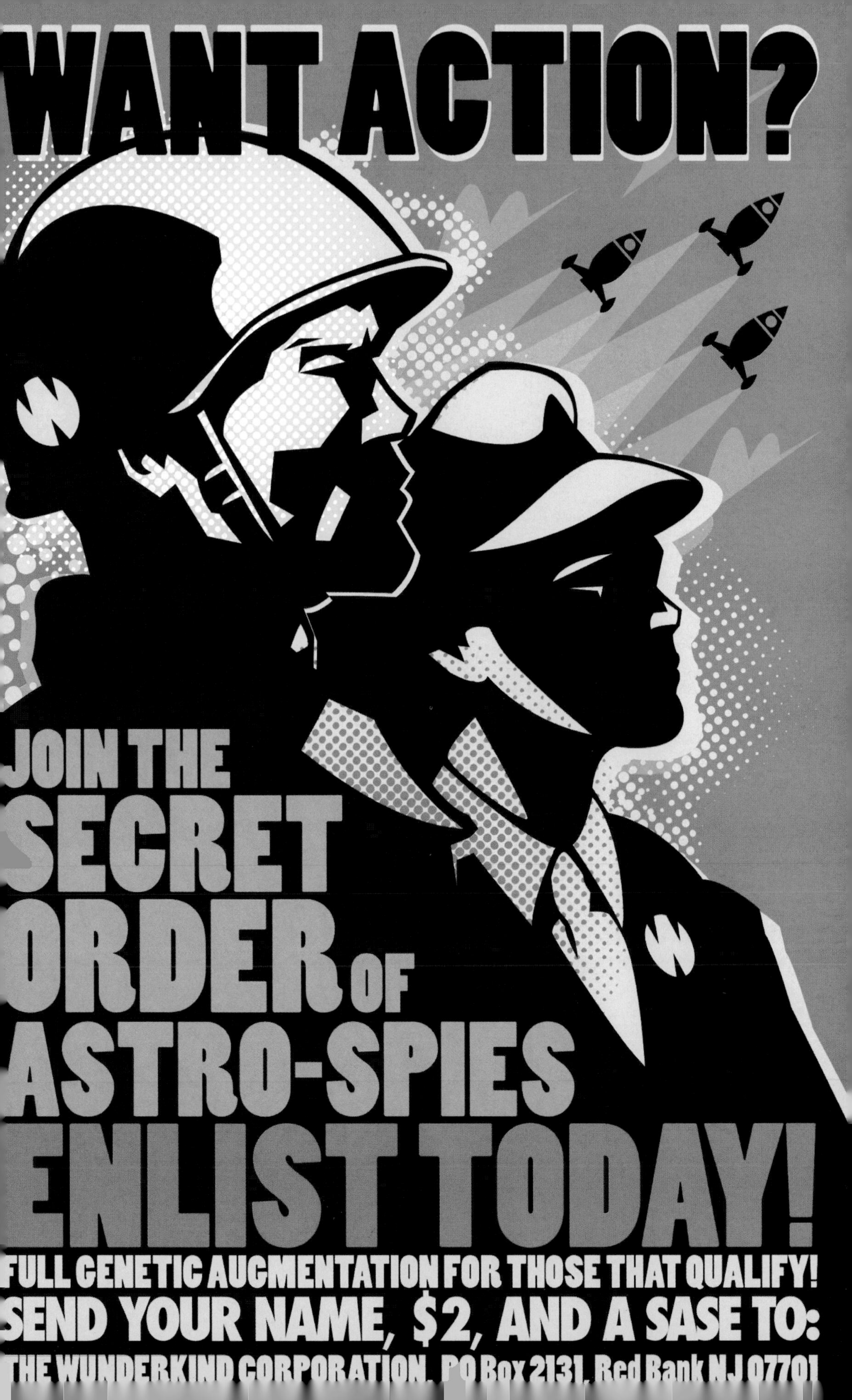
WANT ACTION?
JOIN THE
SECRET
ORDER OF
ASTRO-SPIES
ENLIST TODAY!
FULL GENETIC AUGMENTATION FOR THOSE THAT QUALIFY!
SEND YOUR NAME, $2, AND A SASE TO:
THE WUNDERKIND CORPORATION, PO Box 2131, Red Bank NJ 07701

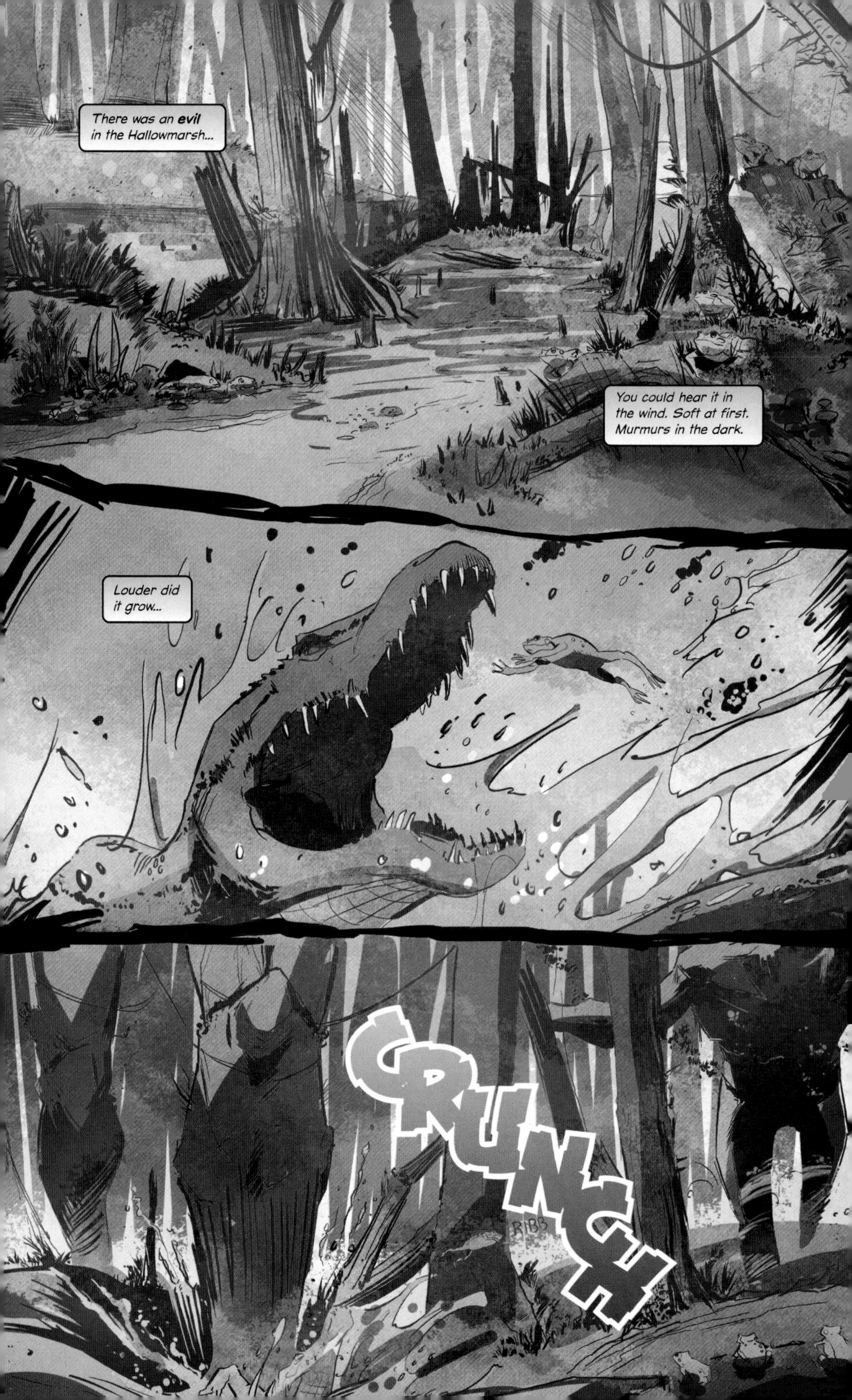
There was an **evil** in the Hallowmarsh...
You could hear it in the wind. Soft at first. Murmurs in the dark.
Louder did it grow...
CRUNCH
RIBB

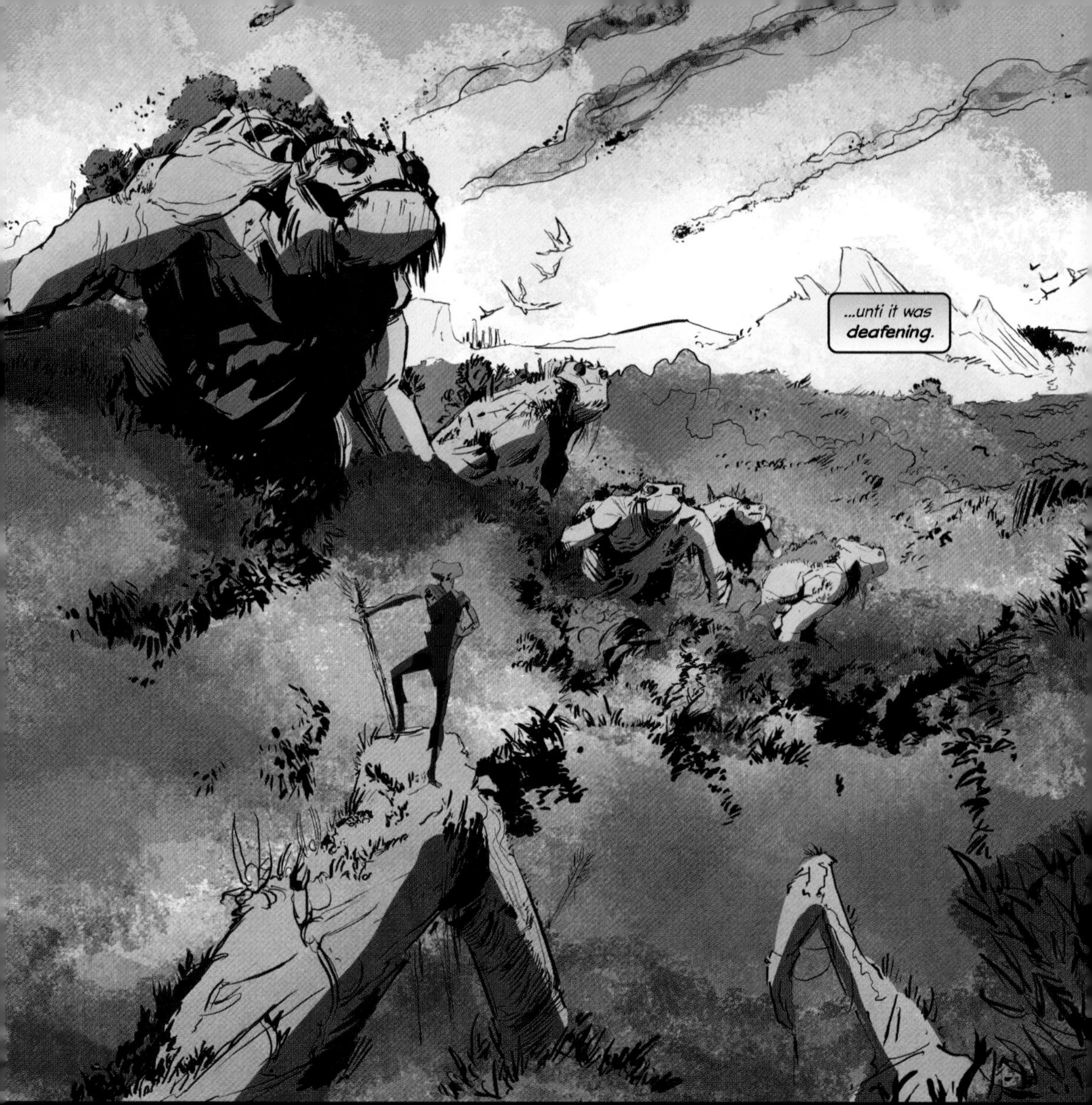
...unti it was **deafening.**

THE FROG RUNNER
A TALE FROM THE PLANET GIGANTIC

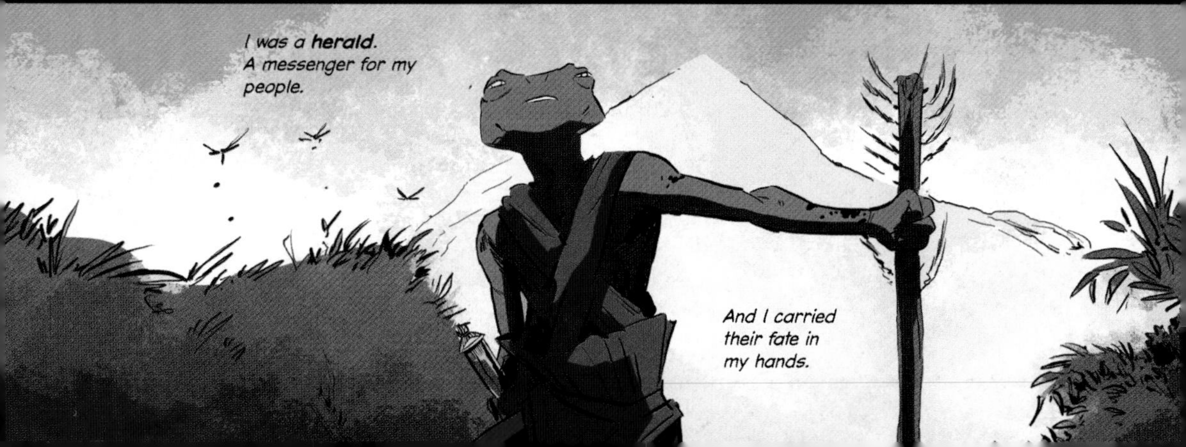
I was a **herald.** A messenger for my people.
And I carried their fate in my hands.

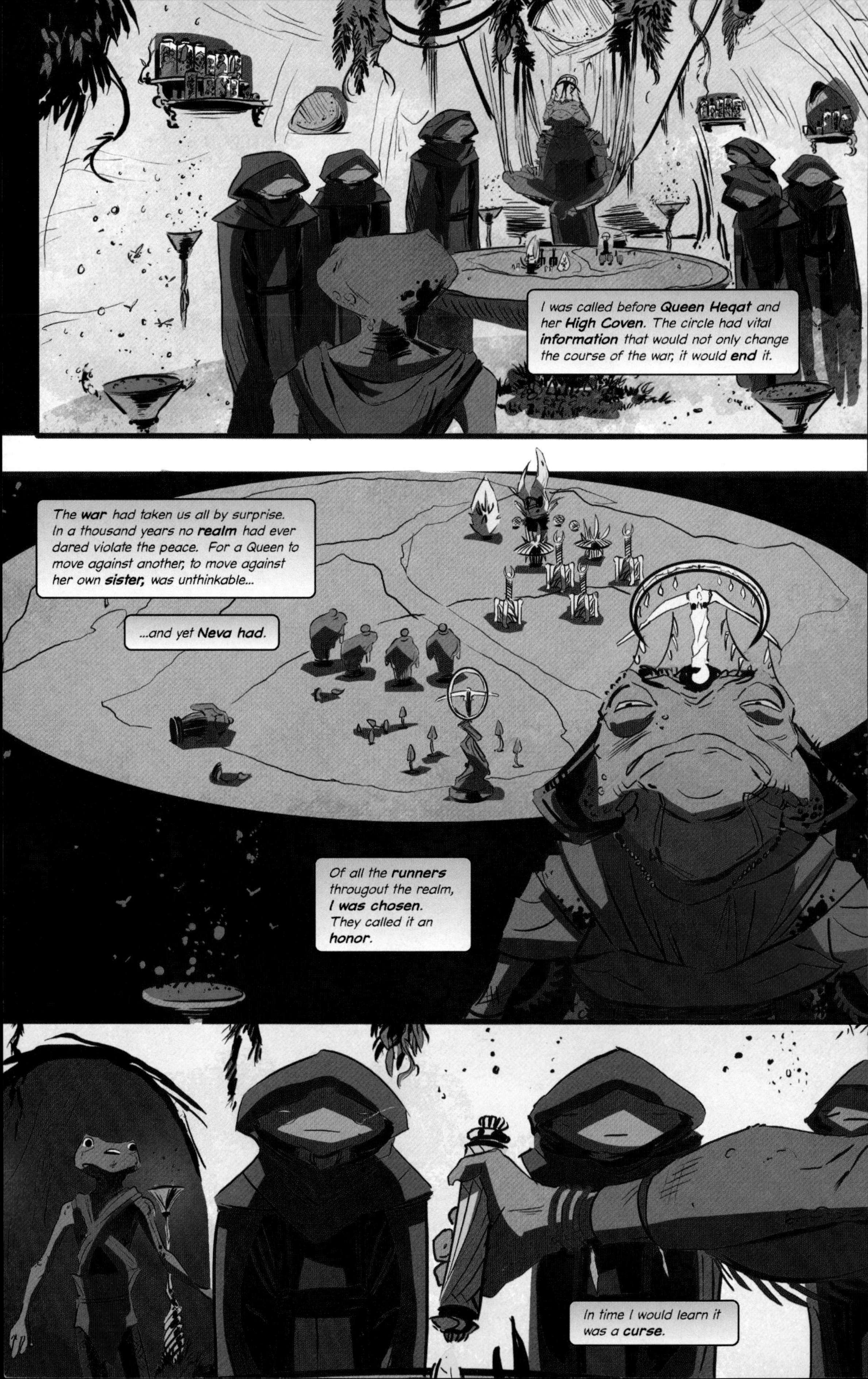
I was called before Queen Heqat and her High Coven. The circle had vital information that would not only change the course of the war, it would end it.
The war had taken us all by surprise. In a thousand years no realm had ever dared violate the peace. For a Queen to move against another, to move against her own sister, was unthinkable...
...and yet Neva had.
Of all the runners througout the realm, I was chosen. They called it an honor.
In time I would learn it was a curse.

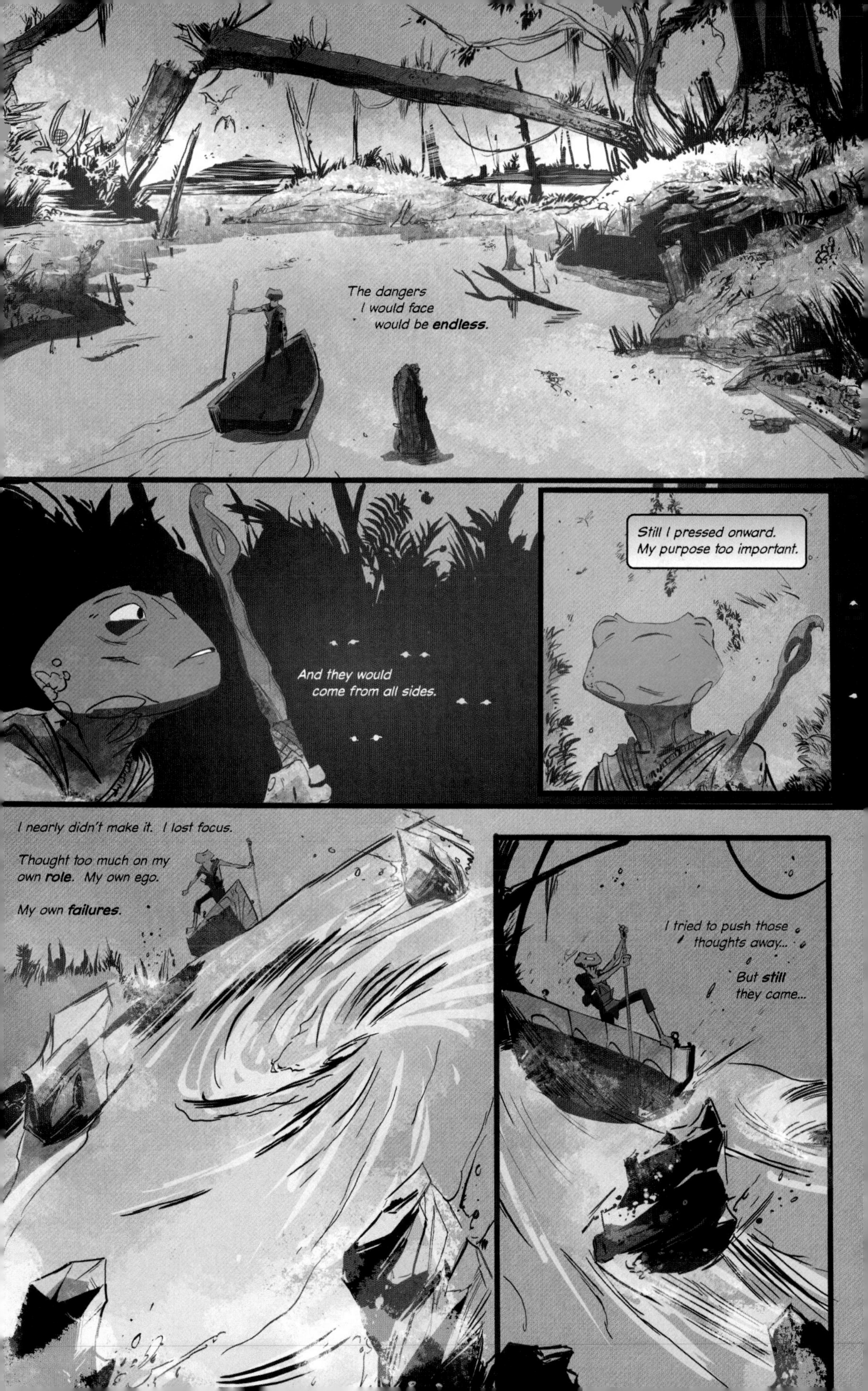
The dangers I would face would be **endless.**
And they would come from all sides.
Still I pressed onward. My purpose too important.
I nearly didn't make it. I lost focus.
Thought too much on my own **role**. My own ego.
My own **failures**.
I tried to push those thoughts away...
But **still** they came...

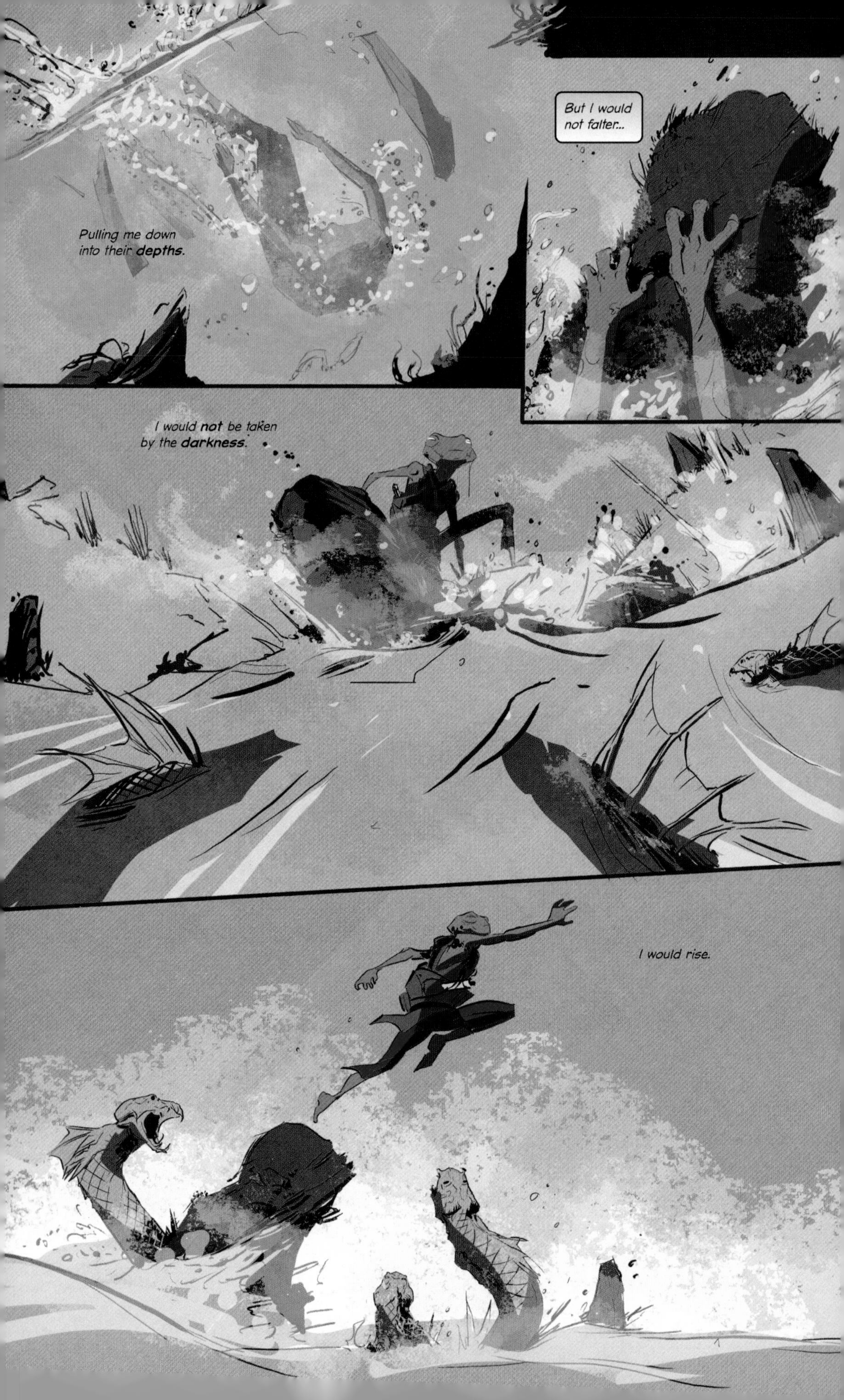

Pulling me down into their **depths**.
But I would not falter...
I would **not** be taken by the **darkness**.
I would rise.

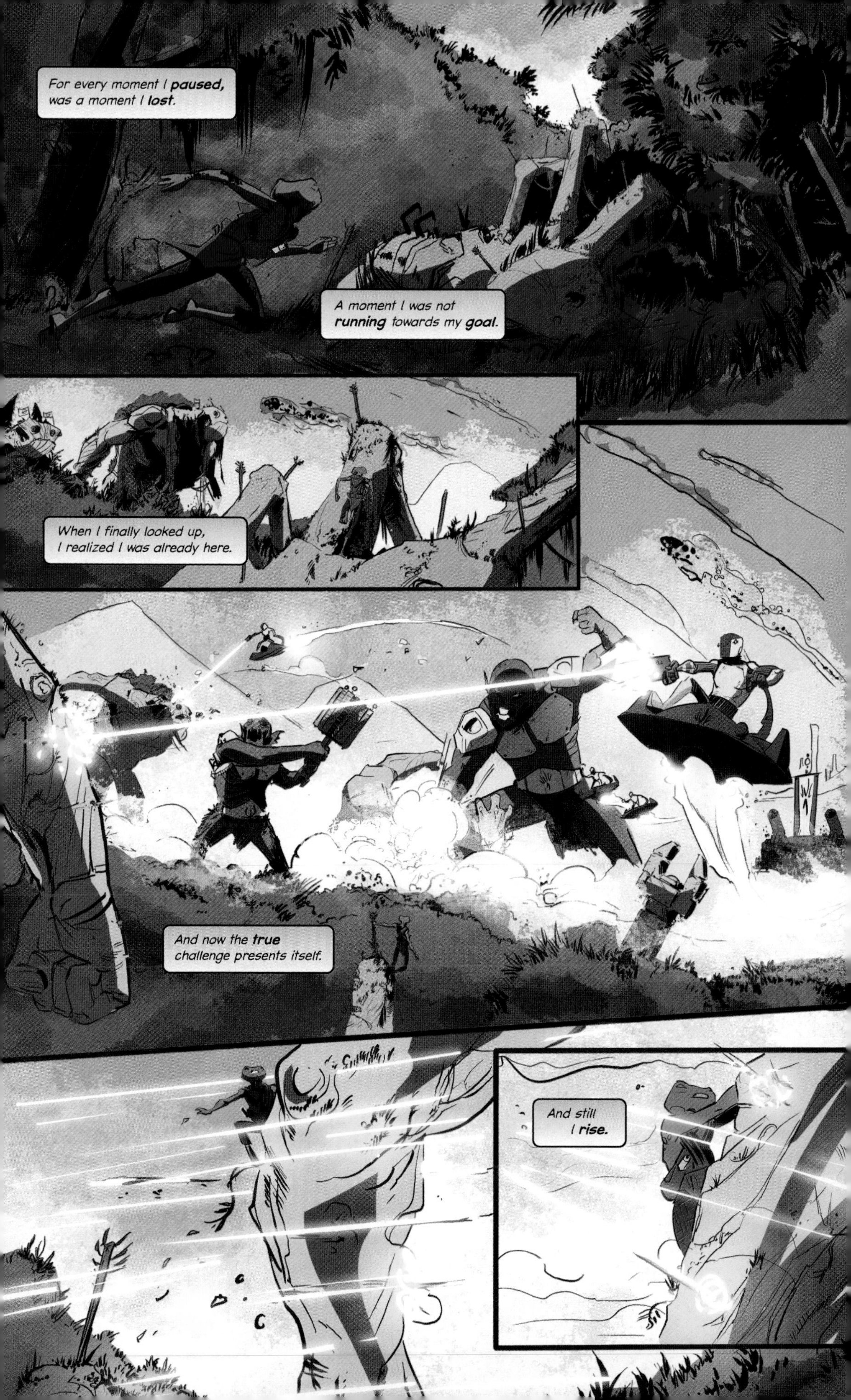
For every moment I **paused,** was a moment I **lost**.
A moment I was not **running** towards my **goal**.
When I finally looked up, I realized I was already here.
And now the **true** challenge presents itself.
And still I **rise.**

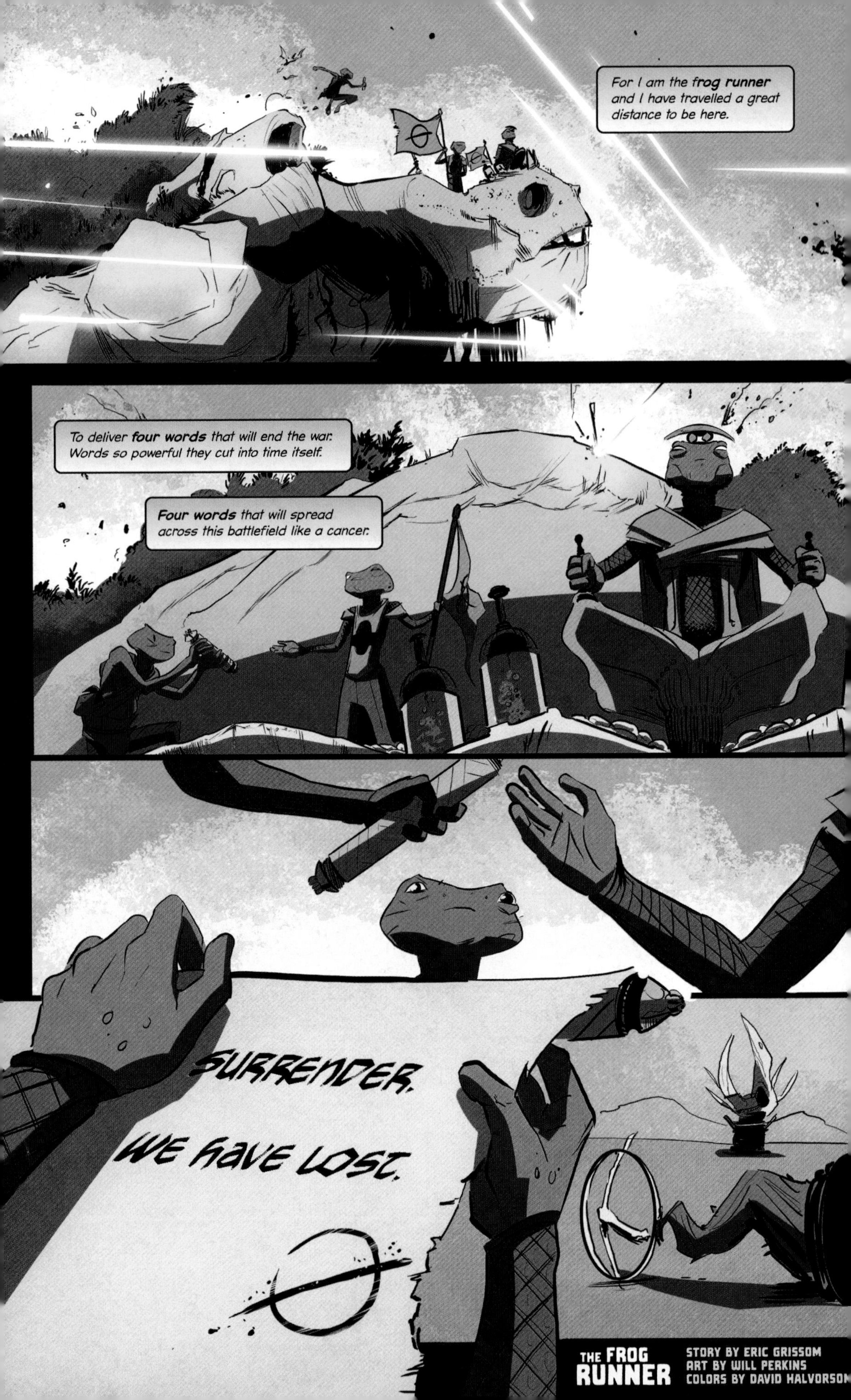

For I am the **frog runner** and I have travelled a great distance to be here.
To deliver **four words** that will end the war. Words so powerful they cut into time itself.
Four words that will spread across this battlefield like a cancer.
SURRENDER.
WE HAVE LOST.
THE FROG RUNNER
STORY BY ERIC GRISSOM
ART BY WILL PERKINS
COLORS BY DAVID HALVORSON

MINECRAFT

The official handbooks packed with guides, exclusive interviews and tips from experts!

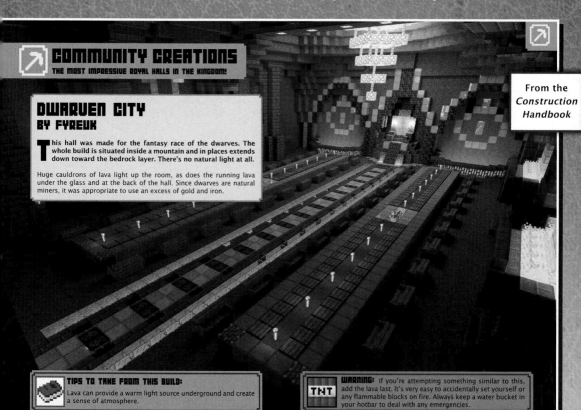

↗ COMMUNITY CREATIONS
THE MOST IMPRESSIVE ROYAL HALLS IN THE KINGDOM!

DWARVEN CITY
BY FYREUK

This hall was made for the fantasy race of the dwarves. The whole build is situated inside a mountain and in places extends down toward the bedrock layer. There's no natural light at all.

Huge cauldrons of lava light up the room, as does the running lava under the glass and at the back of the hall. Since dwarves are natural miners, it was appropriate to use an excess of gold and iron.

From the Construction Handbook

TIPS TO TAKE FROM THIS BUILD:
Lava can provide a warm light source underground and create a sense of atmosphere.

TNT WARNING: If you're attempting something similar to this, add the lava last. It's very easy to accidentally set yourself or any flammable blocks on fire. Always keep a water bucket in your hotbar to deal with any emergencies.

Includes All Four Handbooks!

MINECRAFT
REDSTONE HANDBOOK

MINECRAFT
ESSENTIAL HANDBOOK

MINECRAFT
CONSTRUCTION HANDBOOK

MINECRAFT
COMBAT HANDBOOK

For more tips, visit SCHOLASTIC.COM/MINECRAFT

SCHOLASTIC
open a world of possible

SCHOLASTIC and associated logos are trademarks and/or registered trademarks of Scholastic Inc. © 2014 Mojang. All Rights Reserved. Minecraft is a trademark of Notch Development AB.

READ MORE NOW

Planet Gigantic - Action Lab
www.actionlabcomics.com

00211

7 00465 77246 6

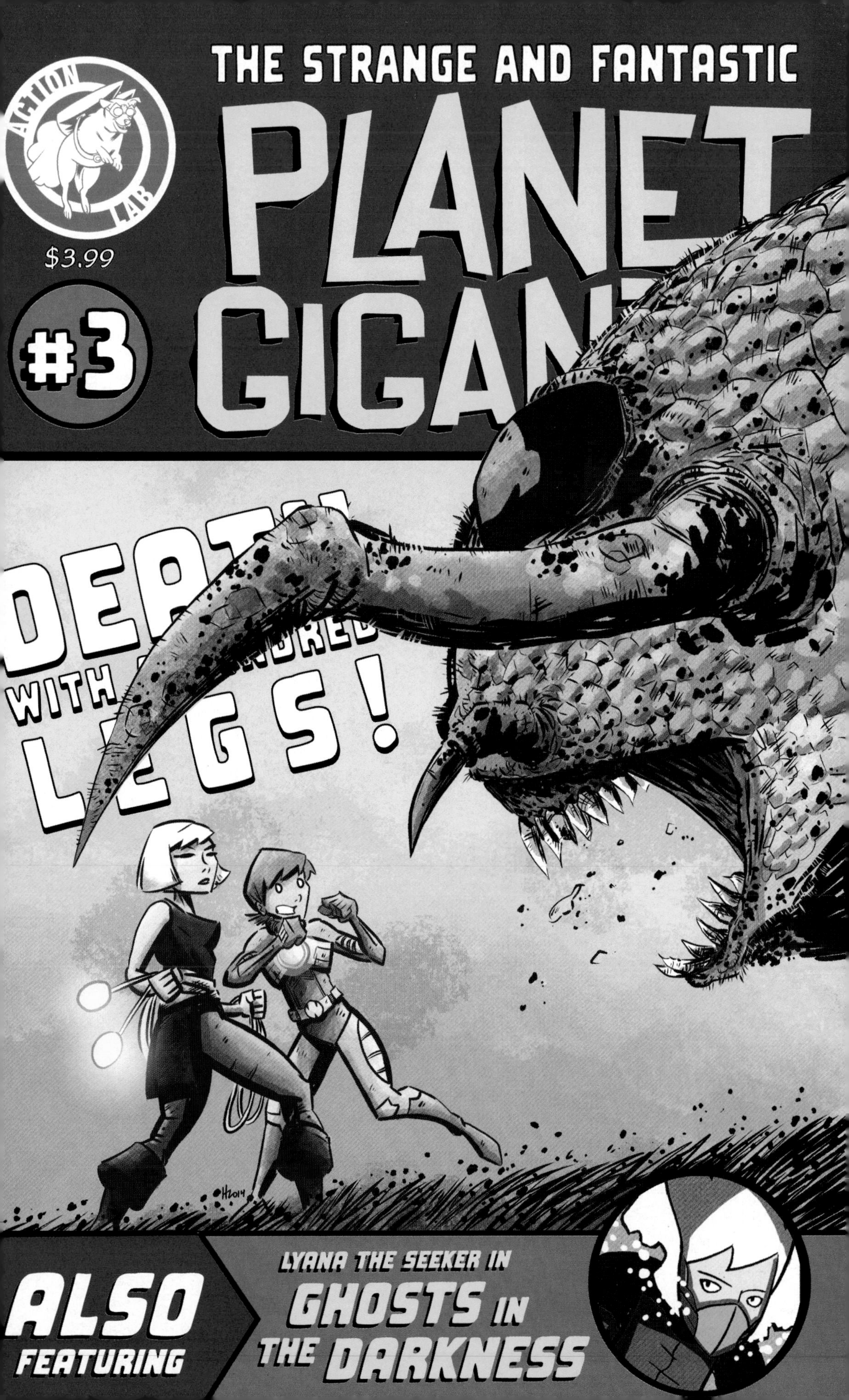
ACTION LAB
$3.99
THE STRANGE AND FANTASTIC
PLANET
GIGAN
#3
DEA
WITH
NDRED
L G S!
ALSO
FEATURING
LYANA THE SEEKER IN
GHOSTS IN
THE DARKNESS

PLANET GIGANTIC

"Death with a Hundred Legs!"
story and letters by ERIC GRISSOM
art and cover by DAVID HALVORSON

"Ghosts in the Darkness"
story and letters by ERIC GRISSOM
art by PHIL SLOAN
colors by DAVID HALVORSON

fonts by COMICRAFT
planetgigantic.com

publisher BRYAN SEATON
president KEVIN FREEMAN
editor-in-chief SHAWN GABBORIN
creative director DAVE DWONCH
co-directors of marketing JAMAL IGLE & KELLY DALE
social media director JIM DIETZ
education outreach director JEREMY WHITLEY
associate editors CHAD CICCONI & COLLEEN BOYD

PLANET GIGANTIC #3. Published by Action Lab Entertainment. Planet Gigantic, its logos and all related characters are TM and © 2014 Eric Grissom and David Halvorson. All rights reserved. The characters and events presented are purely fictional. Any similarities to events or persons living or dead is purely coincidental. No portion of this publication may be reproduced without the written consent from Action Lab Entertainment, Eric Grissom or David Halvorson. For more information visit planetgigantic.com or actionlab.com. Printed in Canada.

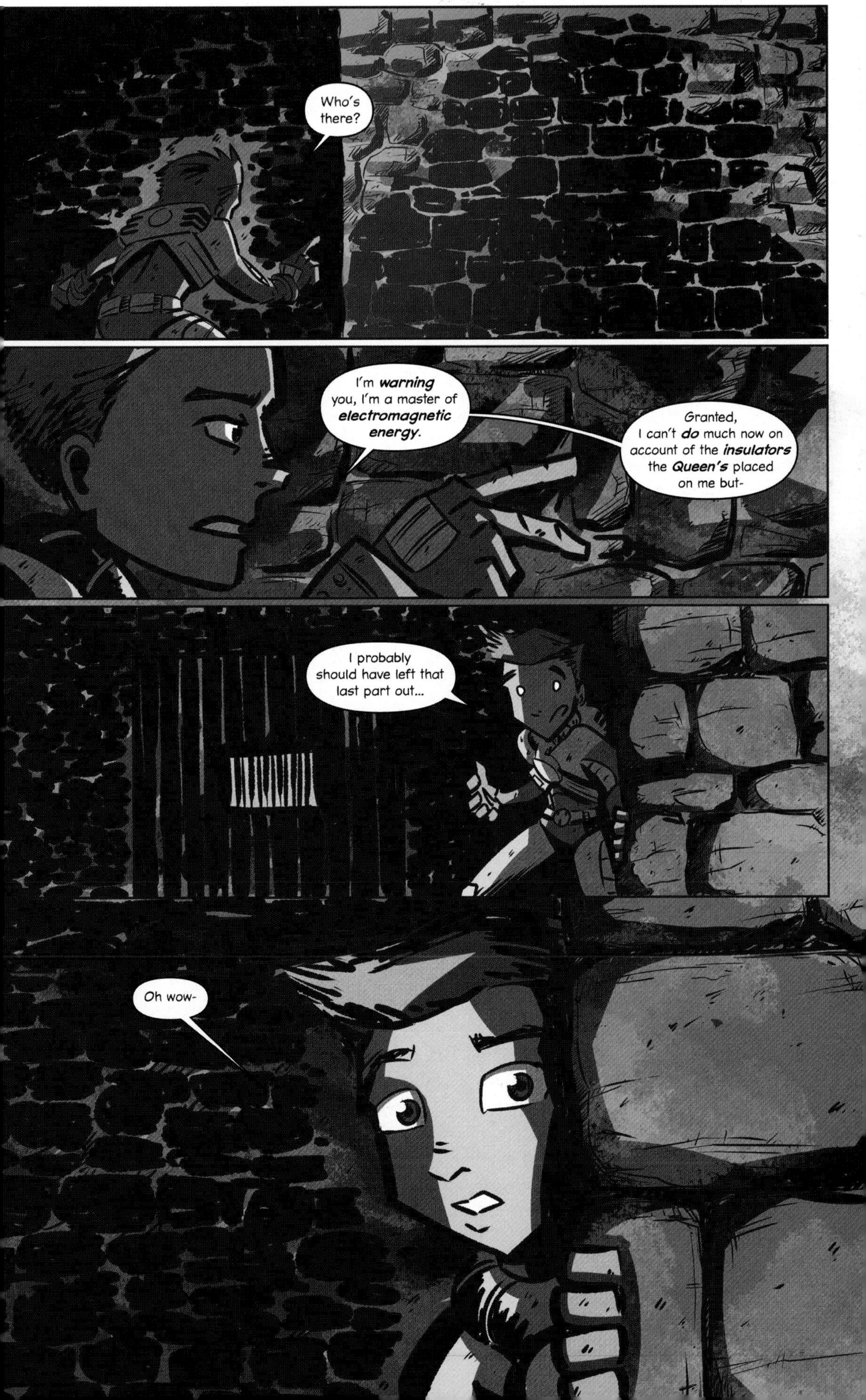
Who's there?
I'm **warning** you, I'm a master of ***electromagnetic*** energy.
Granted, I can't **do** much now on account of the ***insulators*** the ***Queen's*** placed on me but-
I probably should have left that last part out...
Oh wow-

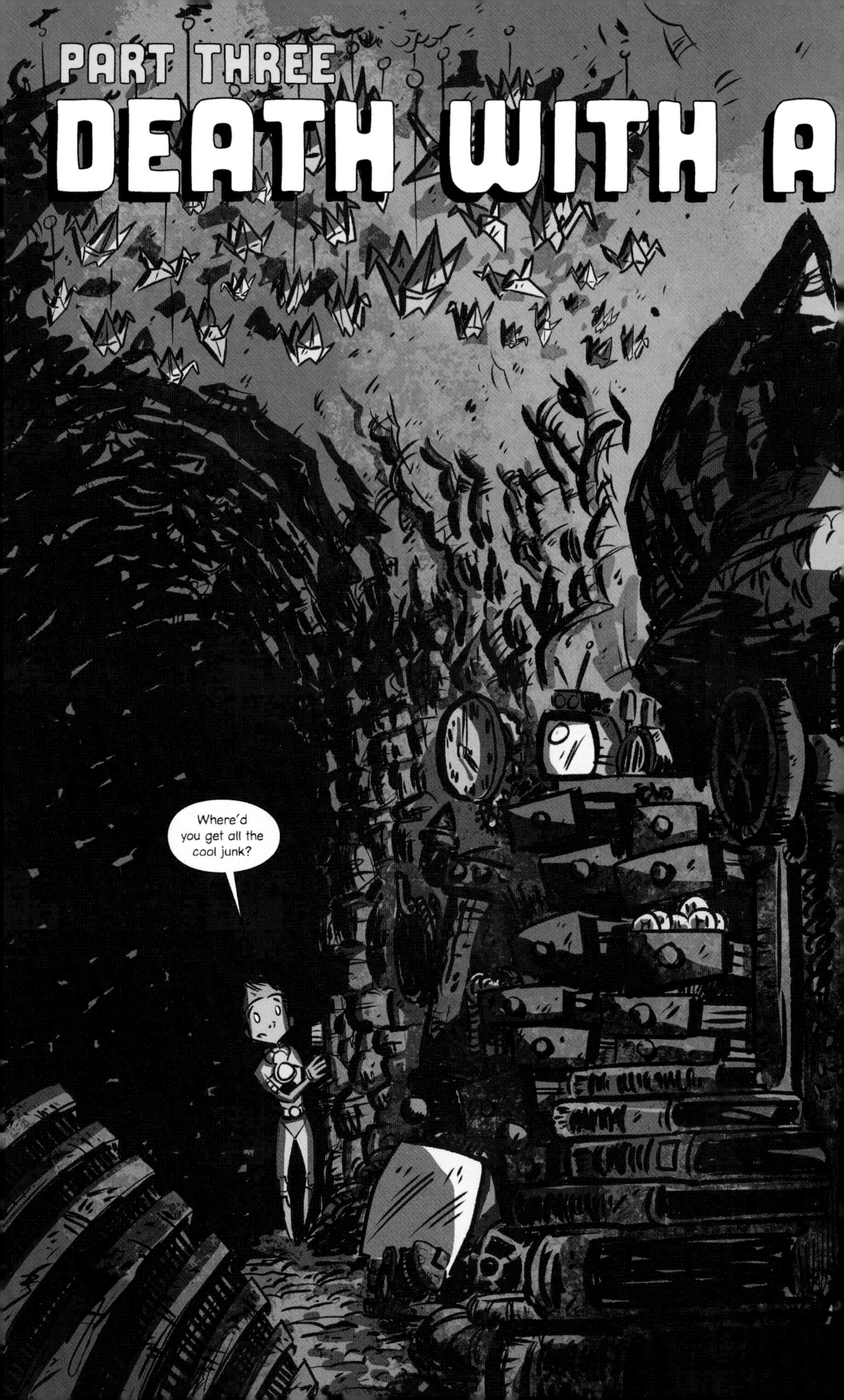
PART THREE
DEATH WITH A
Where'd you get all the cool junk?

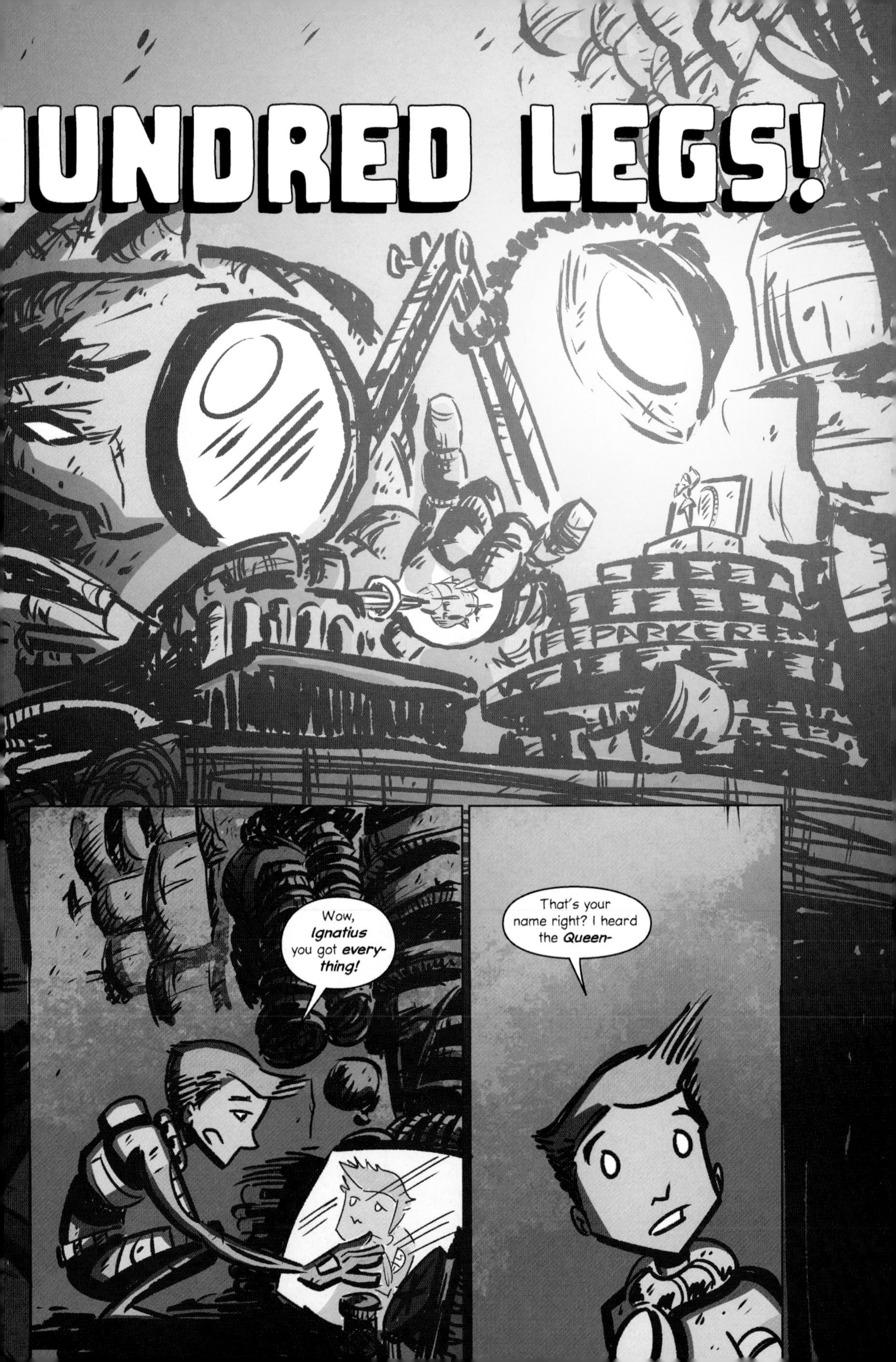
UNDRED LEGS!
PARKER
Wow, Ignatius you got every-thing!
That's your name right? I heard the Queen-

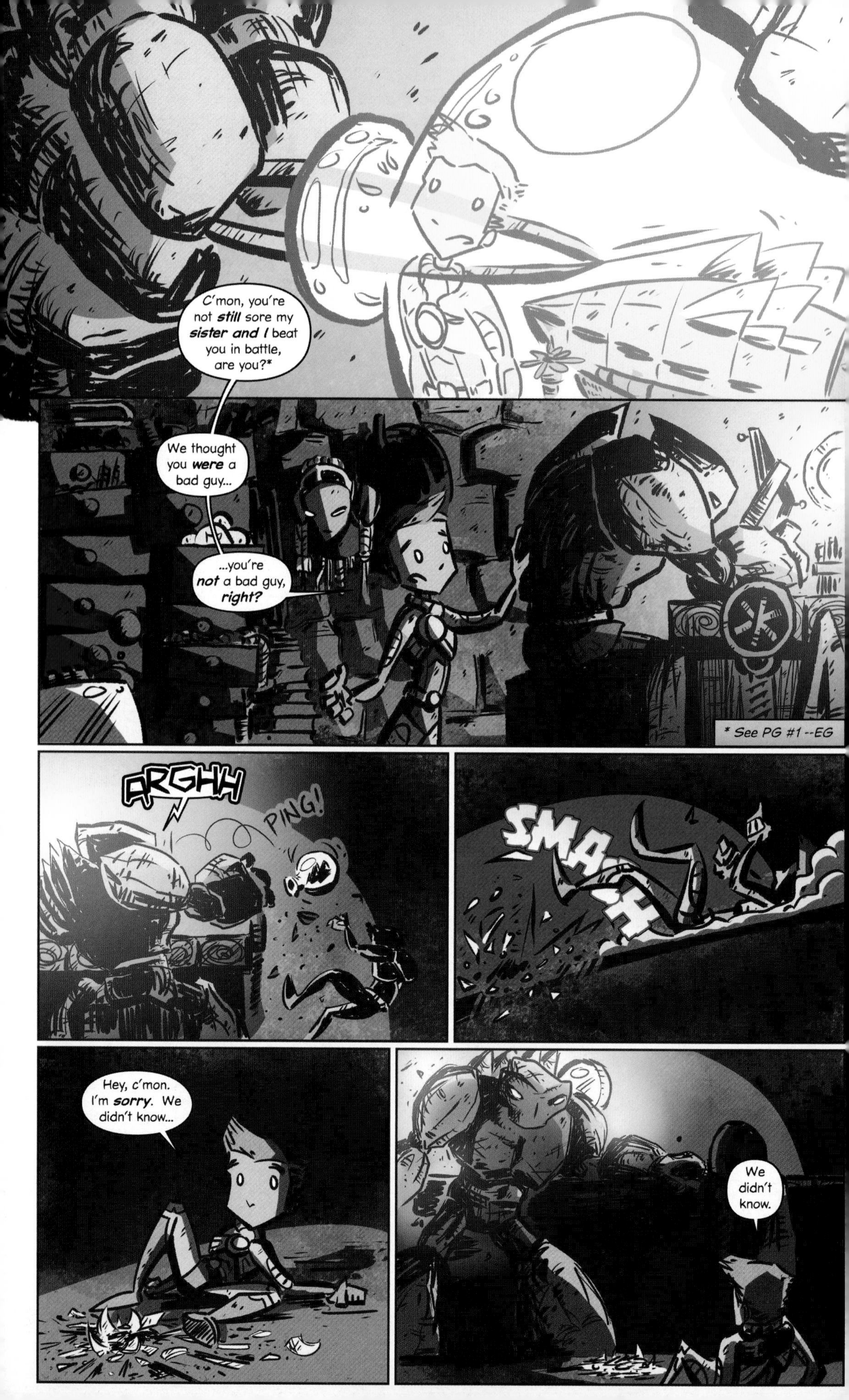
C'mon, you're not still sore my sister and I beat you in battle, are you?*
We thought you were a bad guy...
...you're not a bad guy, right?
* See PG #1 --EG
ARGHH
PING!
SMASH
Hey, c'mon. I'm sorry. We didn't know...
We didn't know.

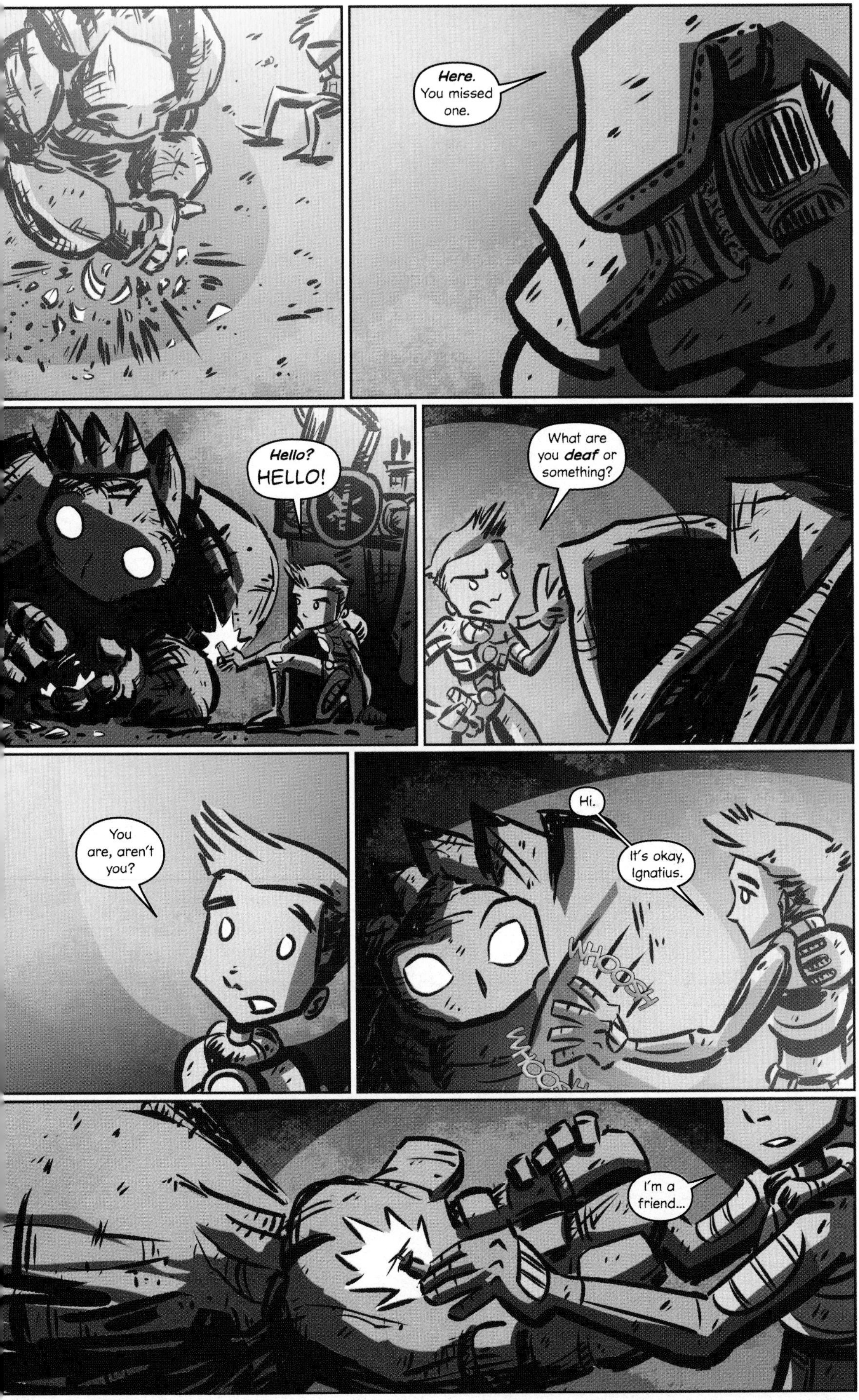
Here. You missed one.
Hello? HELLO!
What are you deaf or something?
You are, aren't you?
Hi.
It's okay, Ignatius.
WHOOSH
WHOOSH
I'm a friend...

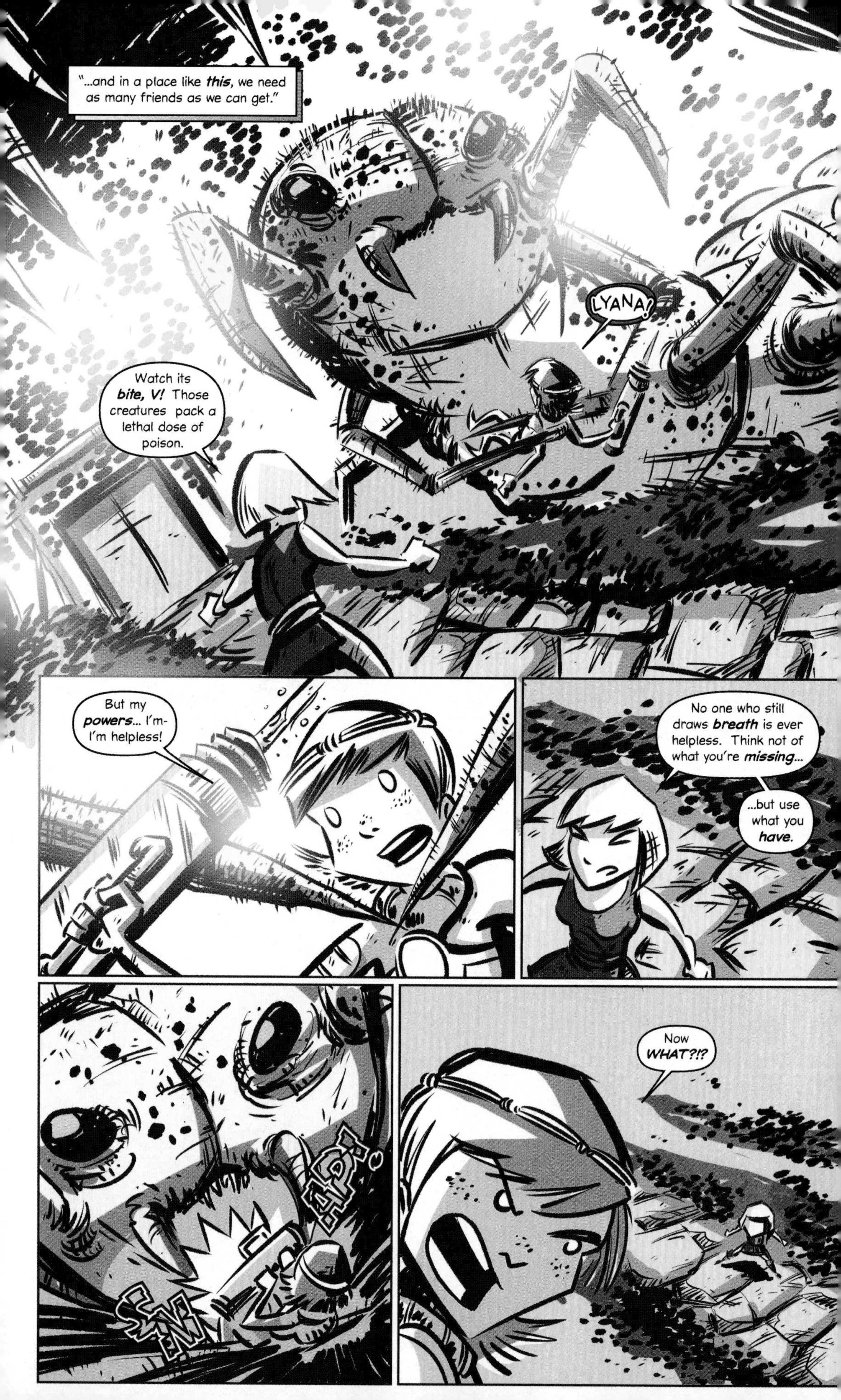
"...and in a place like *this*, we need as many friends as we can get."
LYANA!
Watch its *bite, V!* Those creatures pack a lethal dose of poison.
But my *powers*... I'm-I'm helpless!
No one who still draws *breath* is ever helpless. Think not of what you're *missing*...
...but use what you *have*.
Now *WHAT?!?*

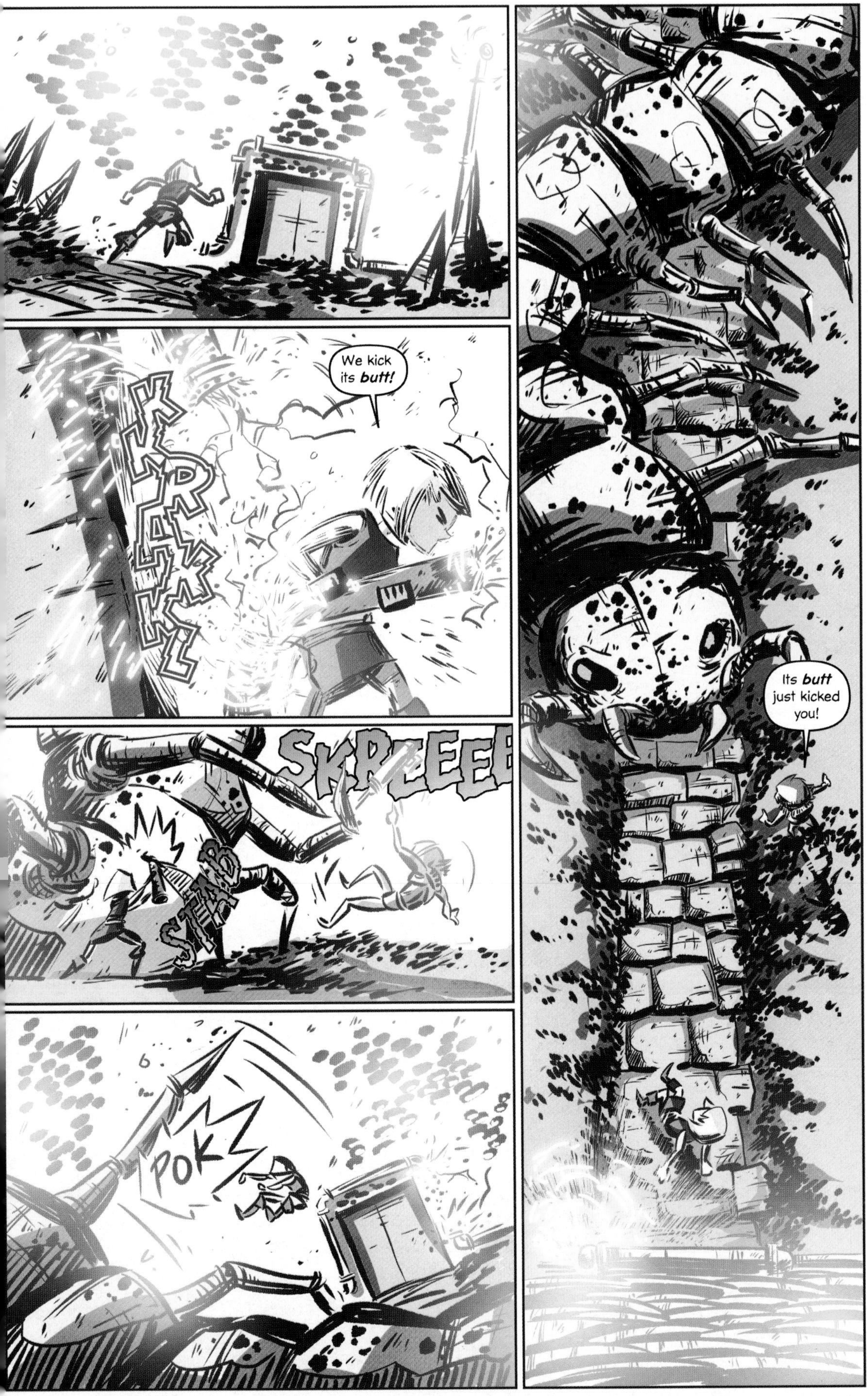
We kick its *butt!*
SKREEE
STAB
POK
Its *butt* just kicked you!

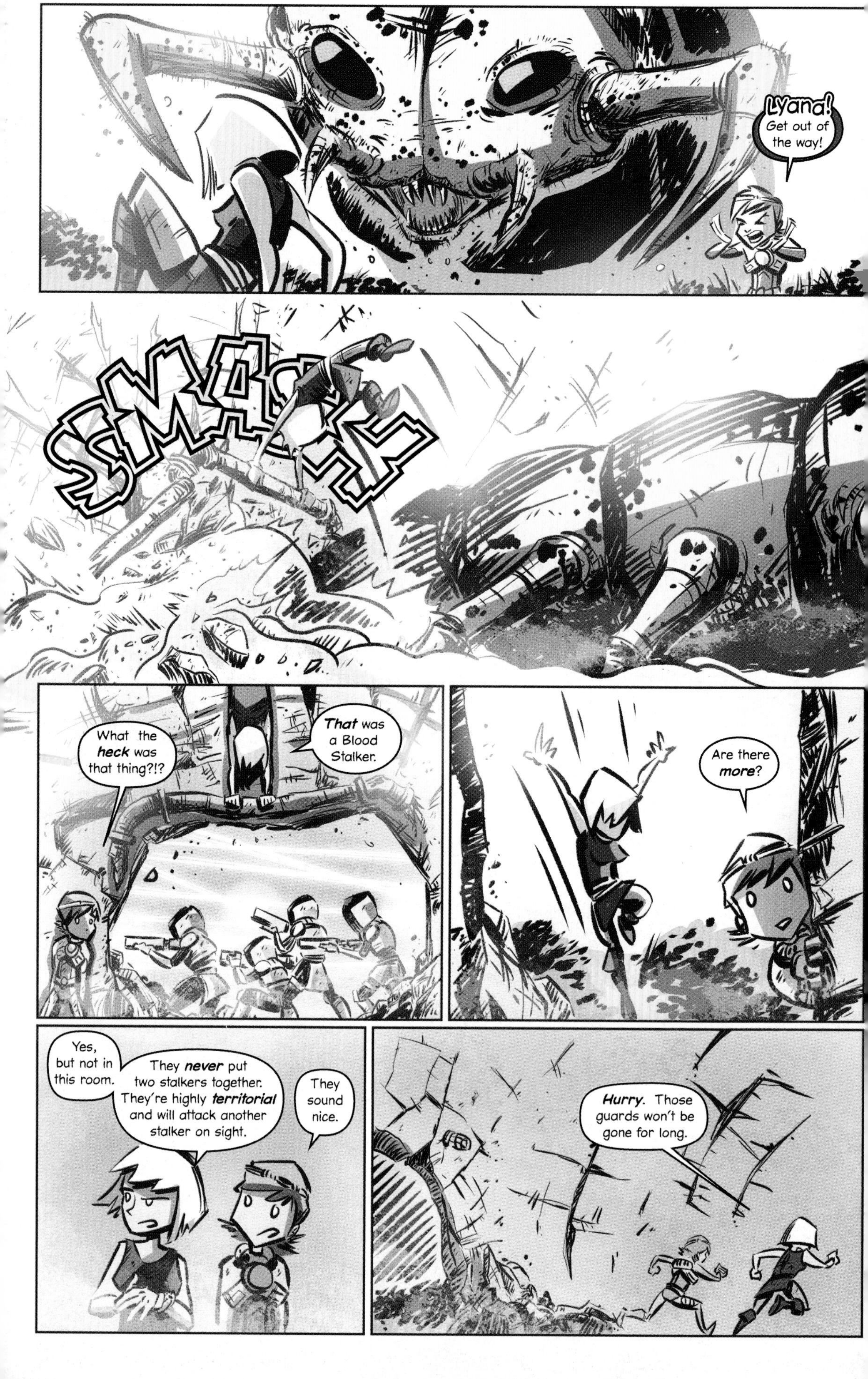

Lyana! Get out of the way!
SMASH
What the heck was that thing?!?
That was a Blood Stalker.
Are there more?
Yes, but not in this room.
They never put two stalkers together. They're highly territorial and will attack another stalker on sight.
They sound nice.
Hurry. Those guards won't be gone for long.

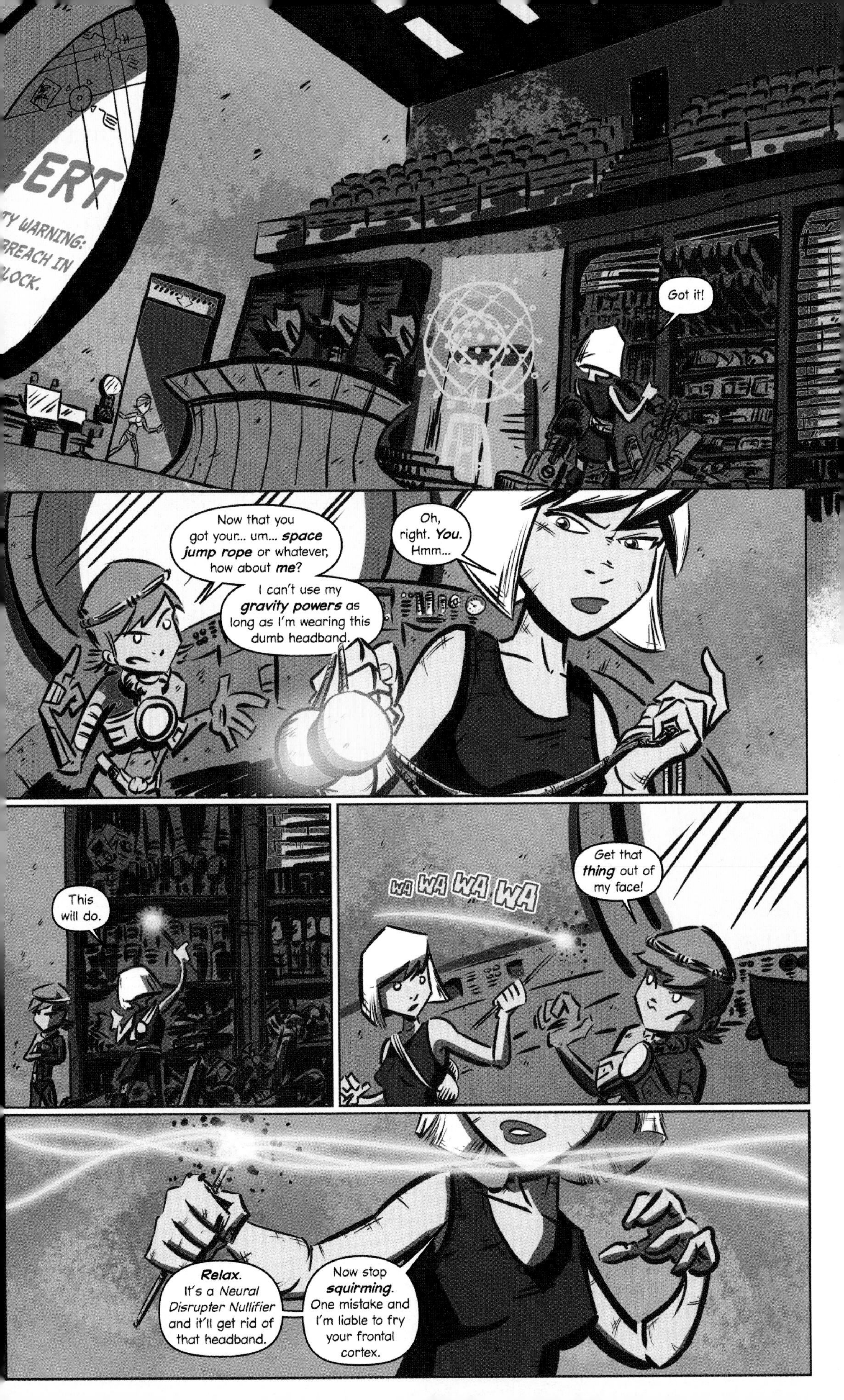

ERT
TY WARNING:
REACH IN
LOCK.
Got it!
Now that you got your... um... *space jump rope* or whatever, how about *me*?
I can't use my *gravity powers* as long as I'm wearing this dumb headband.
Oh, right. *You*. Hmm...
This will do.
WA WA WA WA
Get that *thing* out of my face!
Relax. It's a *Neural Disrupter Nullifier* and it'll get rid of that headband.
Now stop *squirming*. One mistake and I'm liable to fry your frontal cortex.

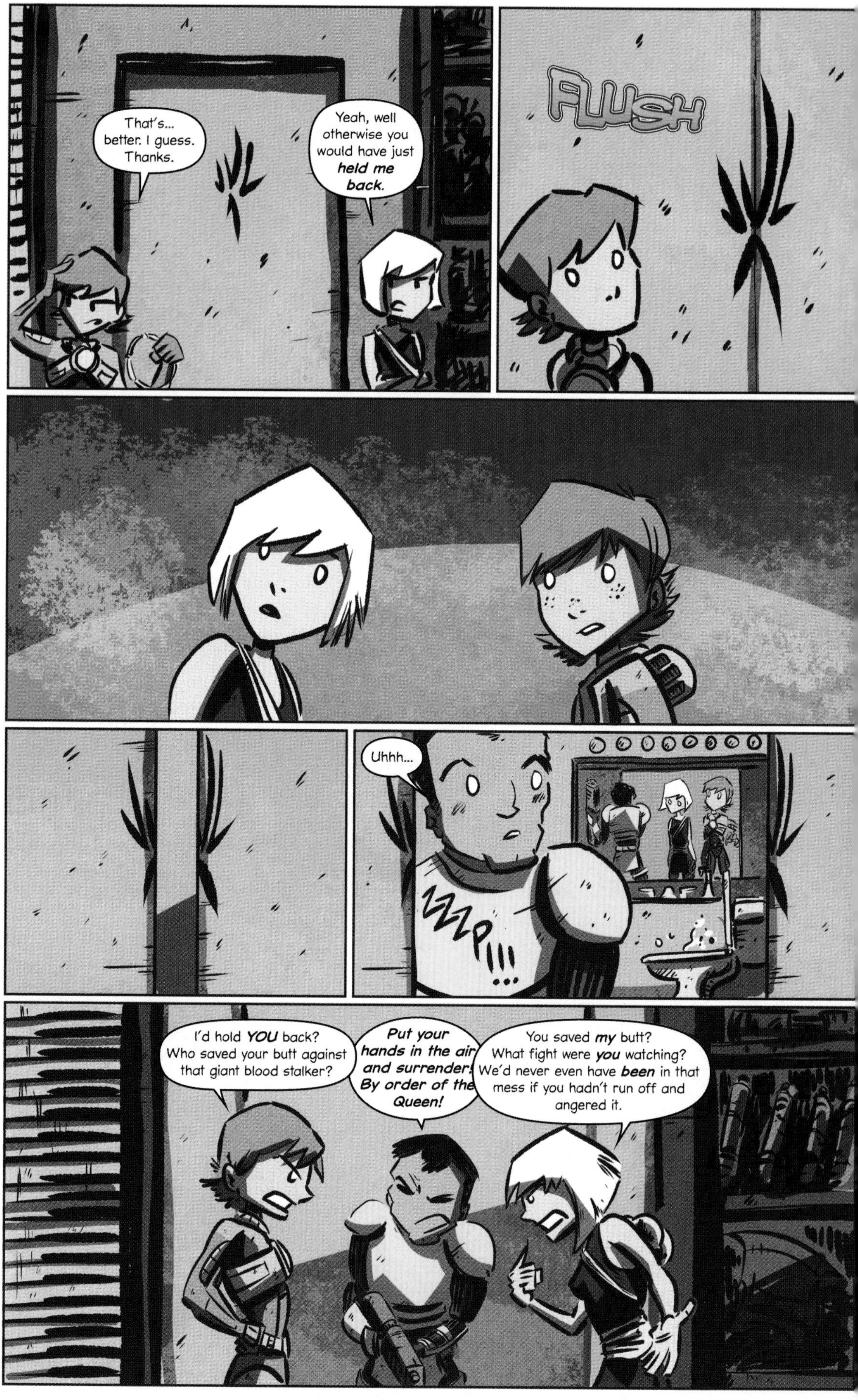
That's... better. I guess. Thanks.
Yeah, well otherwise you would have just **held me back**.
FLUSH
Uhhh...
ZZZP!!!...
I'd hold *YOU* back? Who saved your butt against that giant blood stalker?
Put your hands in the air and surrender! By order of the Queen!
You saved *my* butt? What fight were *you* watching? We'd never even have *been* in that mess if you hadn't run off and angered it.

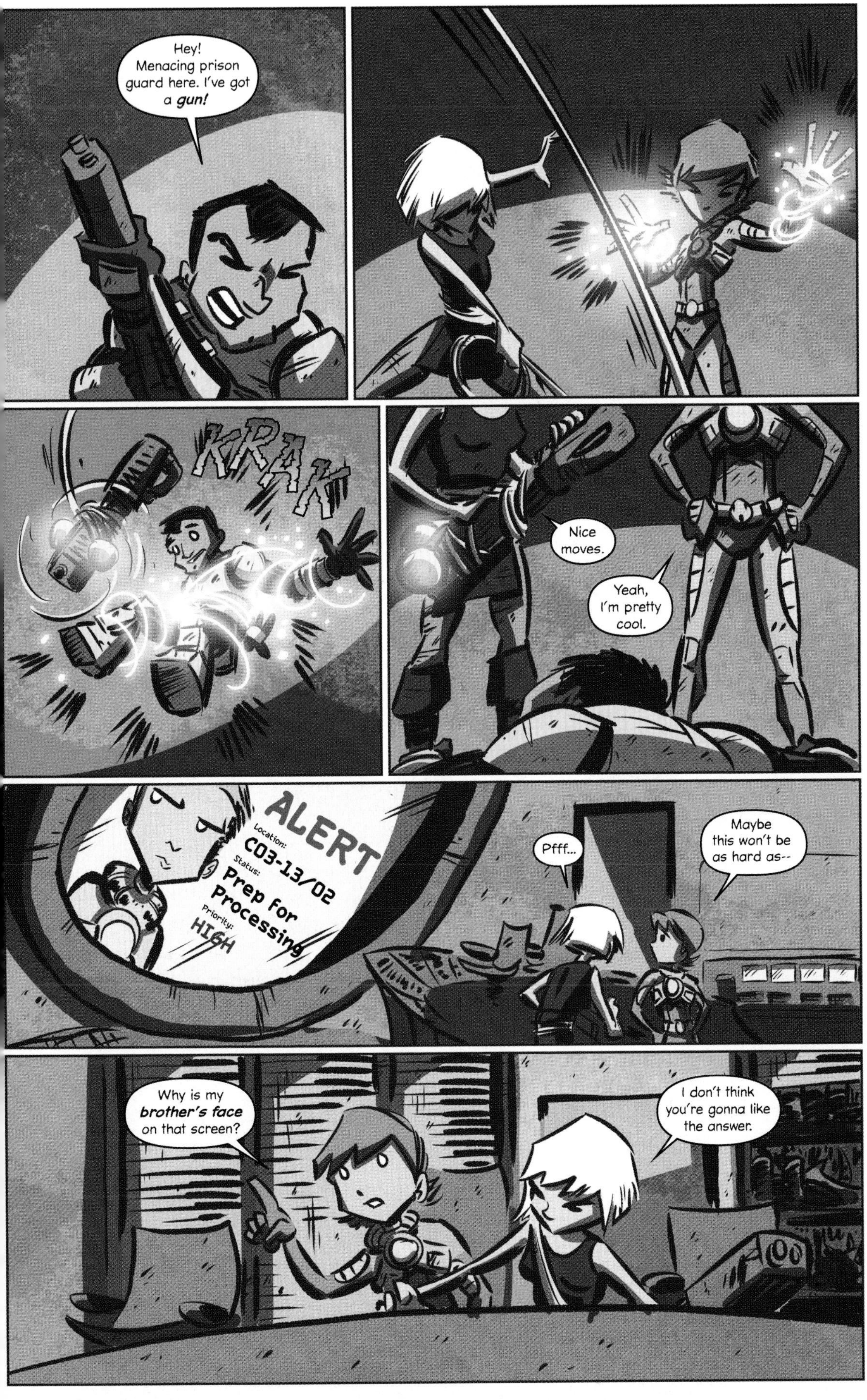
Hey! Menacing prison guard here. I've got a *gun!*
KRAK
Nice moves.
Yeah, I'm pretty cool.
ALERT
Location: C03-13/02
Status: Prep for Processing
Priority: HIGH
Pfff...
Maybe this won't be as hard as--
Why is my ***brother's face*** on that screen?
I don't think you're gonna like the answer.

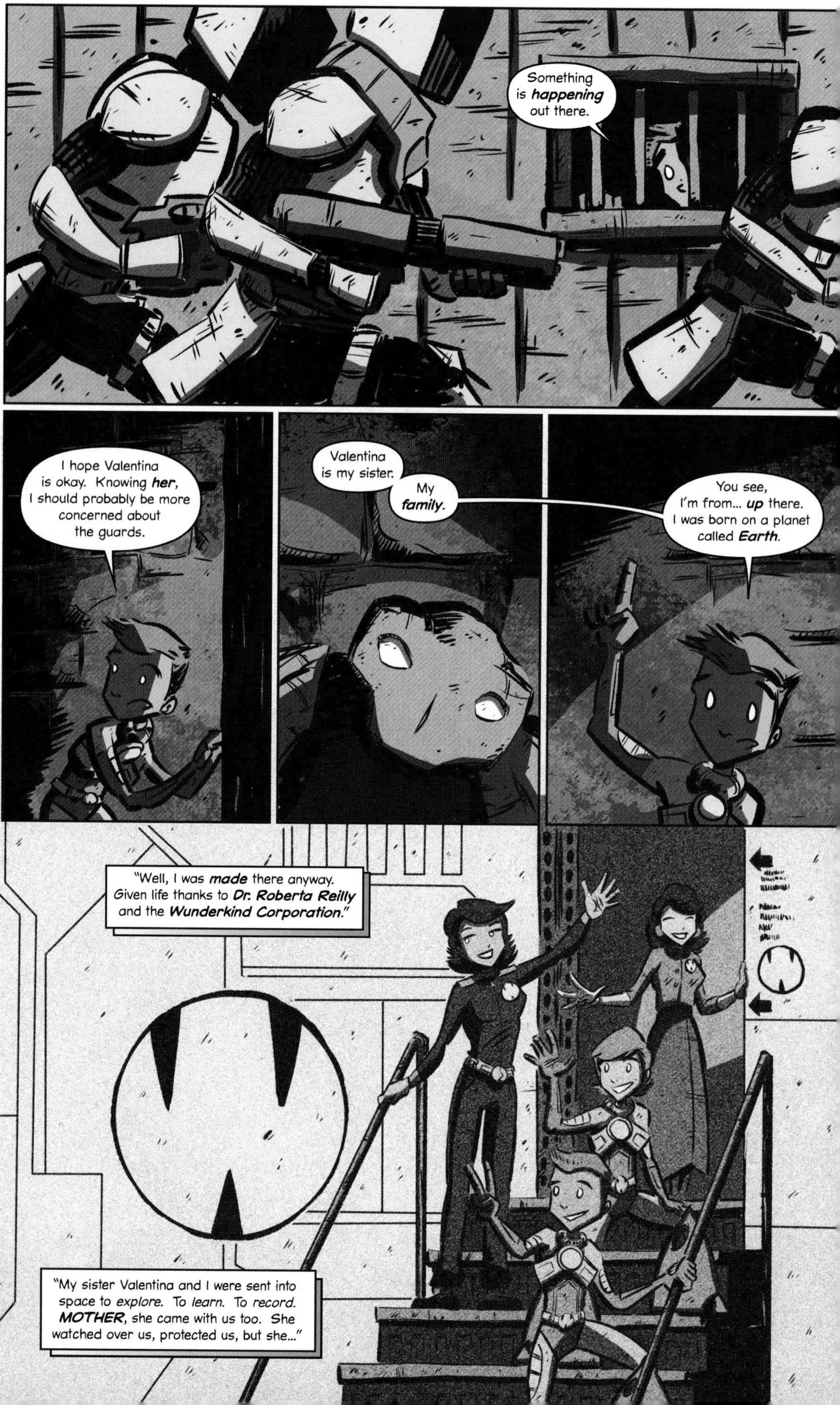

Something is **happening** out there.
I hope Valentina is okay. Knowing **her**, I should probably be more concerned about the guards.
Valentina is my sister.
My **family**.
You see, I'm from... **up** there. I was born on a planet called **Earth**.
"Well, I was **made** there anyway. Given life thanks to **Dr. Roberta Reilly** and the **Wunderkind Corporation**."
"My sister Valentina and I were sent into space to *explore*. To *learn*. To *record*. **MOTHER**, she came with us too. She watched over us, protected us, but she..."

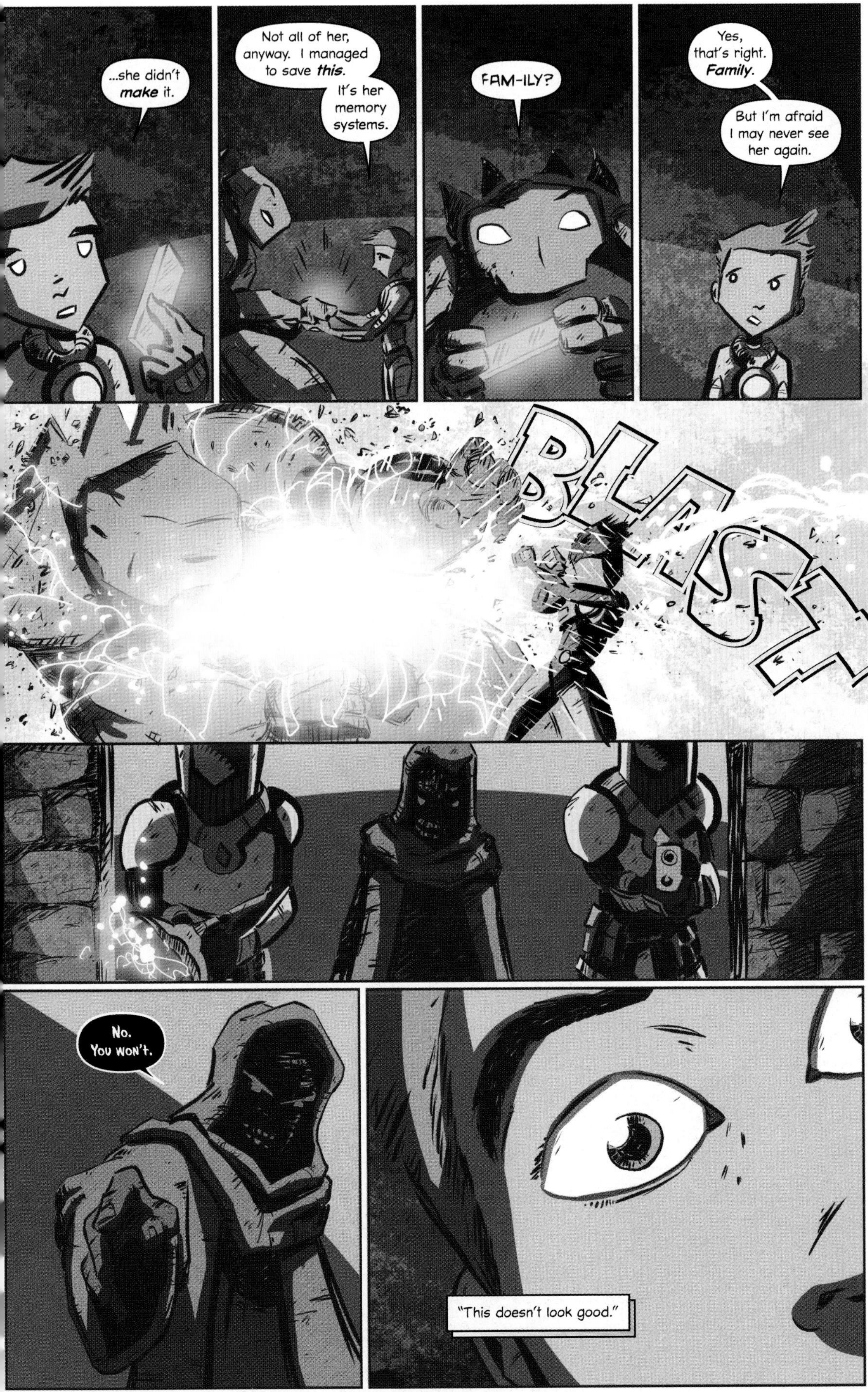
...she didn't make it.
Not all of her, anyway. I managed to save this.
It's her memory systems.
FAM-ILY?
Yes, that's right. Family.
But I'm afraid I may never see her again.
BLAST
No. You won't.
"This doesn't look good."

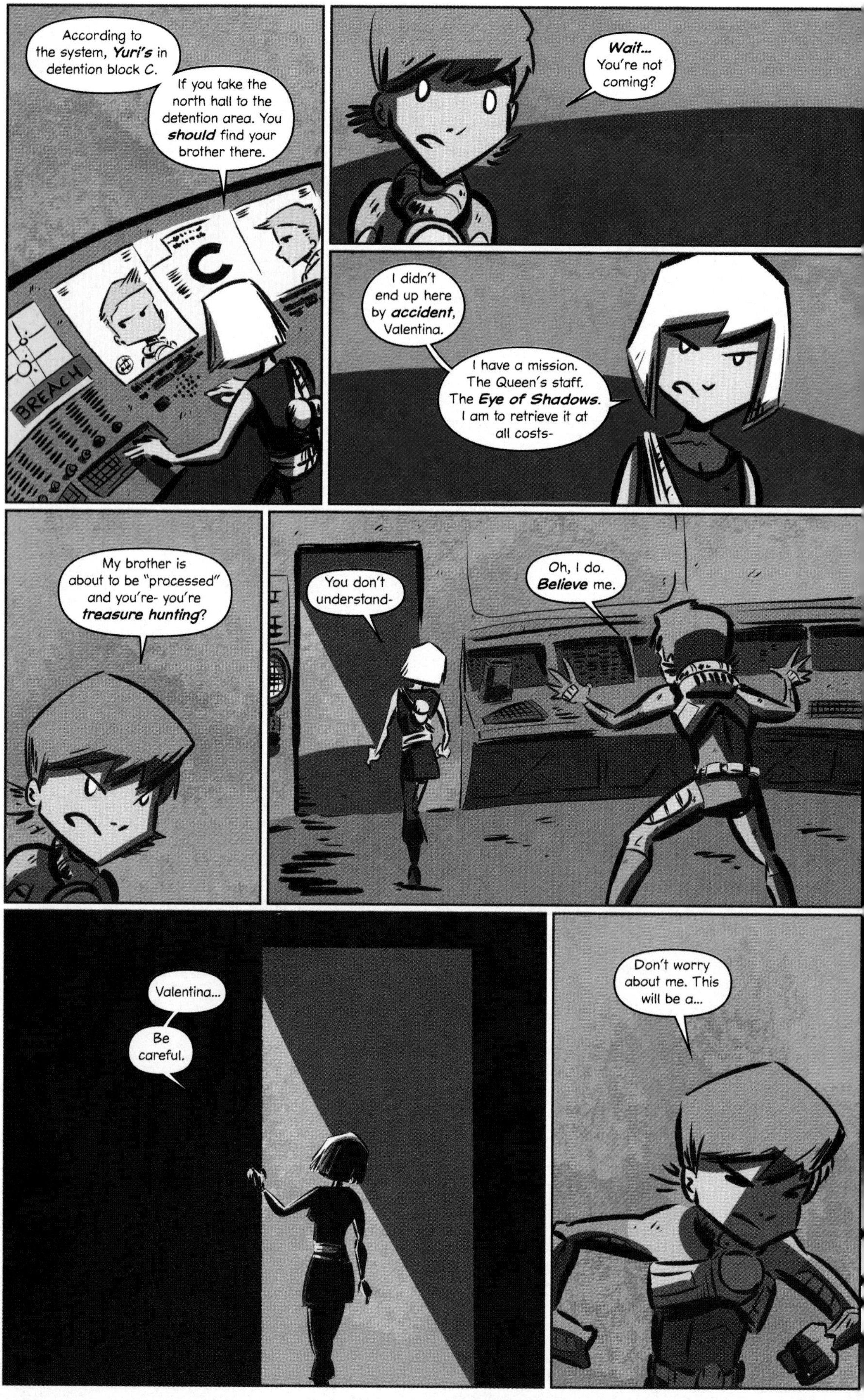
According to the system, Yuri's in detention block C.
If you take the north hall to the detention area. You should find your brother there.
BREACH
Wait... You're not coming?
I didn't end up here by accident, Valentina.
I have a mission. The Queen's staff. The Eye of Shadows. I am to retrieve it at all costs-
My brother is about to be "processed" and you're- you're treasure hunting?
You don't understand-
Oh, I do. Believe me.
Valentina...
Be careful.
Don't worry about me. This will be a...

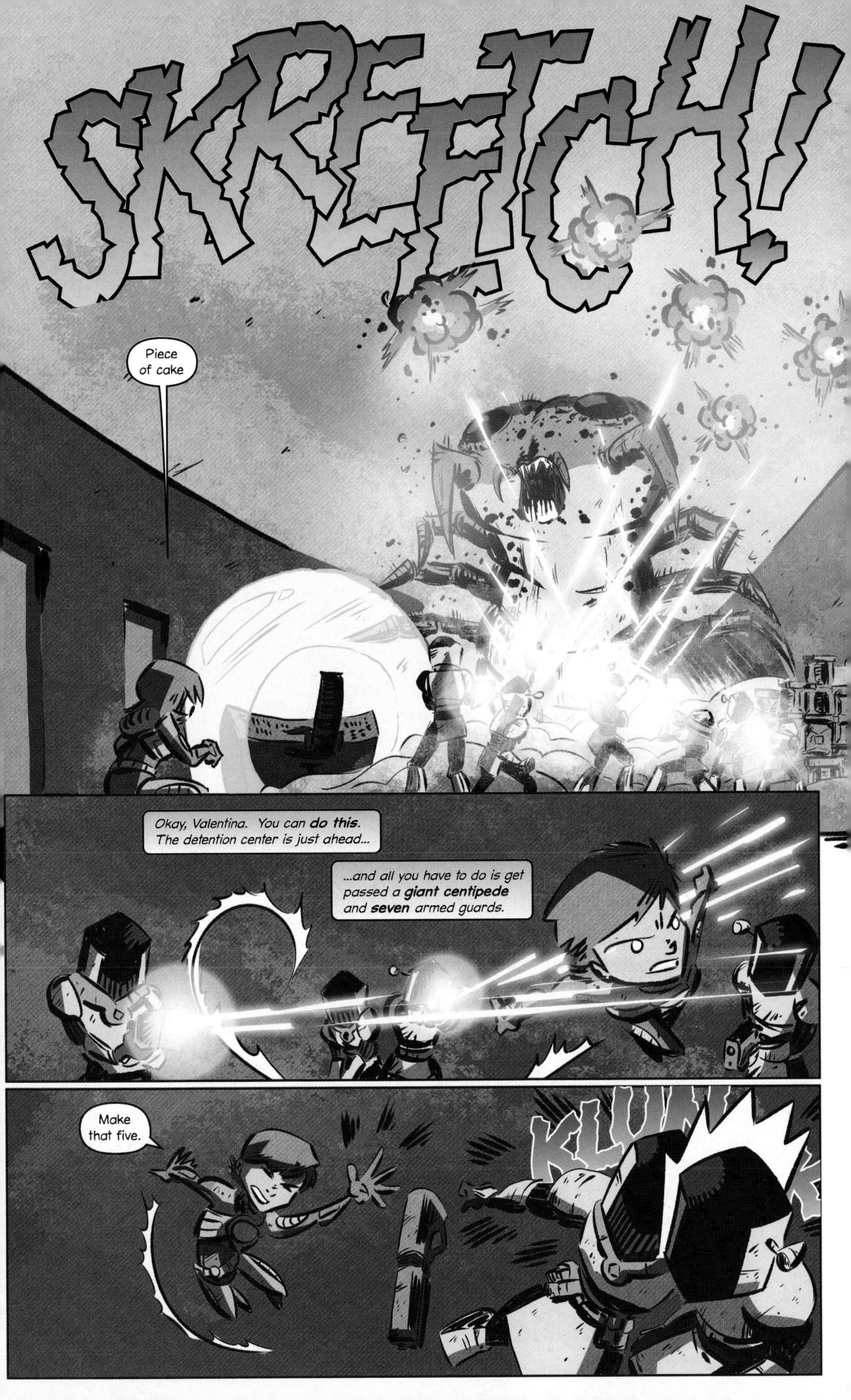
SKREETCH!
Piece of cake
Okay, Valentina. You can **do this**. The detention center is just ahead...
...and all you have to do is get passed a **giant centipede** and **seven** armed guards.
Make that five.

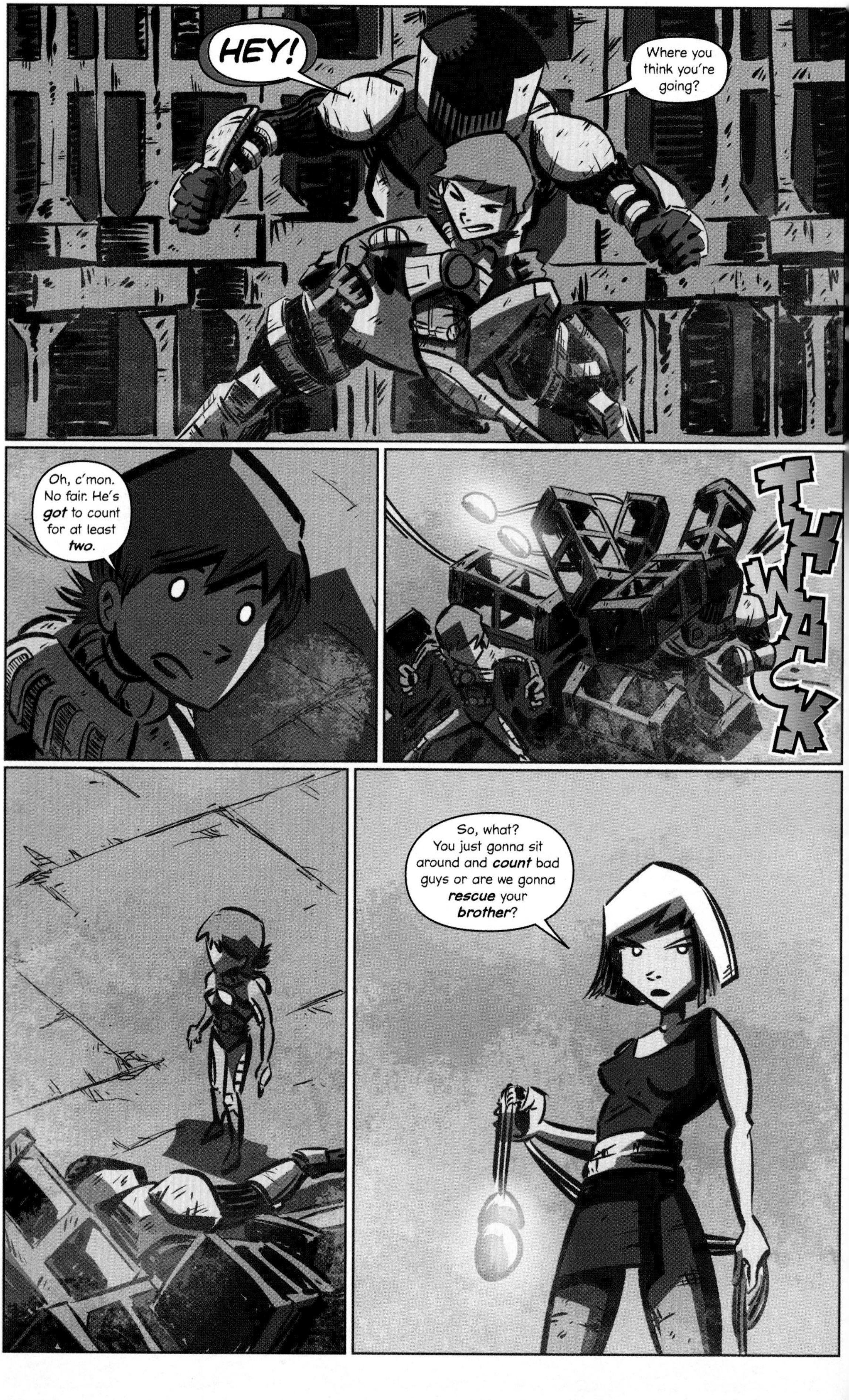
HEY!
Where you think you're going?
Oh, c'mon. No fair. He's got to count for at least two.
THWACK
So, what? You just gonna sit around and count bad guys or are we gonna rescue your brother?

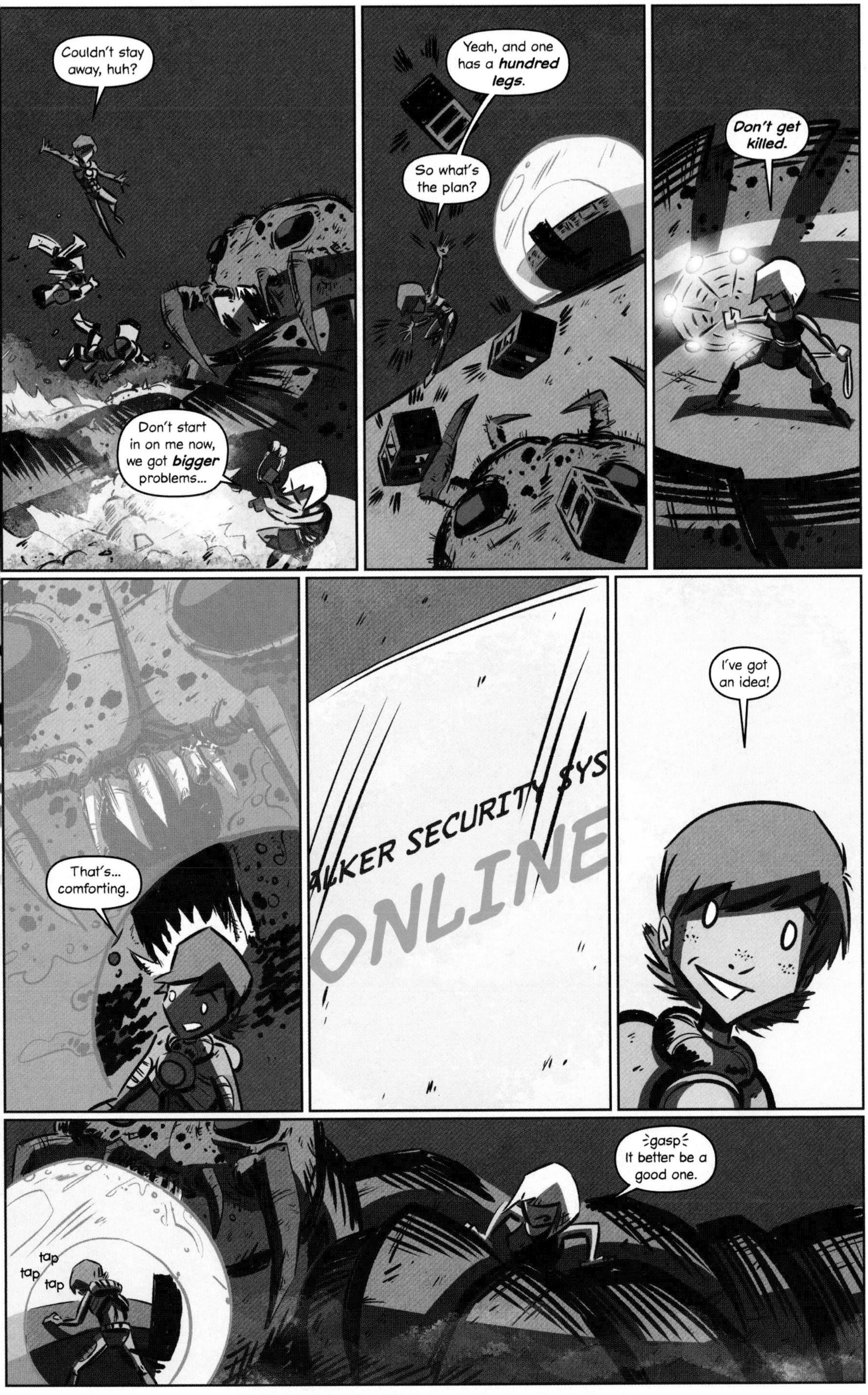
Couldn't stay away, huh?
Don't start in on me now, we got **bigger** problems...
Yeah, and one has a **hundred legs**.
So what's the plan?
Don't get killed.
That's... comforting.
ALKER SECURITY SYS
ONLINE
I've got an idea!
gasp
It better be a good one.
tap
tap
tap

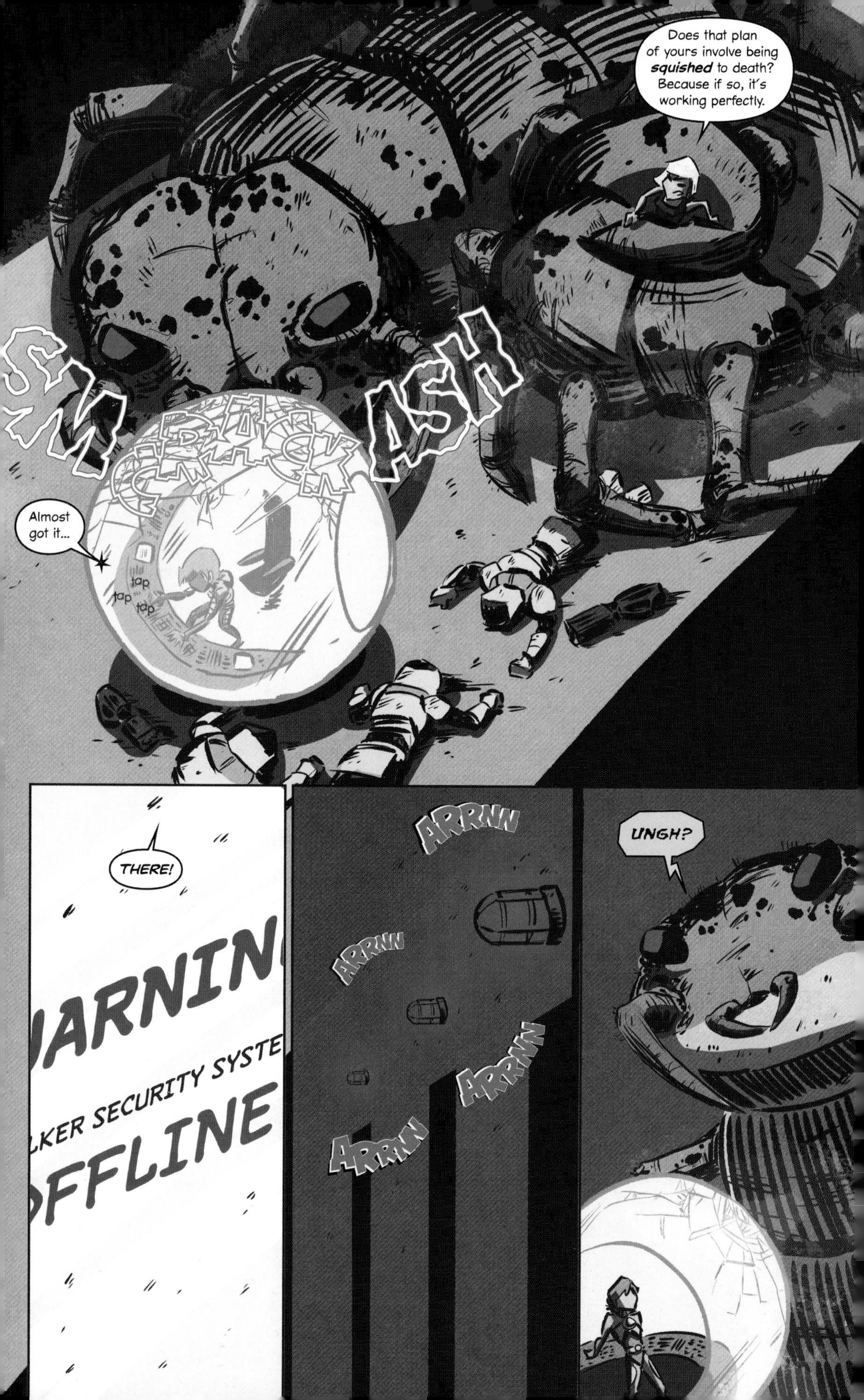
Does that plan of yours involve being *squished* to death? Because if so, it's working perfectly.
SMASH
CRACK
Almost got it...
tap tap tap
THERE!
WARNING
LKER SECURITY SYSTE
OFFLINE
ARRNN
ARRNN
ARRNN
ARRNN
UNGH?

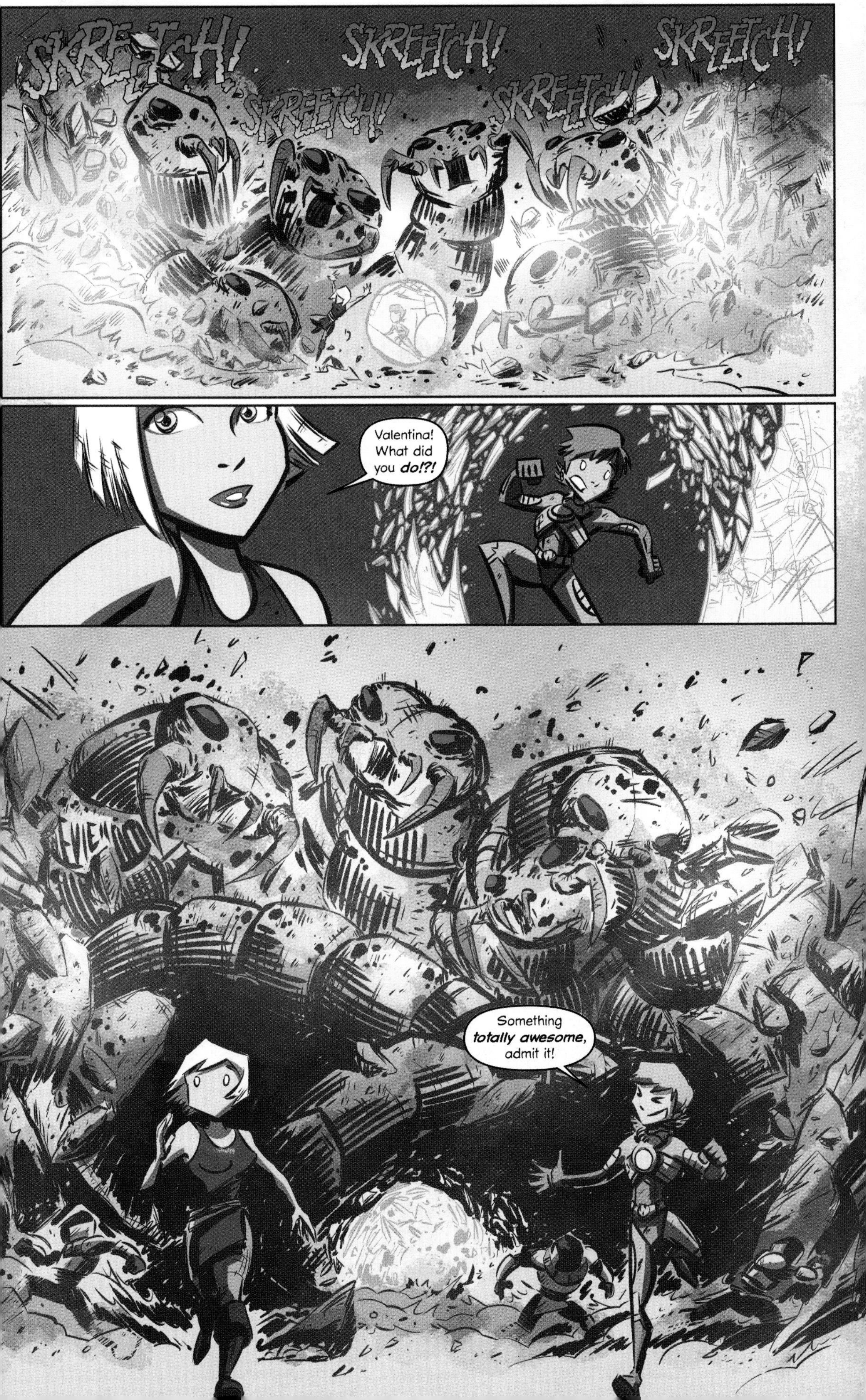
SKREETCH!
SKREETCH!
SKREETCH!
SKREETCH!
SKREETCH!
Valentina! What did you *do!?!*
Something ***totally awesome,*** admit it!

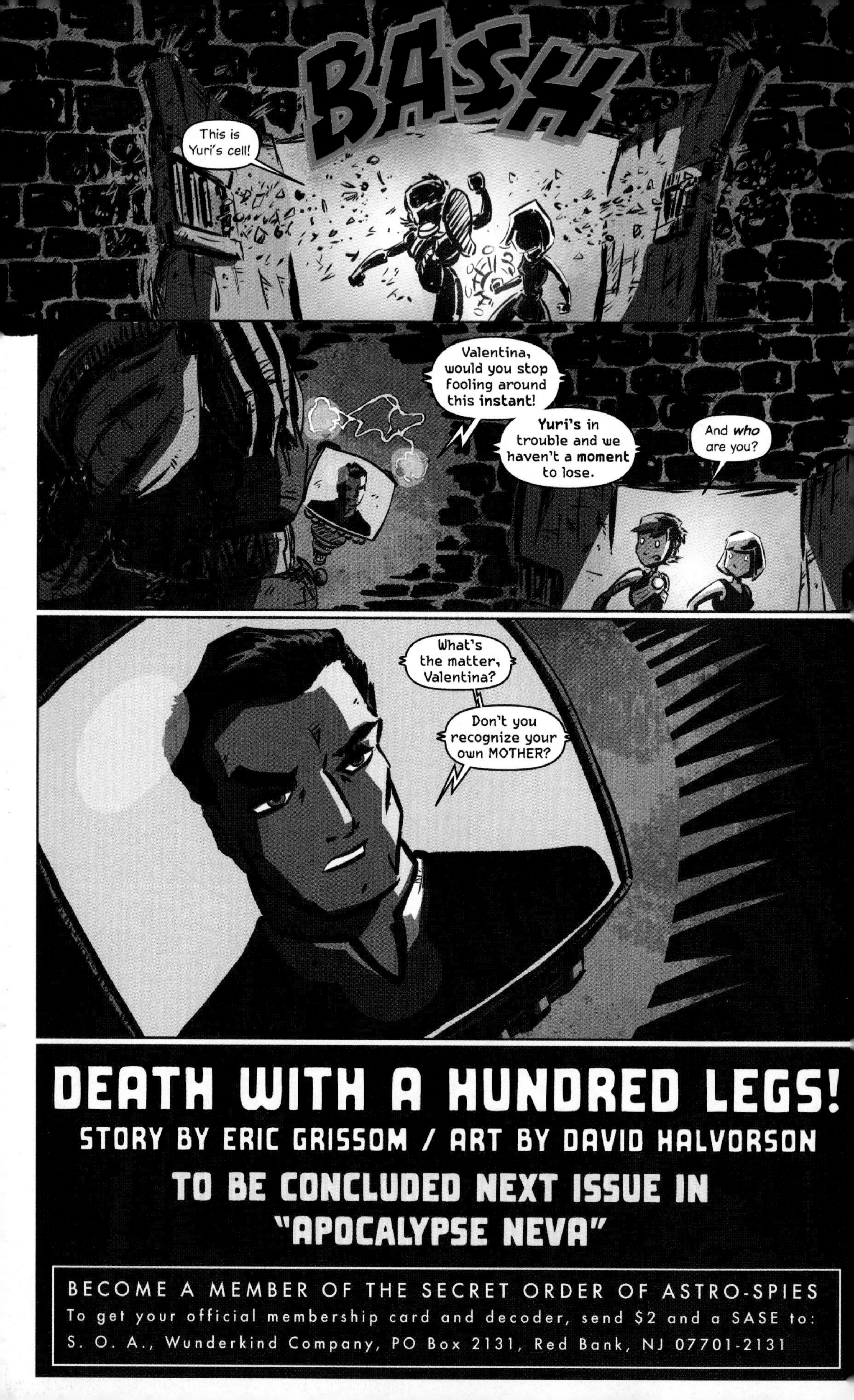
BASH
This is Yuri's cell!
Valentina, would you stop fooling around this instant!
Yuri's in trouble and we haven't a moment to lose.
And who are you?
What's the matter, Valentina?
Don't you recognize your own MOTHER?

DEATH WITH A HUNDRED LEGS!

STORY BY ERIC GRISSOM / ART BY DAVID HALVORSON

TO BE CONCLUDED NEXT ISSUE IN "APOCALYPSE NEVA"

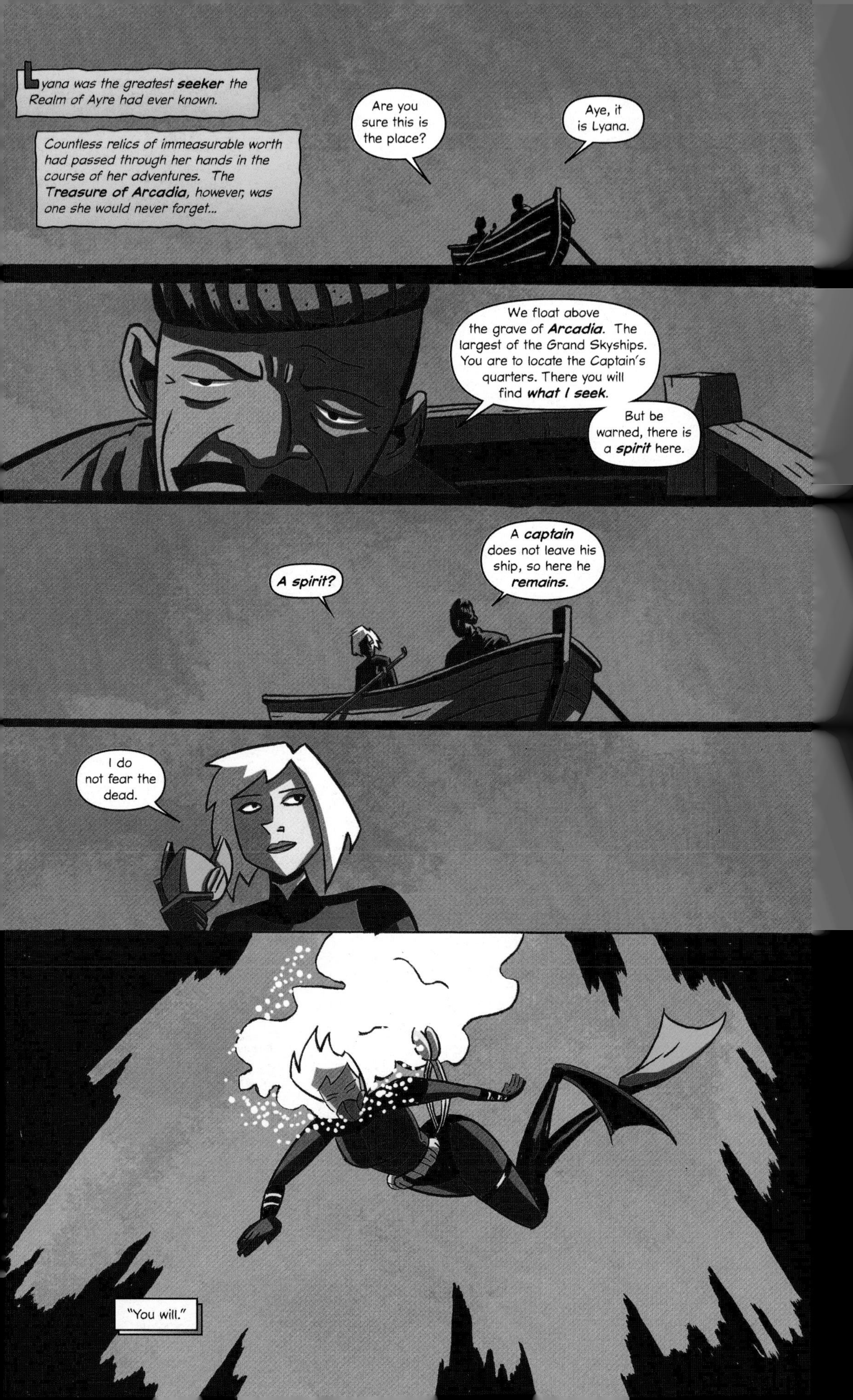
Lyana was the greatest seeker the Realm of Ayre had ever known.
Countless relics of immeasurable worth had passed through her hands in the course of her adventures. The Treasure of Arcadia, however, was one she would never forget...
Are you sure this is the place?
Aye, it is Lyana.
We float above the grave of Arcadia. The largest of the Grand Skyships. You are to locate the Captain's quarters. There you will find what I seek.
But be warned, there is a spirit here.
A spirit?
A captain does not leave his ship, so here he remains.
I do not fear the dead.
"You will."

GHOSTS IN THE DARKNESS

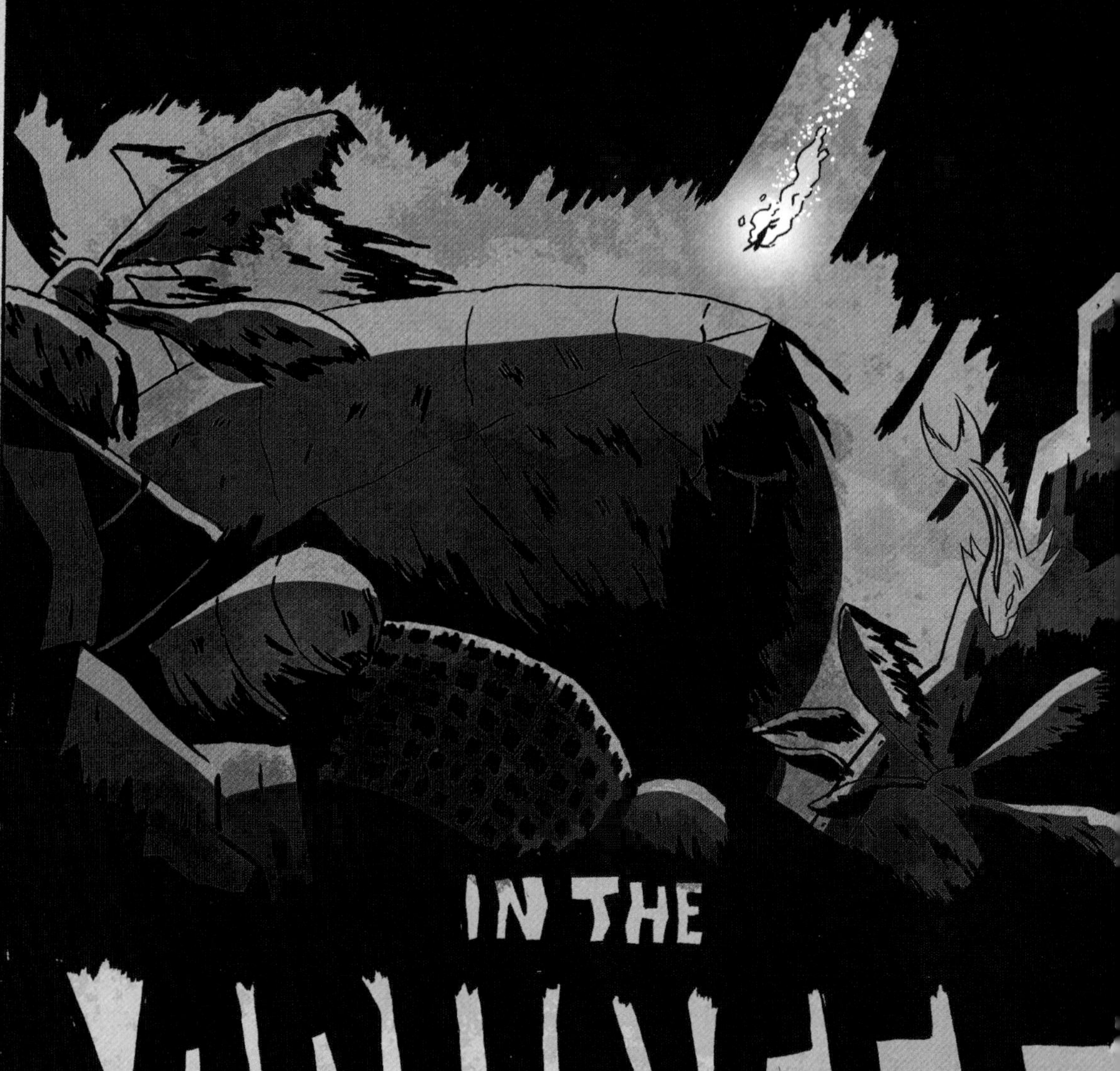

A TALE FROM THE PLANET GIGANTIC

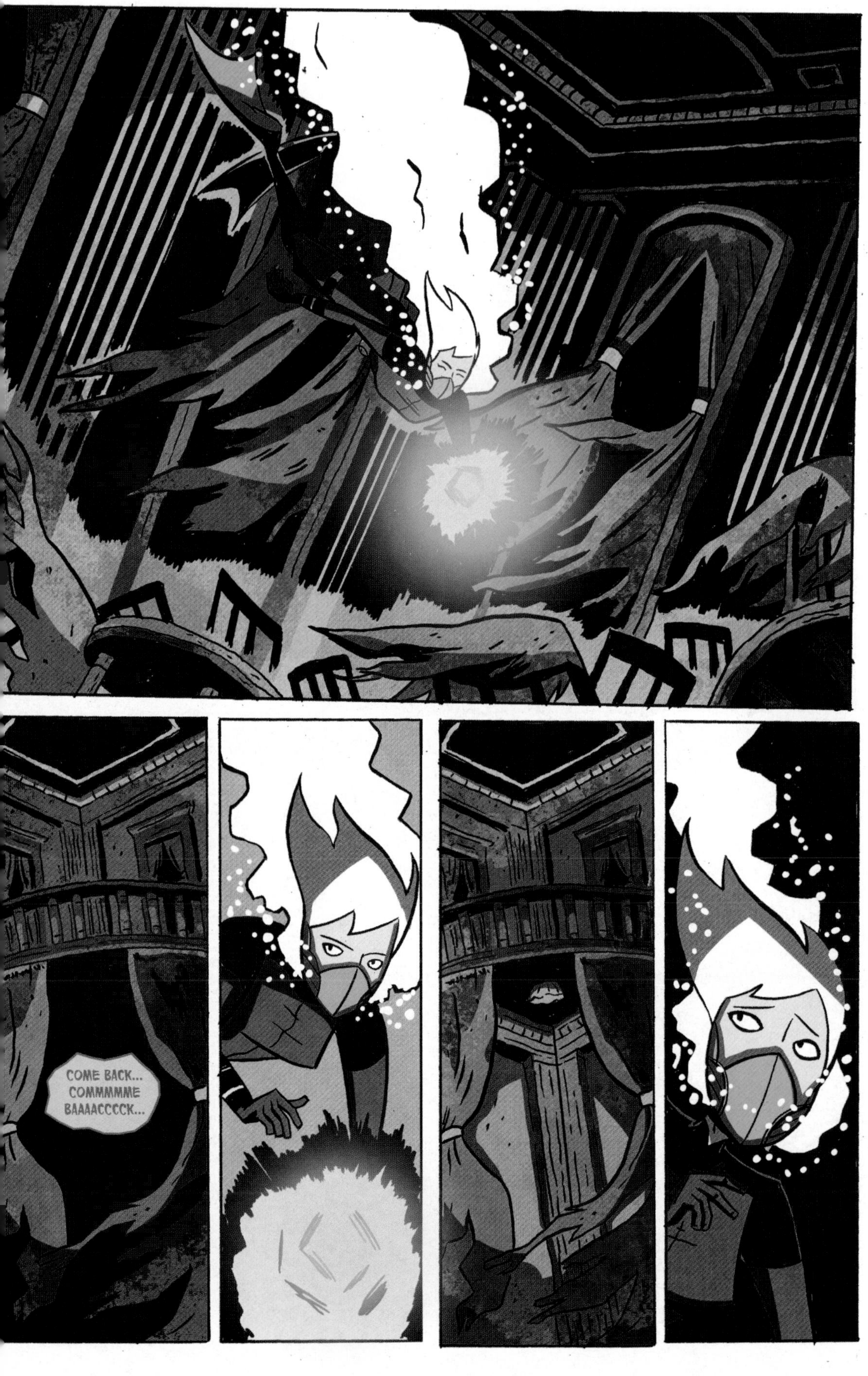
COME BACK... COMMMMME BAAAACCCCK...

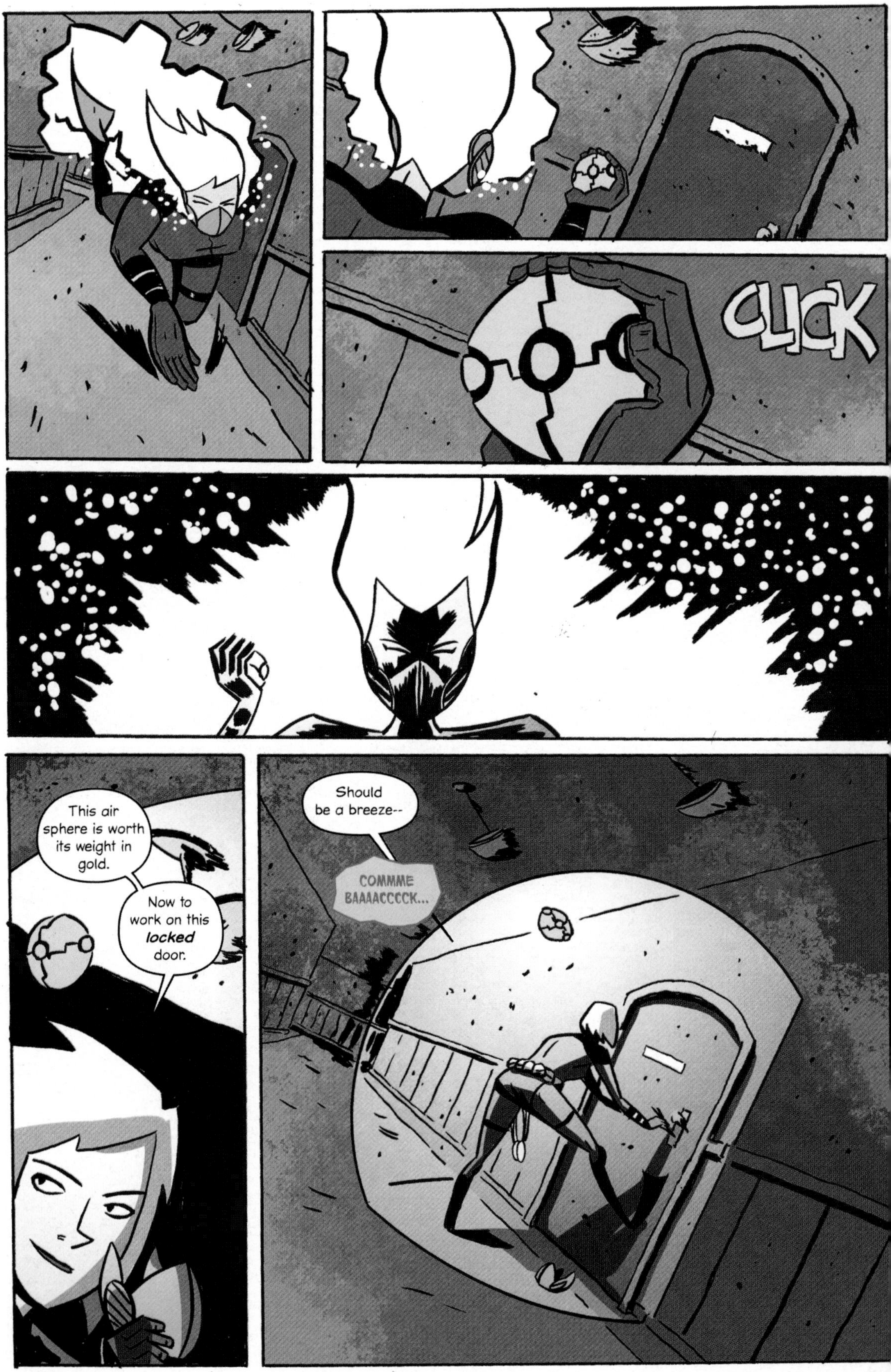
CLICK
This air sphere is worth its weight in gold.
Now to work on this *locked* door.
Should be a breeze--
COMMME BAAAACCCCK...

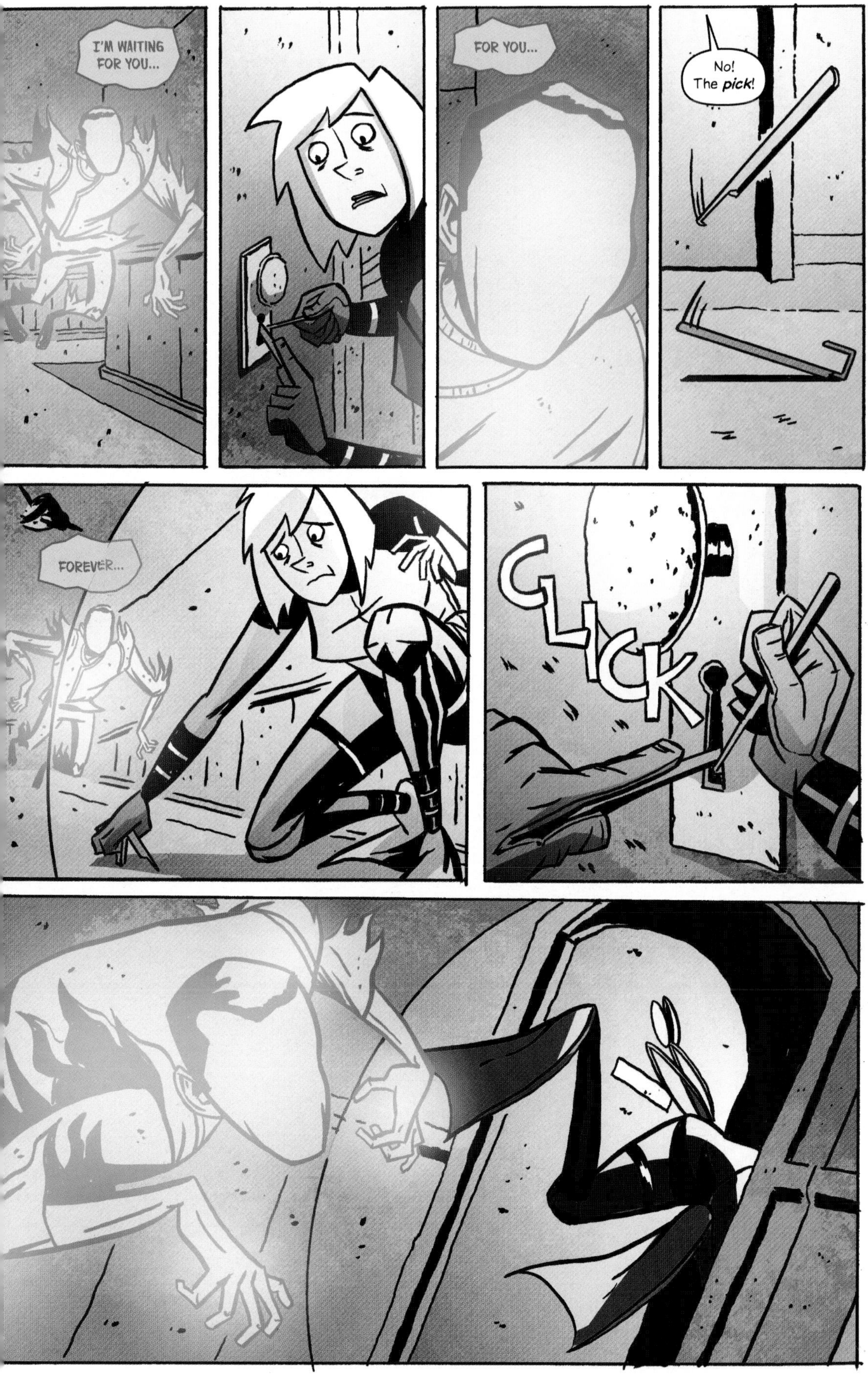
I'M WAITING FOR YOU...
FOR YOU...
No! The pick!
FOREVER...
CLICK

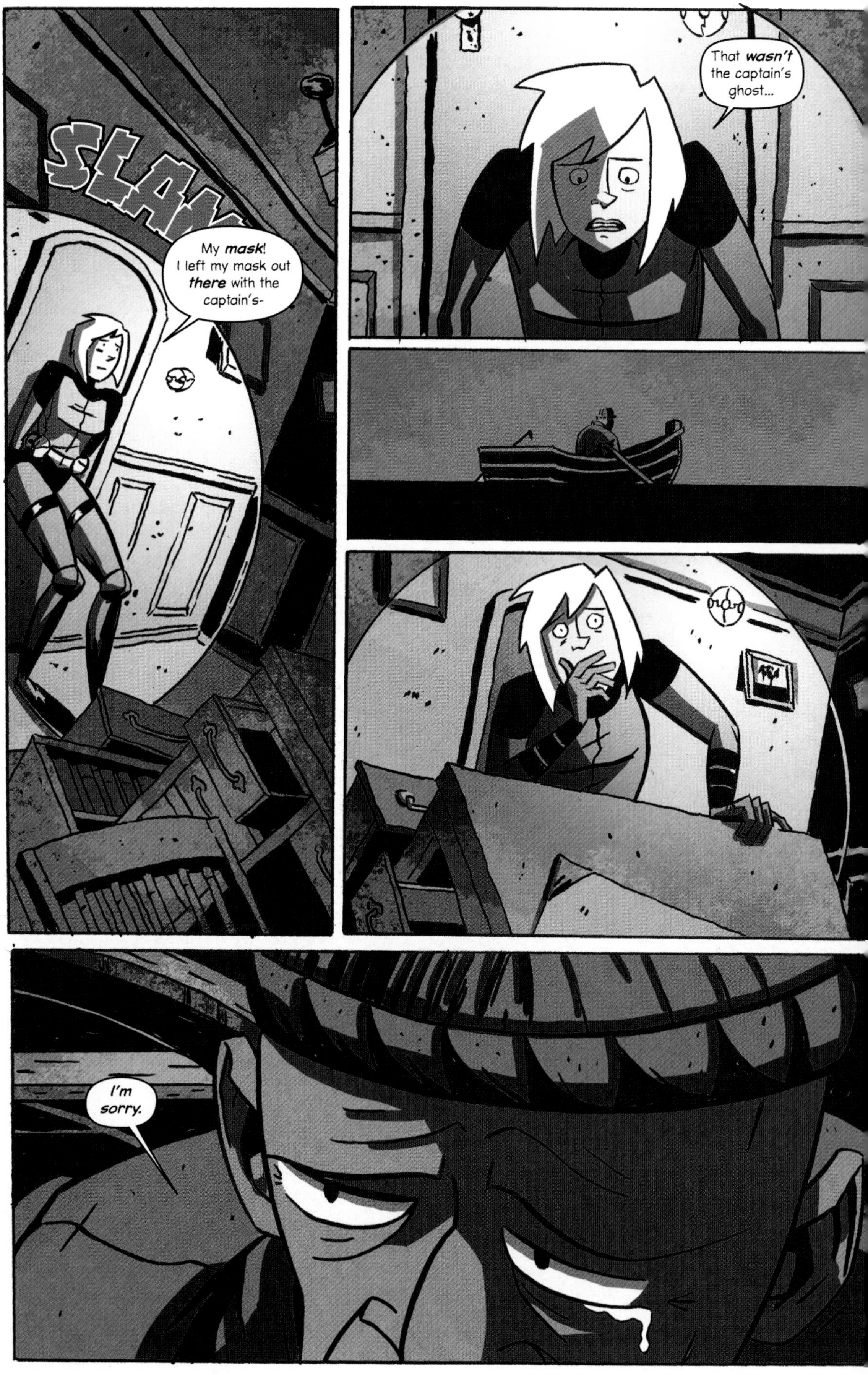
SLAM
My *mask*! I left my mask out *there* with the captain's-
That *wasn't* the captain's ghost...
I'm sorry.

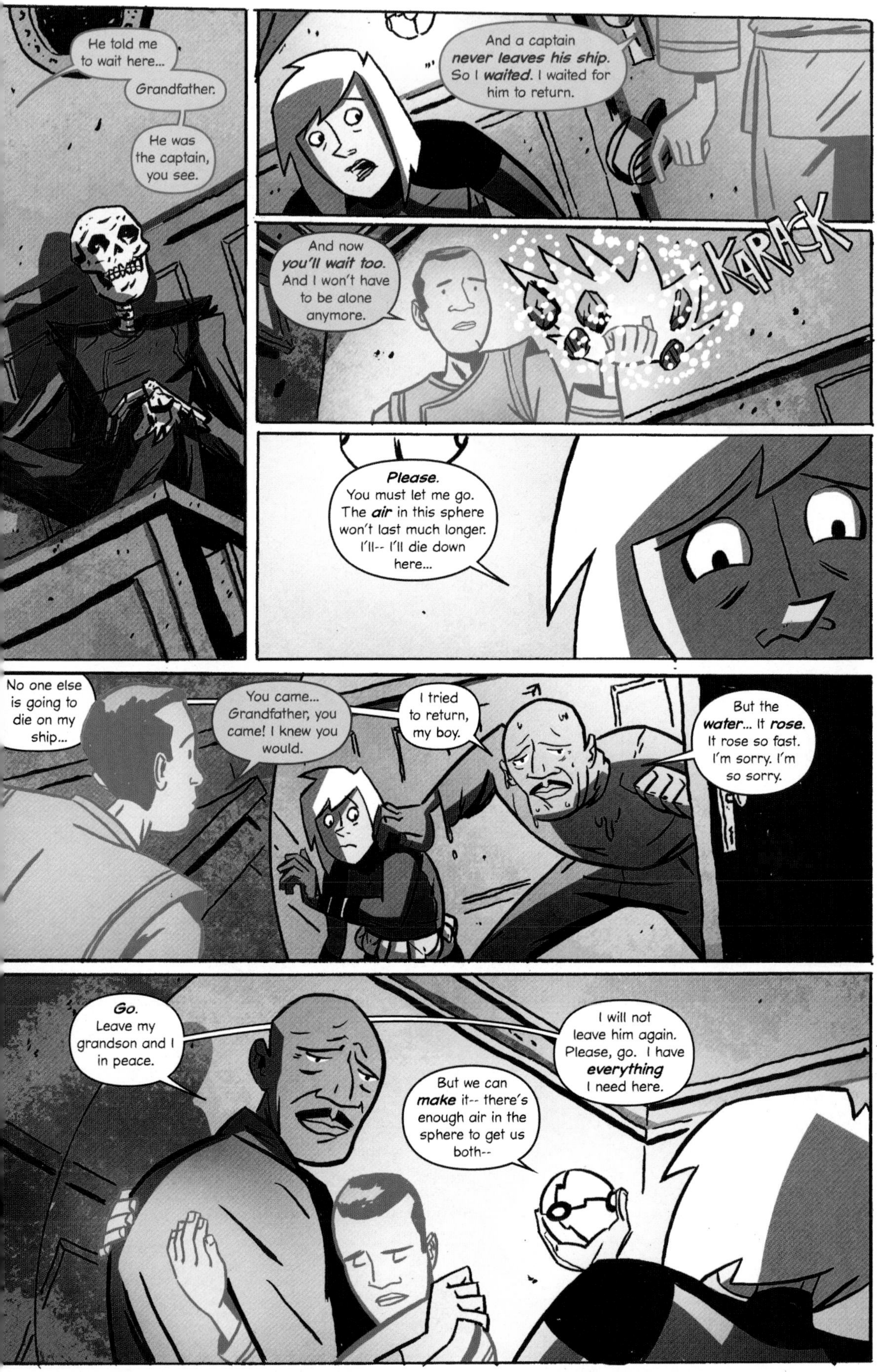
He told me to wait here...
Grandfather.
He was the captain, you see.
And a captain never leaves his ship. So I waited. I waited for him to return.
And now you'll wait too. And I won't have to be alone anymore.
KARACK
Please. You must let me go. The air in this sphere won't last much longer. I'll-- I'll die down here...
No one else is going to die on my ship...
You came... Grandfather, you came! I knew you would.
I tried to return, my boy.
But the water... It rose. It rose so fast. I'm sorry. I'm so sorry.
Go. Leave my grandson and I in peace.
I will not leave him again. Please, go. I have everything I need here.
But we can make it-- there's enough air in the sphere to get us both--

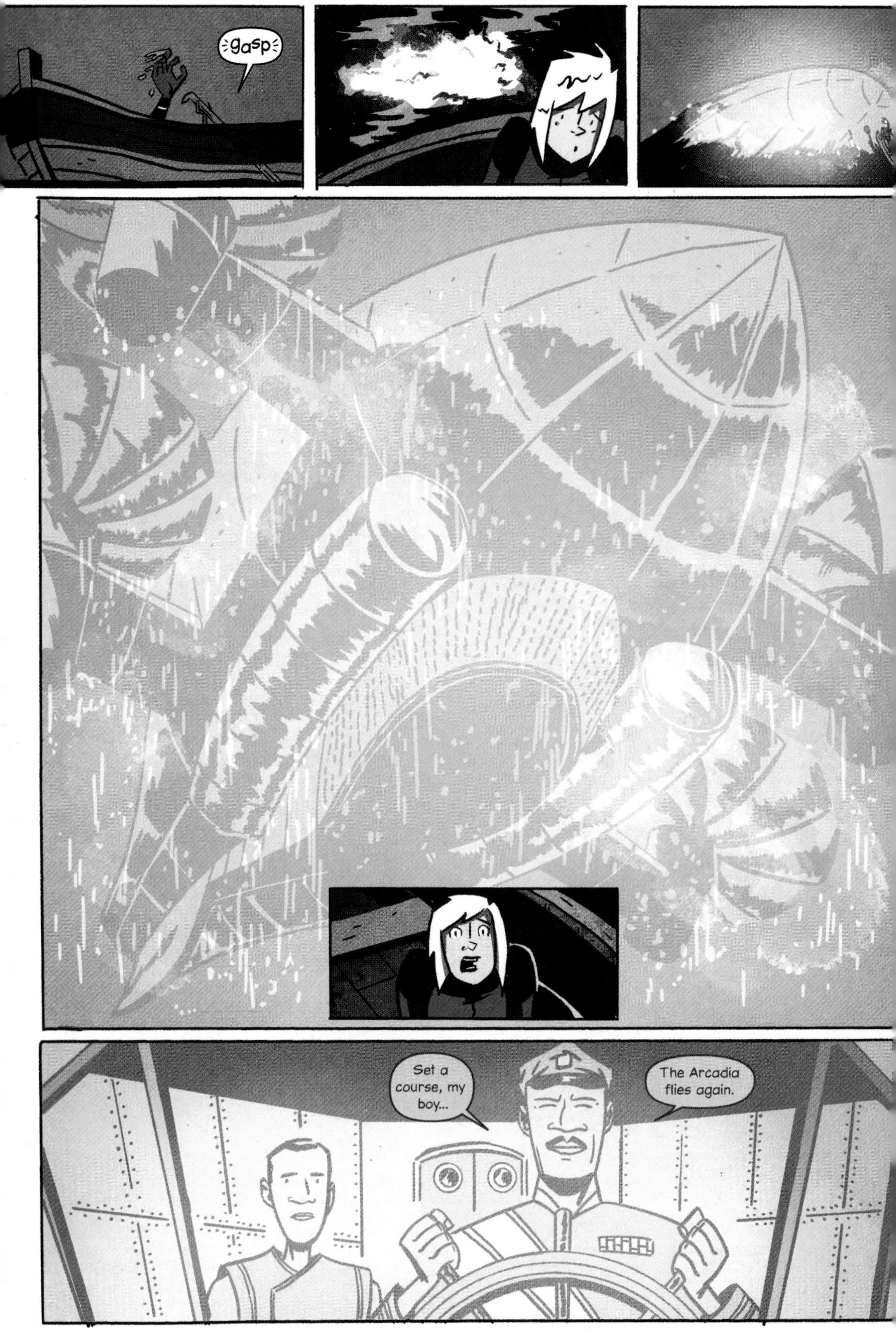
gasp
Set a course, my boy...
The Arcadia flies again.

GHOSTS IN THE DARKNESS

STORY BY ERIC GRISSOM / ART BY PHIL SLOAN / COLORS BY DAVID HALVORSON

MUNCHKIN®

MILLIONS OF GAMES SOLD! BILLIONS OF MONSTERS SLAIN!

1. KICK DOWN THE DOOR

LEVEL 20
PLUTONIUM DRAGON
Will not pursue anyone of Level 5 or below.

Bad Stuff: You are toasted and eaten. You are dead.

2 Levels   5 Treasures

2. FIGHT THE MONSTER

+5 BONUS
Usable by Wizard Only
STAFF OF NAPALM

+2 BONUS
BOOTS OF
BUTT-KICKING

LEVEL 20
...ONIUM DRAGON
...pursue anyone of Level 5 or

1 Hand   800 Gold Pieces   400 Gold Pieces   5 Treasures

3. GRAB THE TREASURE

MAGIC MISSILE
Use during any combat. +5 to either side. Usable once only.

POTION OF GENERAL
STUDLINESS

300 Gold Pieces   GO UP A LEVEL

4. REACH LEVEL 10 AND WIN

WIZARD

Flight Spell: You may discard up to 3 cards after rolling the die to Run Away; each one gives you a +1 bonus to flee.

Charm Spell: You may discard your whole hand (minimum 3 cards) to charm a single Monster instead of fighting it. Discard the Monster and take its Treasure, but don't gain levels. If there are other monsters in the combat, fight them normally.

Class

LEVEL 10
NET TROLL
He has no special powers, and he's really mad about it.

Bad Stuff: Screws up the game states by forcing you to let the [owner] of the highest Level take any item (each) from you.

3 Treasures

Go down in the dungeon. Fight every monster you meet. Stab your rivals in the back and steal their stuff. Grab the treasure and run!

MUNCHKIN
KILL THE MONSTERS • STEAL THE TREASURE • STAB YOUR BUDDY

GAME DESIGN BY
STEVE JACKSON

ILLUSTRATED BY
JOHN KOVALIC

STEVE JACKSON GAMES

FIND *MUNCHKIN* TODAY AT COMIC SHOPS, GAME STORES AND SELECT MAJOR RETAILER

STEVE JACKSON GAM
munchkin.sjgames.com

JOIN THE PARTY!

Like and follow us on Facebook at
facebook.com/sjgames

Follow **@sj...**
on Twi...

Find other *Munchkin* players at **gamerfinder.sjgames...**

New *Munchkin* sequels and supplements come o... the time . . . mix and match them for a *completel...* dungeon crawl! Learn all about *Munchkin* a... **worldofmunchkin.com**

READ MORE NOW

Planet Gigantic - Action Lab
www.actionlabcomics.com

00311

7 00465 77246 6

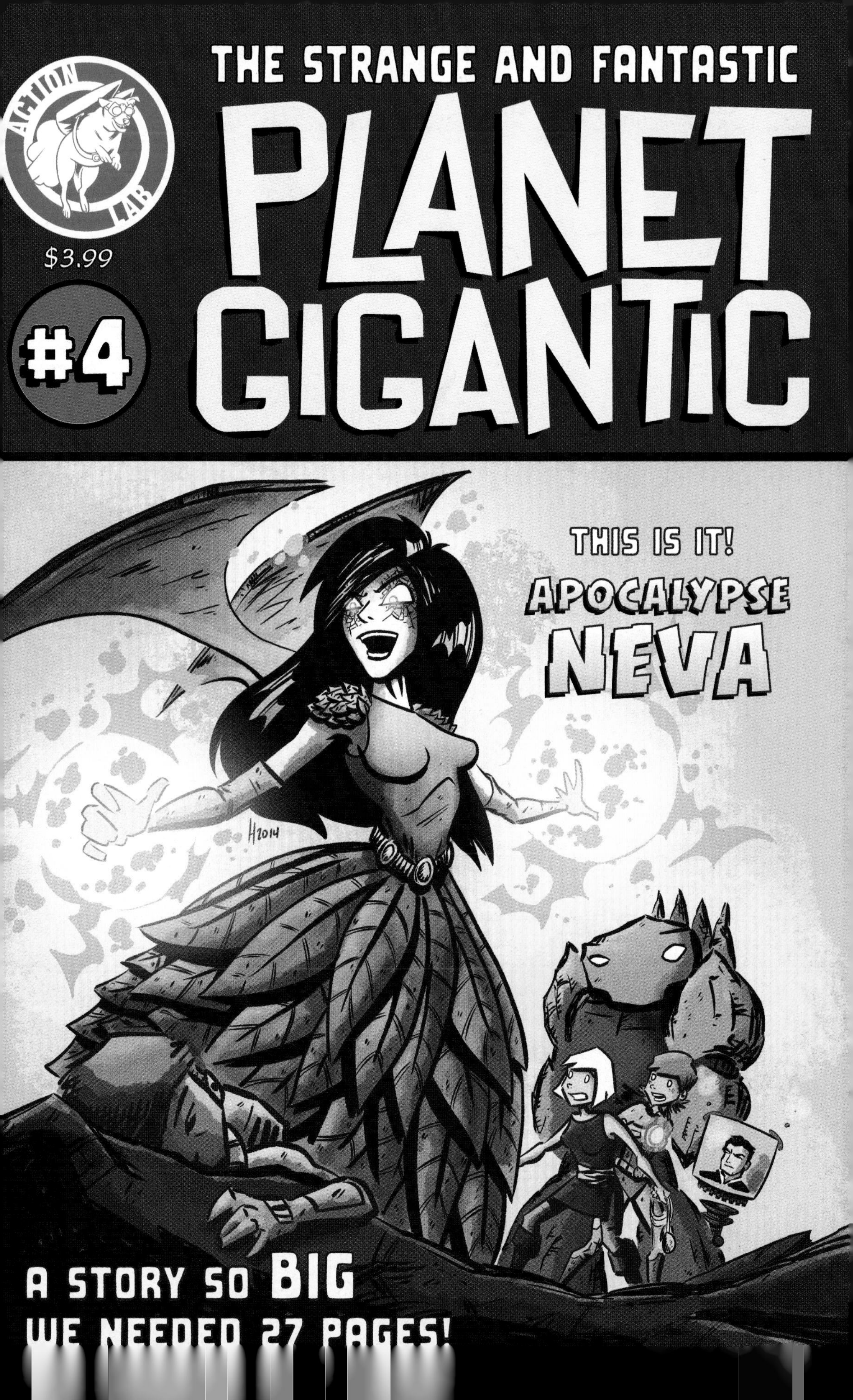
ACTION LAB
$3.99
#4
THE STRANGE AND FANTASTIC
PLANET GIGANTIC
THIS IS IT!
APOCALYPSE NEVA
H2014
A STORY SO BIG
WE NEEDED 27 PAGES!

PLANET GIGANTIC

"Apocalypse Neva"
story and letters by ERIC GRISSOM
art and cover by DAVID HALVORSON

fonts by COMICRAFT
planetgigantic.com

publisher BRYAN SEATON
president KEVIN FREEMAN
editor-in-chief SHAWN GABBORIN
creative director DAVE DWONCH
co-directors of marketing JAMAL IGLE & KELLY DALE
social media director JIM DIETZ
education outreach director JEREMY WHITLEY
associate editors CHAD CICCONI & COLLEEN BOYD

PLANET GIGANTIC #4, January 2015. Published by Action Lab Entertainment. Planet Gigantic, its logos and all related cahracters are TM and copyright 2014 Eric Grissom and David Halvorson. All rights reserved. The characters and events presented are purely fictional. Any similarities to events or persons living or dead is purely cuincidental. No portion of this publication may be reproduced without the written consent from Action Lab Entertainment, Eric Grissom or David Halvorson. Printed in Canada. First Printing. For more information visit planetgigantic.com or actionlab.com

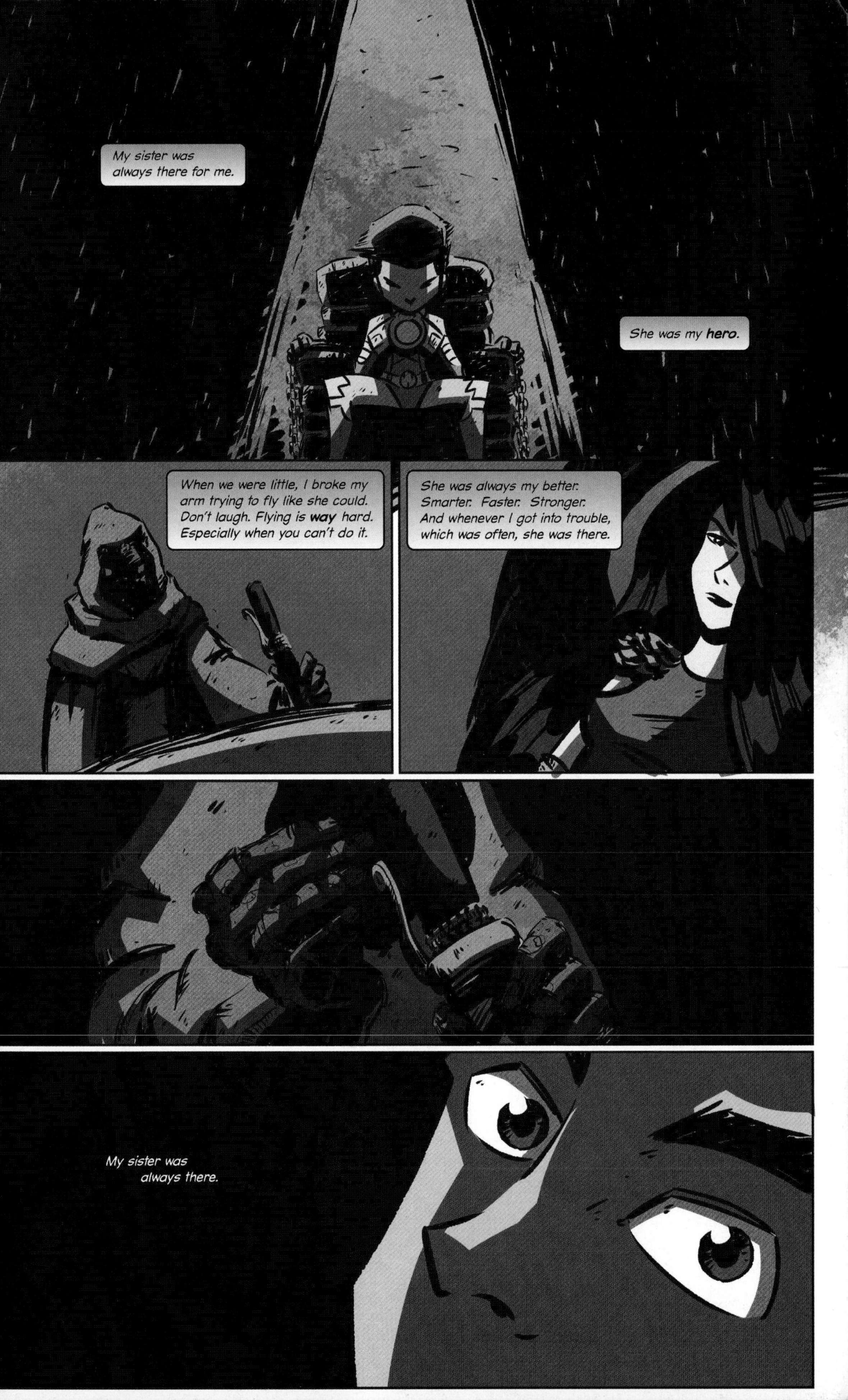
My sister was always there for me.
She was my **hero**.
When we were little, I broke my arm trying to fly like she could. Don't laugh. Flying is **way** hard. Especially when you can't do it.
She was always my better. Smarter. Faster. Stronger. And whenever I got into trouble, which was often, she was there.
My sister was always there.

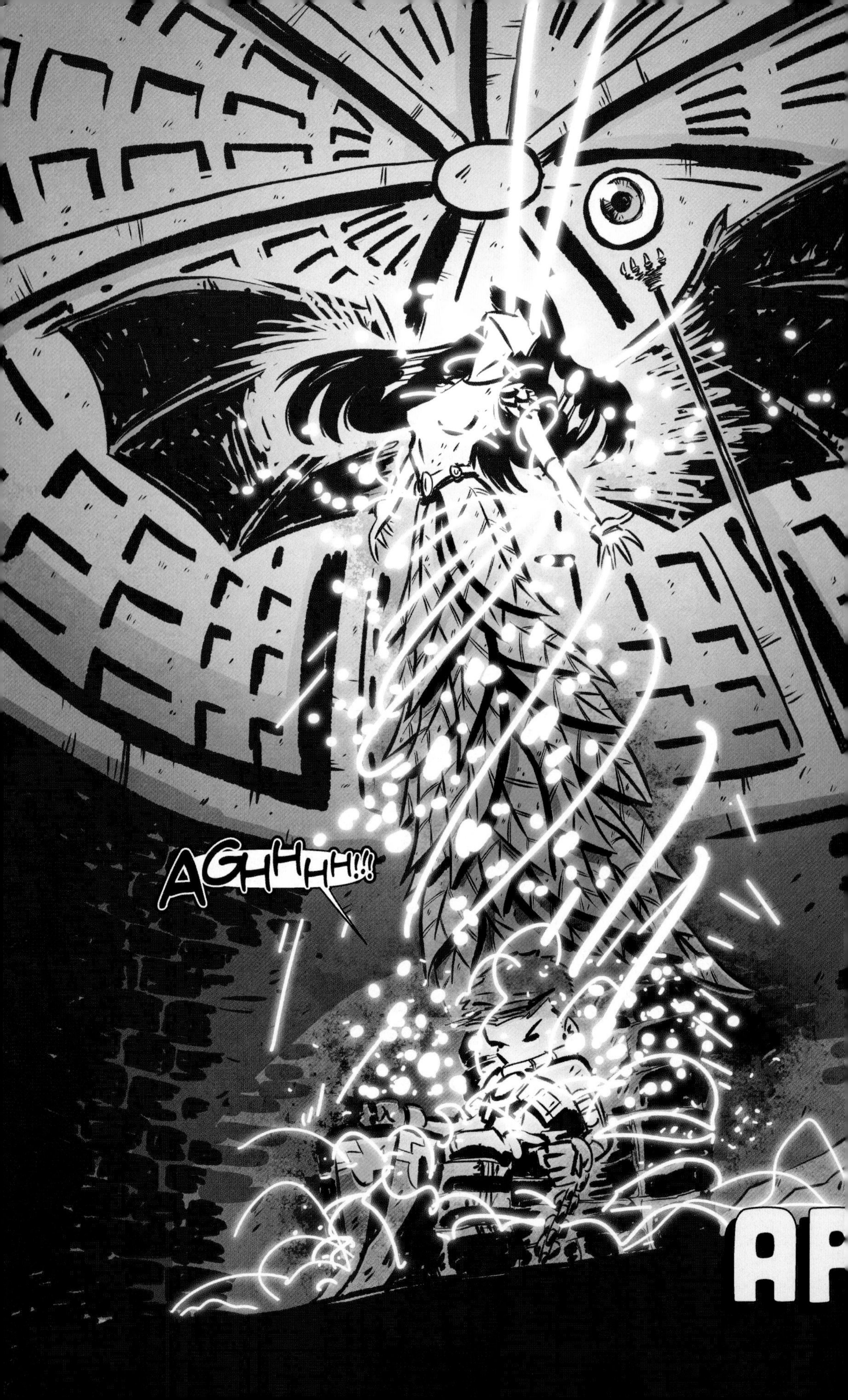
AGHHHH!!!

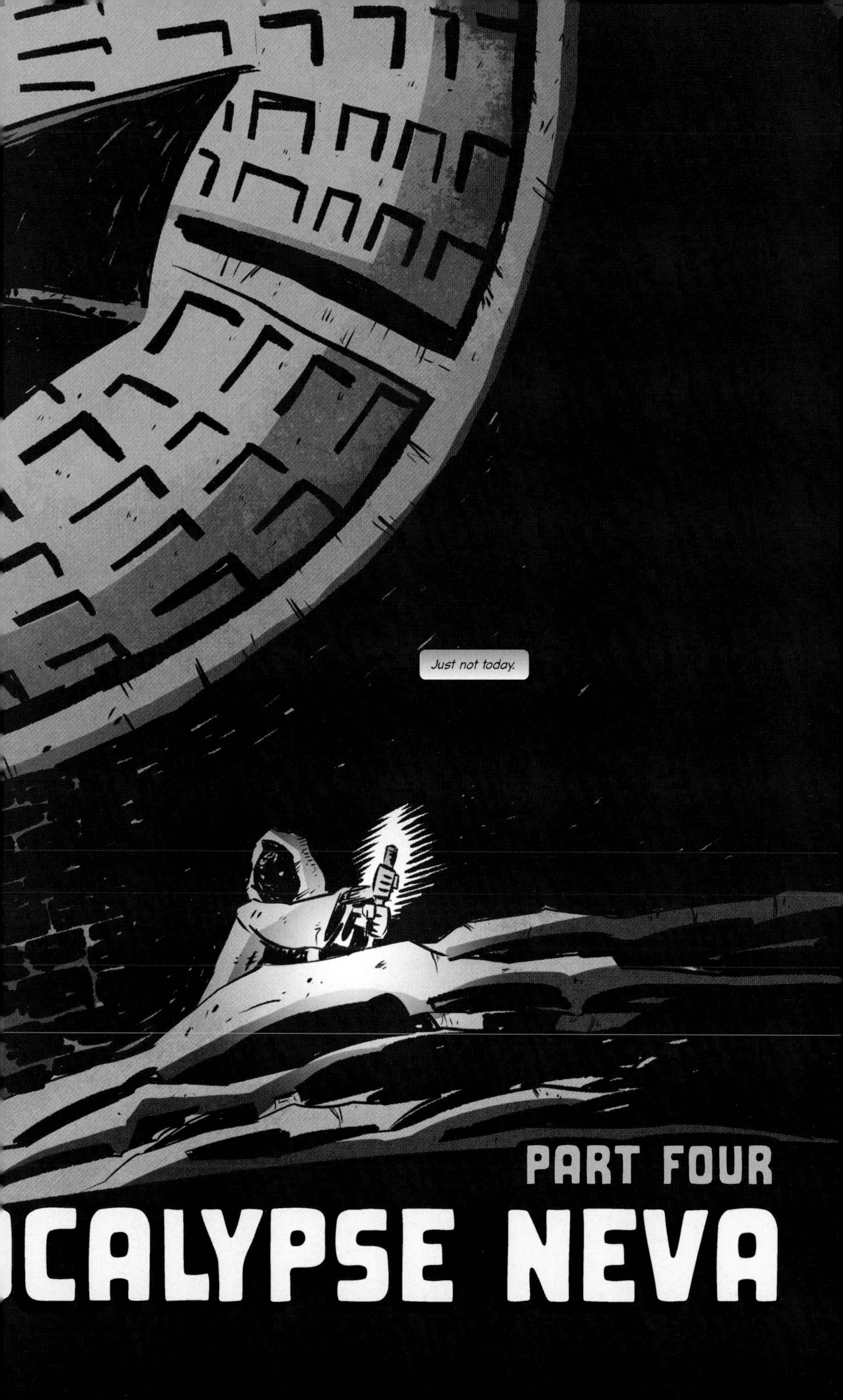
Just not today.
PART FOUR
CALYPSE NEVA

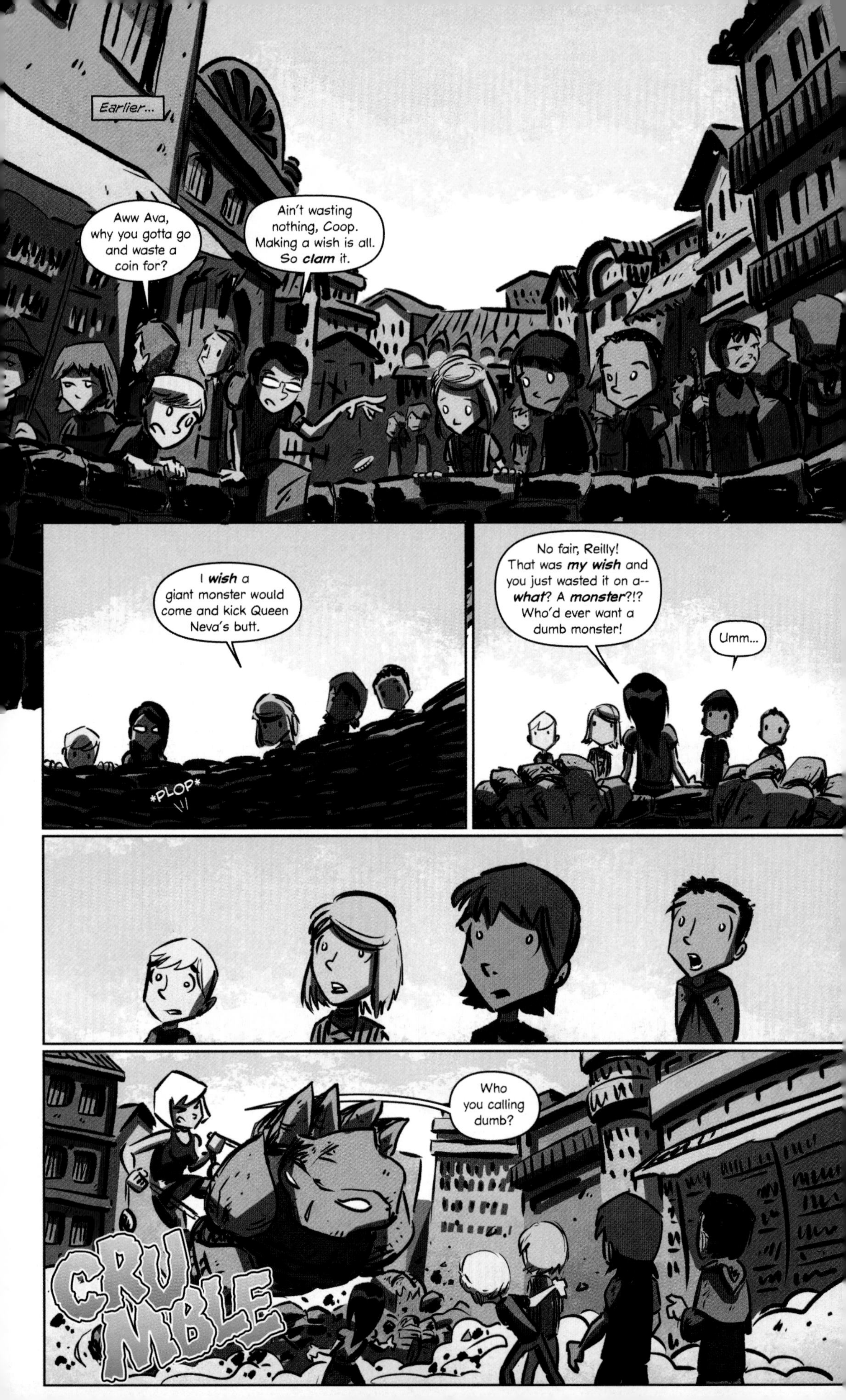

Earlier...
Aww Ava, why you gotta go and waste a coin for?
Ain't wasting nothing, Coop. Making a wish is all. So **clam** it.
I **wish** a giant monster would come and kick Queen Neva's butt.
PLOP
No fair, Reilly! That was **my wish** and you just wasted it on a-- **what**? A **monster**?!? Who'd ever want a dumb monster!
Umm...
Who you calling dumb?
CRUMBLE

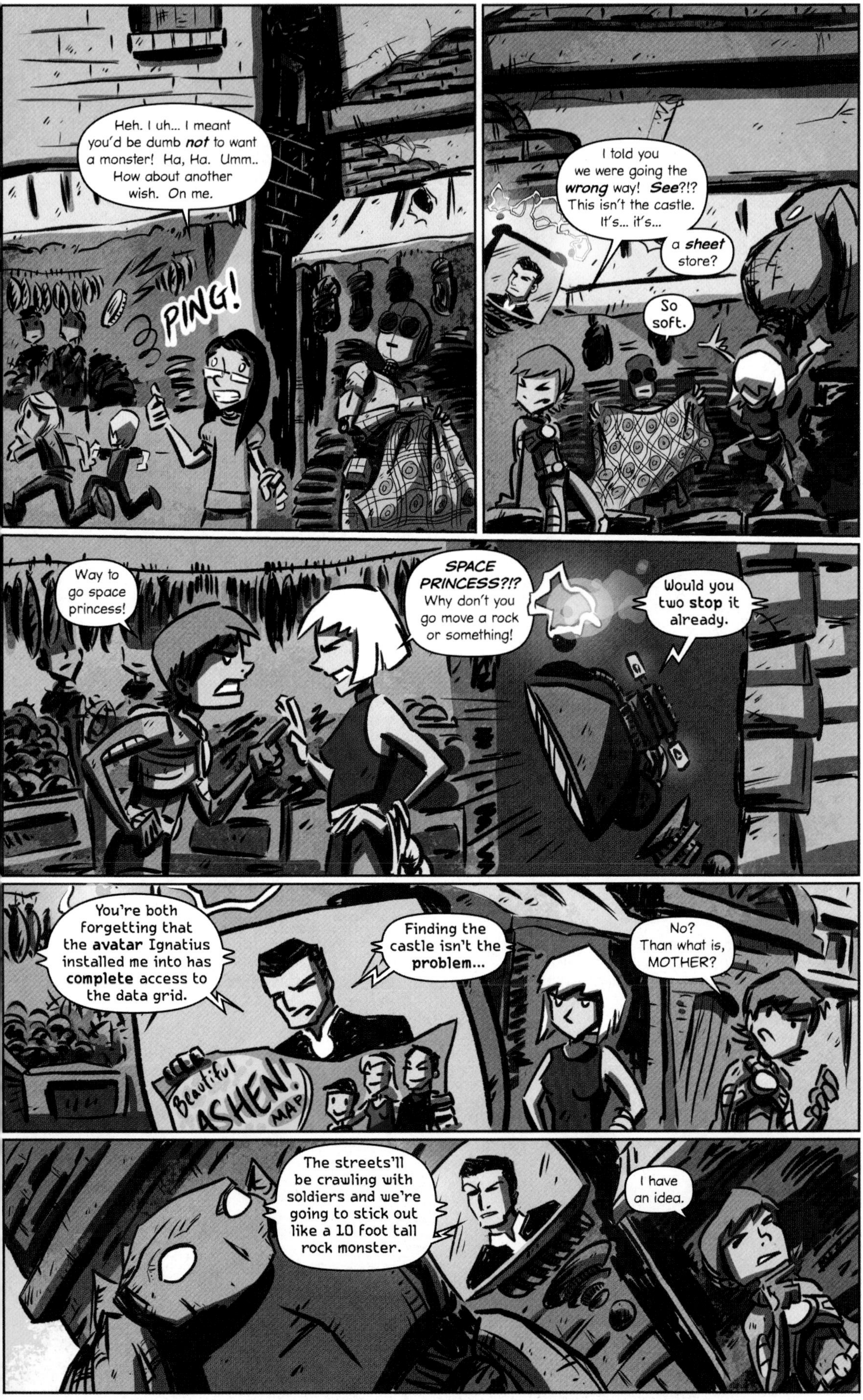
Heh. I uh... I meant you'd be dumb *not* to want a monster! Ha, Ha. Umm.. How about another wish. On me.
PING!
I told you we were going the *wrong* way! *See*?!? This isn't the castle. It's... it's...
a *sheet* store?
So soft.
Way to go space princess!
SPACE PRINCESS?!? Why don't you go move a rock or something!
Would you two **stop** it already.
You're both forgetting that the **avatar** Ignatius installed me into has **complete** access to the data grid.
Finding the castle isn't the **problem...**
No? Than what is, MOTHER?
Beautiful ASHEN! MAP
The streets'll be crawling with soldiers and we're going to stick out like a 10 foot tall rock monster.
I have an idea.

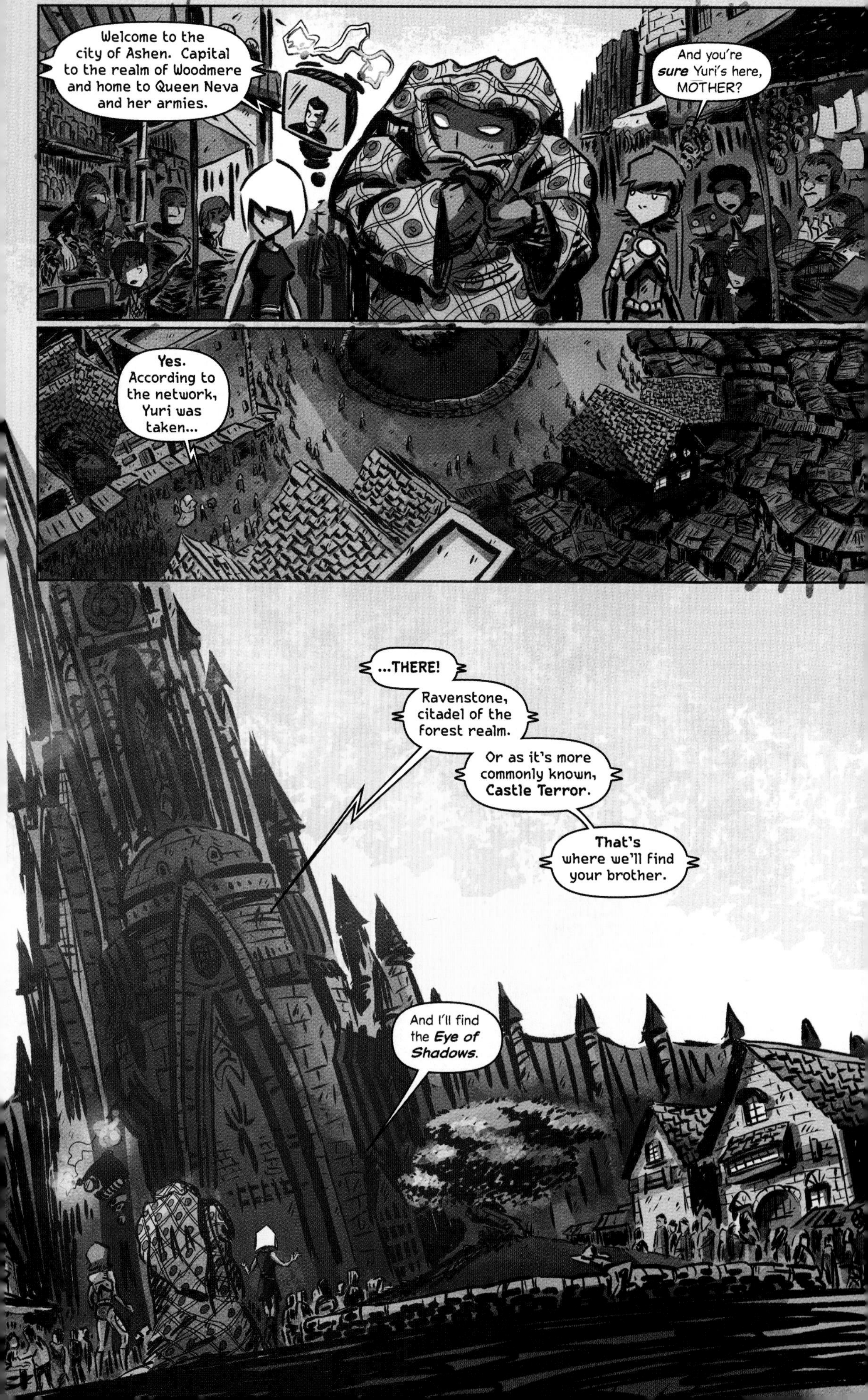
Welcome to the city of Ashen. Capital to the realm of Woodmere and home to Queen Neva and her armies.
And you're *sure* Yuri's here, MOTHER?
Yes. According to the network, Yuri was taken...
...THERE!
Ravenstone, citadel of the forest realm.
Or as it's more commonly known, **Castle Terror**.
That's where we'll find your brother.
And I'll find the ***Eye of Shadows***.

The front gate isn't far ahead... Let's do this.

I don't think that's such a good idea. The gate is *heavily* guarded and worse yet, they have *hoppers*.

And they have *your brother!* We have to be smart and we have to be *fast.* Yuri is being scheduled for some kind of... *procedure.*

But we've got *Iggy's raw power!*

She's going to steal his soul.

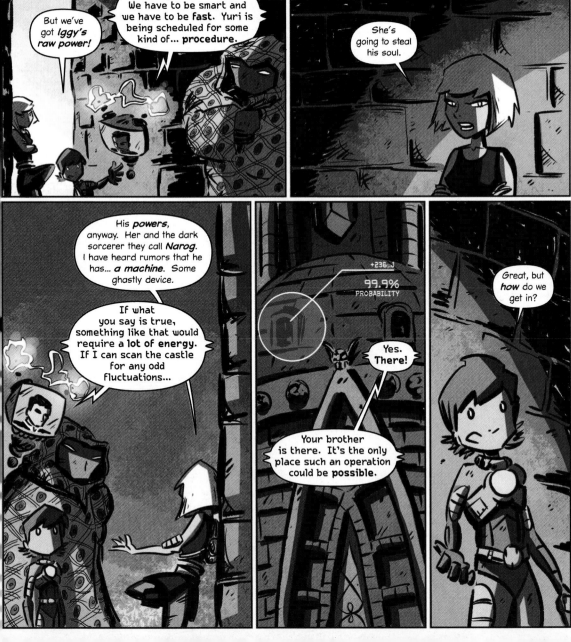

His *powers,* anyway. Her and the dark sorcerer they call *Narog.* I have heard rumors that he has... *a machine.* Some ghastly device.

If what you say is true, something like that would require a lot of energy. If I can scan the castle for any odd fluctuations...

+236µJ

99.9% PROBABILITY

Yes. There!

Your brother is there. It's the only place such an operation could be *possible.*

Great, but *how* do we get in?

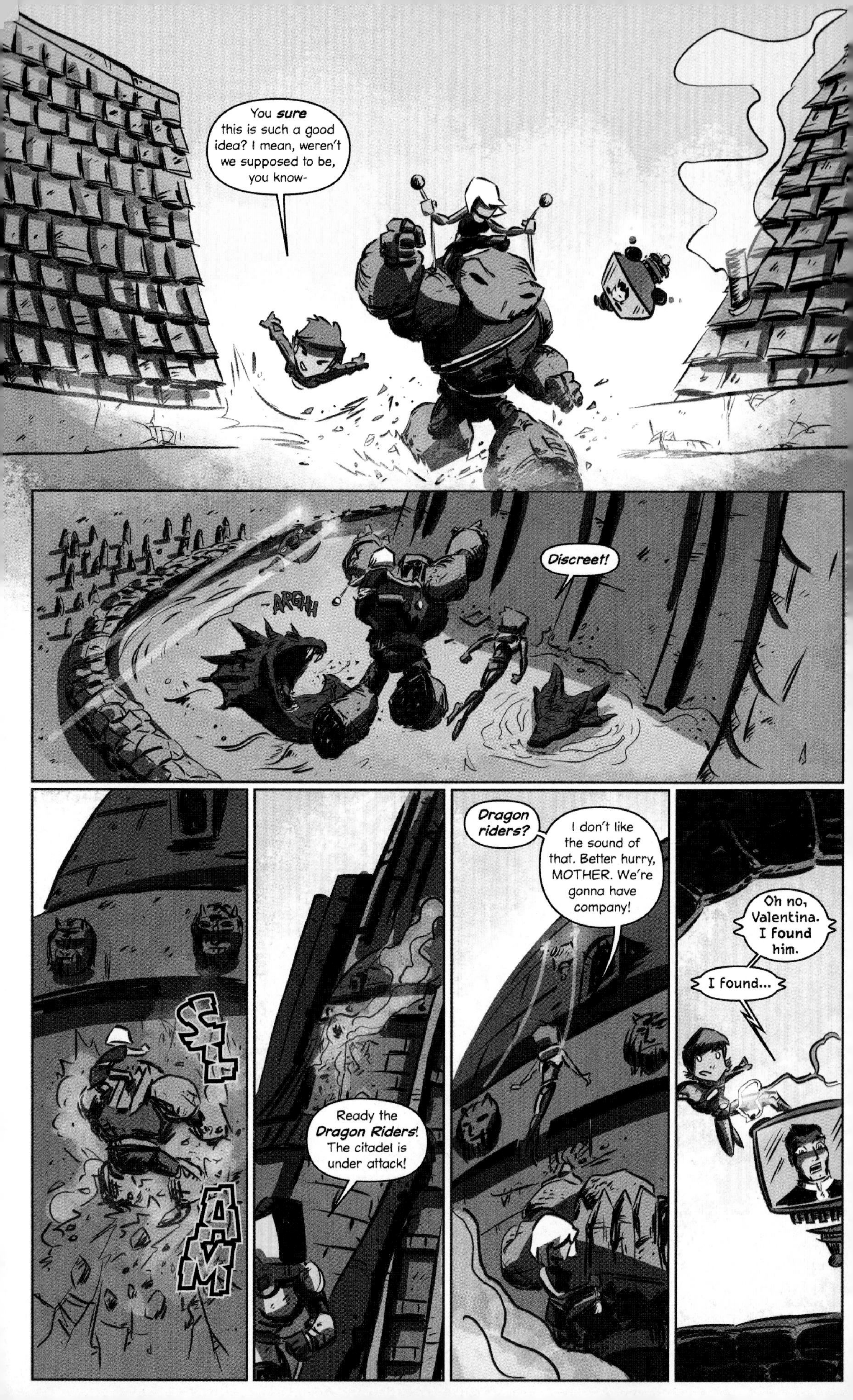
You *sure* this is such a good idea? I mean, weren't we supposed to be, you know-
ARGHH
Discreet!
SLAM
Ready the *Dragon Riders*! The citadel is under attack!
Dragon riders?
I don't like the sound of that. Better hurry, MOTHER. We're gonna have company!
Oh no, Valentina. I found him.
I found...

YUR!!

Get away from my brother!

No! YOU FOOL!

SMASH

Do you realize what you've done! You've set a time bomb in motion! This whole place is going to explode.

Narog is right. The transfer engine is caught in an exponential loop. We haven't much time.

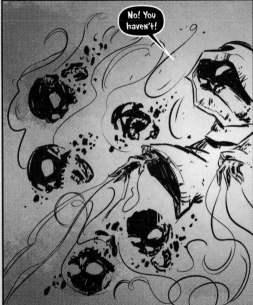

No! You haven't!

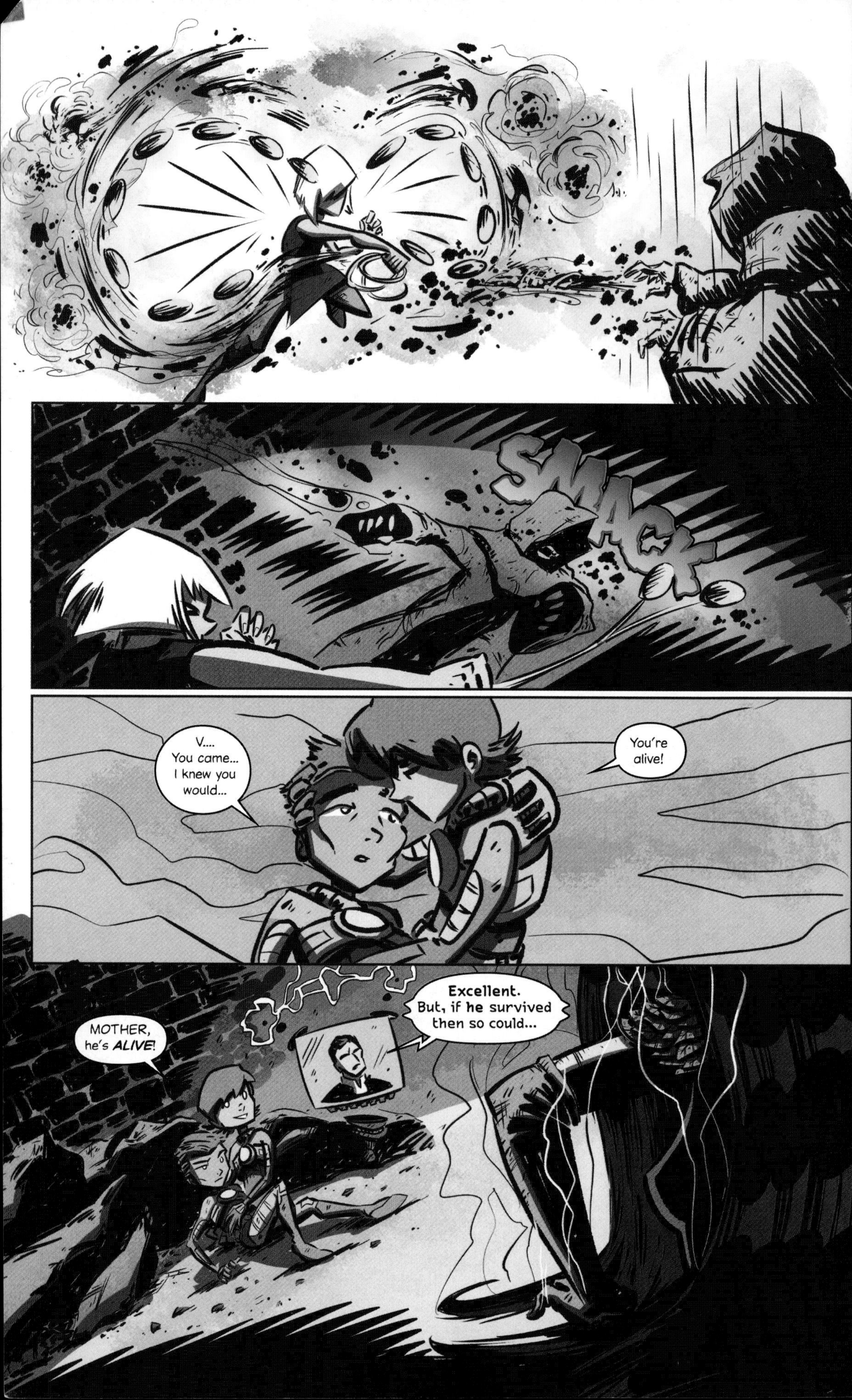
SMACK
V....
You came...
I knew you
would...
You're
alive!
MOTHER,
he's ***ALIVE***!
Excellent.
But, if **he** survived
then so could...

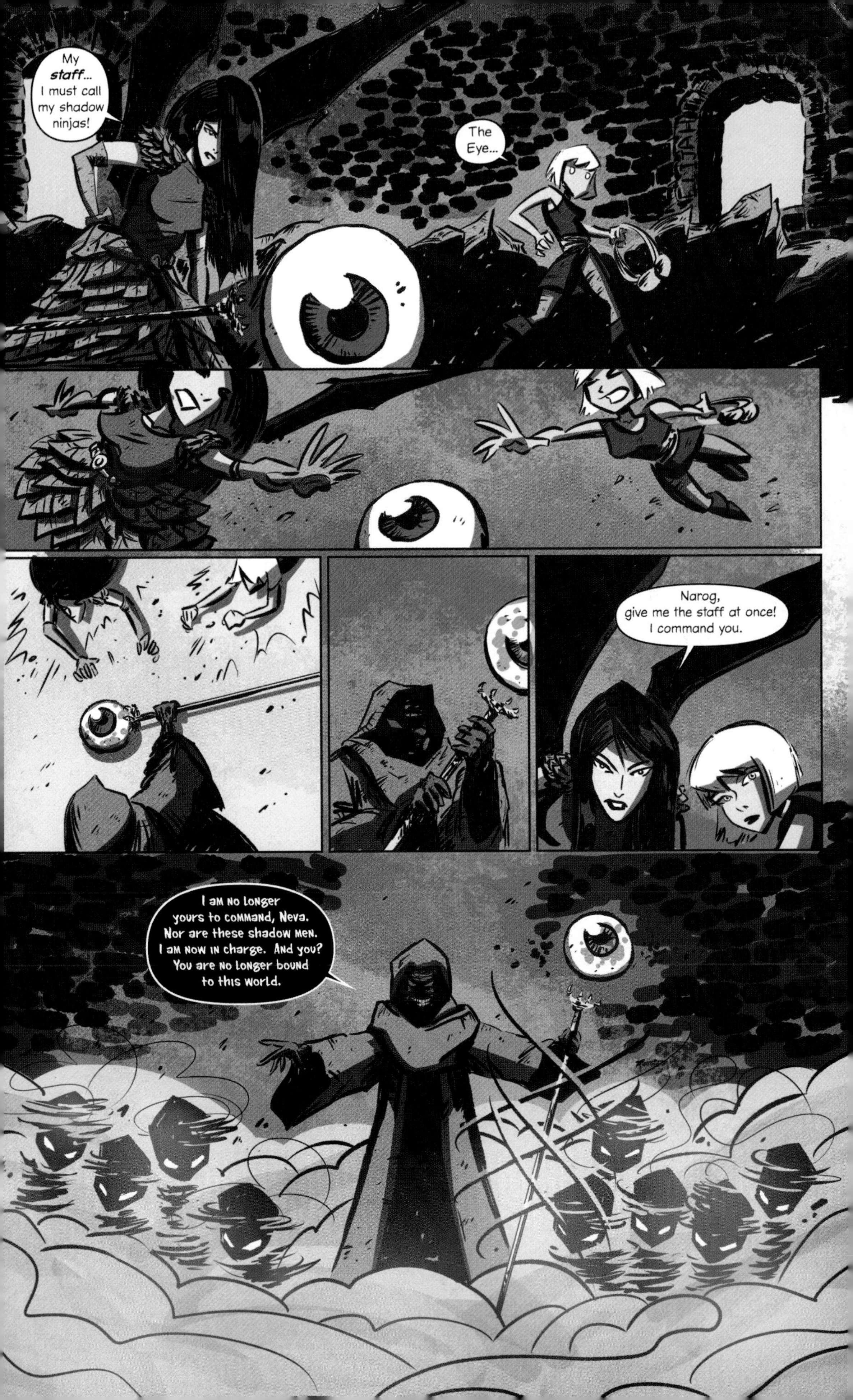
My staff... I must call my shadow ninjas!
The Eye...
Narog, give me the staff at once! I command you.
I am no longer yours to command, Neva. Nor are these shadow men. I am now in charge. And you? You are no longer bound to this world.

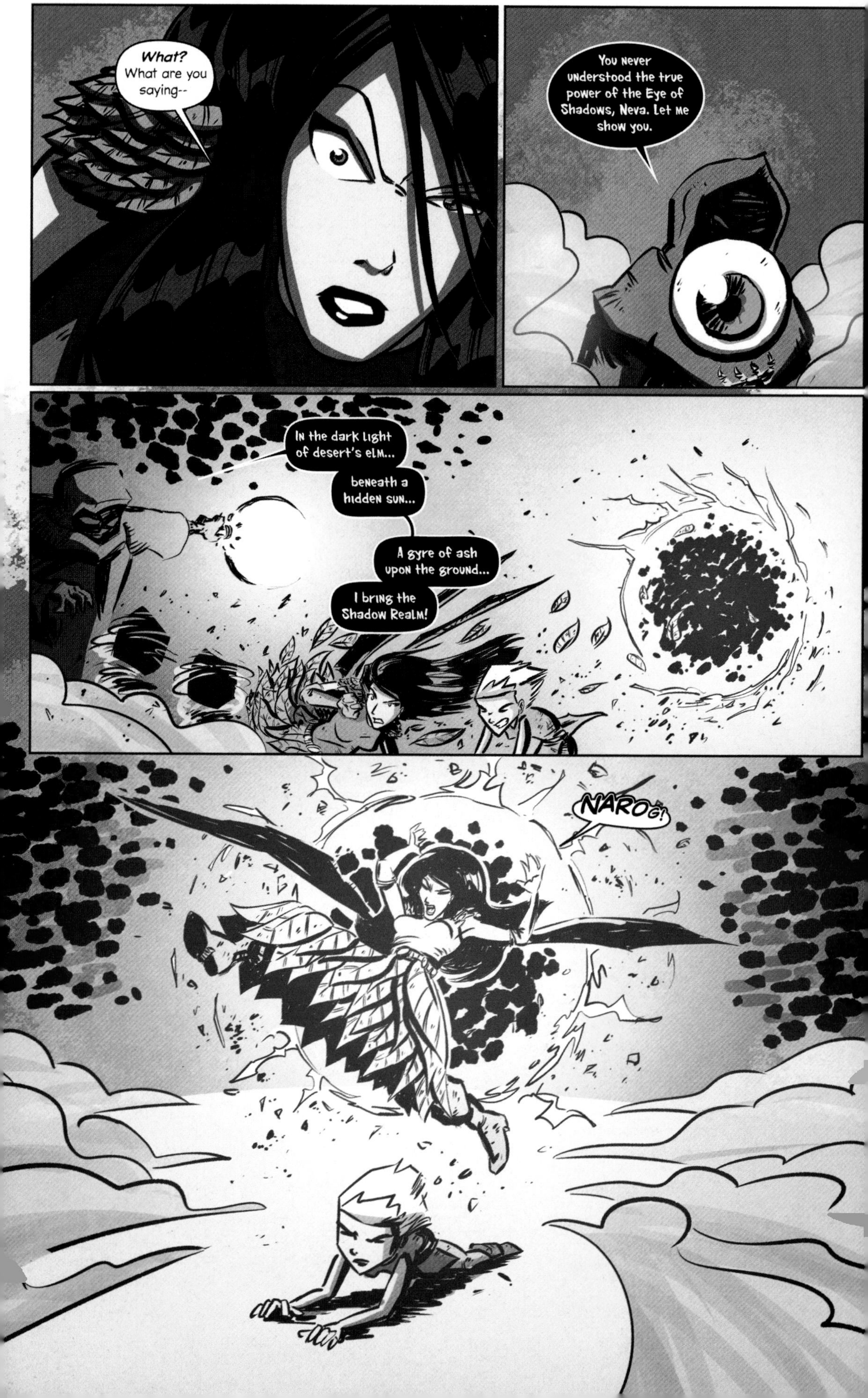
What? What are you saying--
You never understood the true power of the Eye of Shadows, Neva. Let me show you.
In the dark light of desert's elm...
beneath a hidden sun...
A gyre of ash upon the ground...
I bring the Shadow Realm!
NAROG!

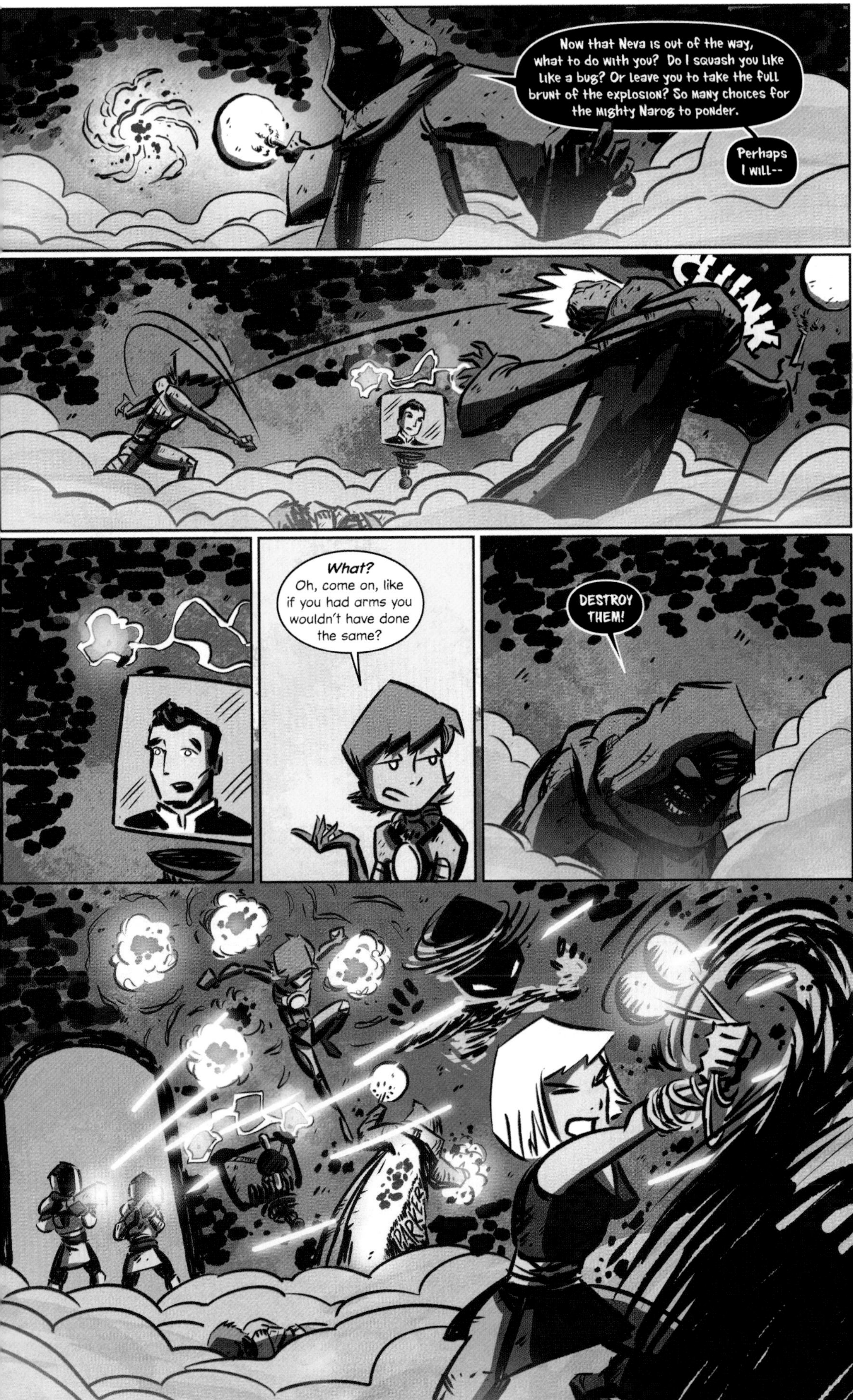
Now that Neva is out of the way, what to do with you? Do I squash you like like a bug? Or leave you to take the full brunt of the explosion? So many choices for the mighty Narog to ponder.
Perhaps I will--
CLINK
What?
Oh, come on, like if you had arms you wouldn't have done the same?
DESTROY THEM!

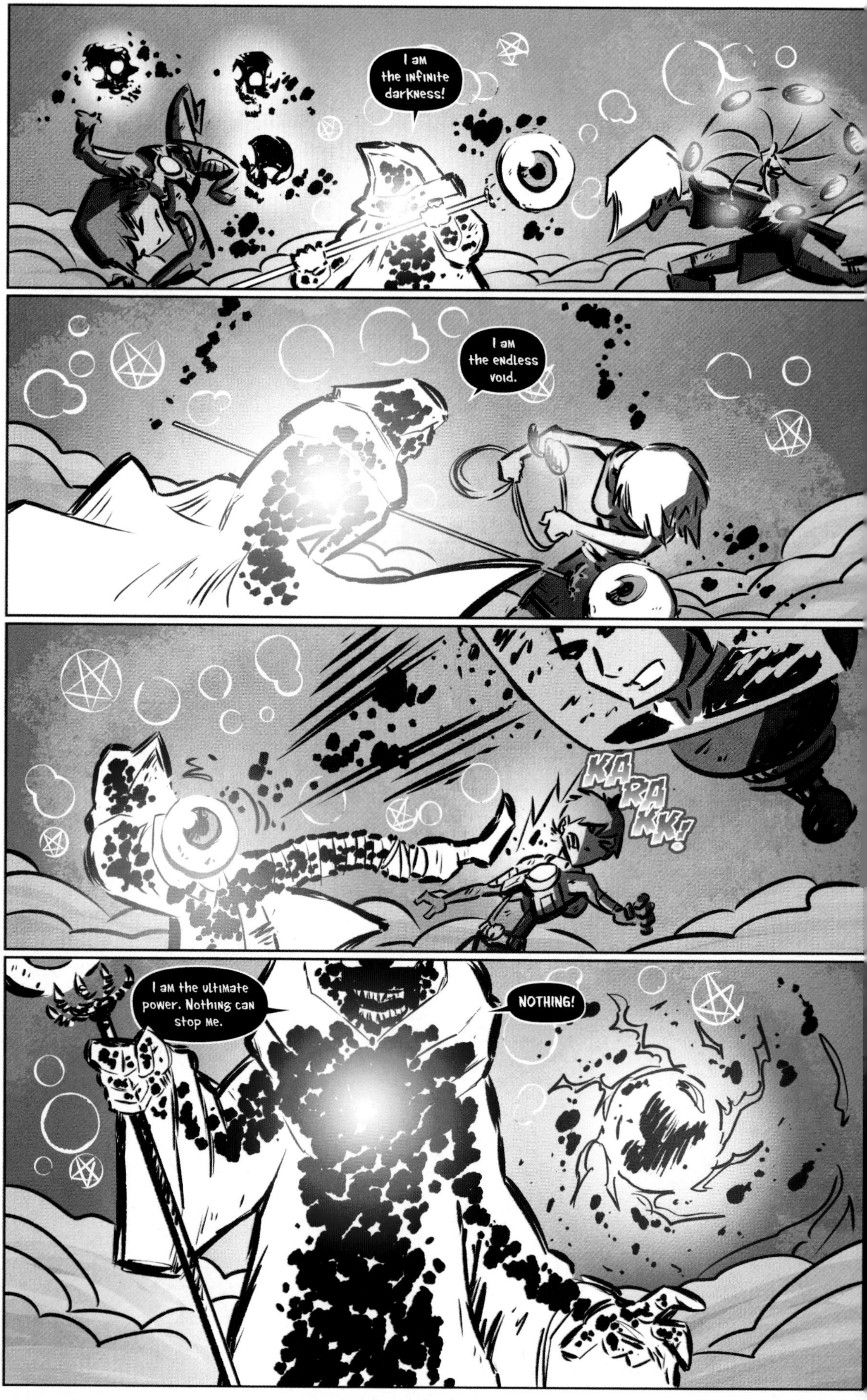
I am the infinite darkness!
I am the endless void.
KARAKK!
I am the ultimate power. Nothing can stop me.
NOTHING!

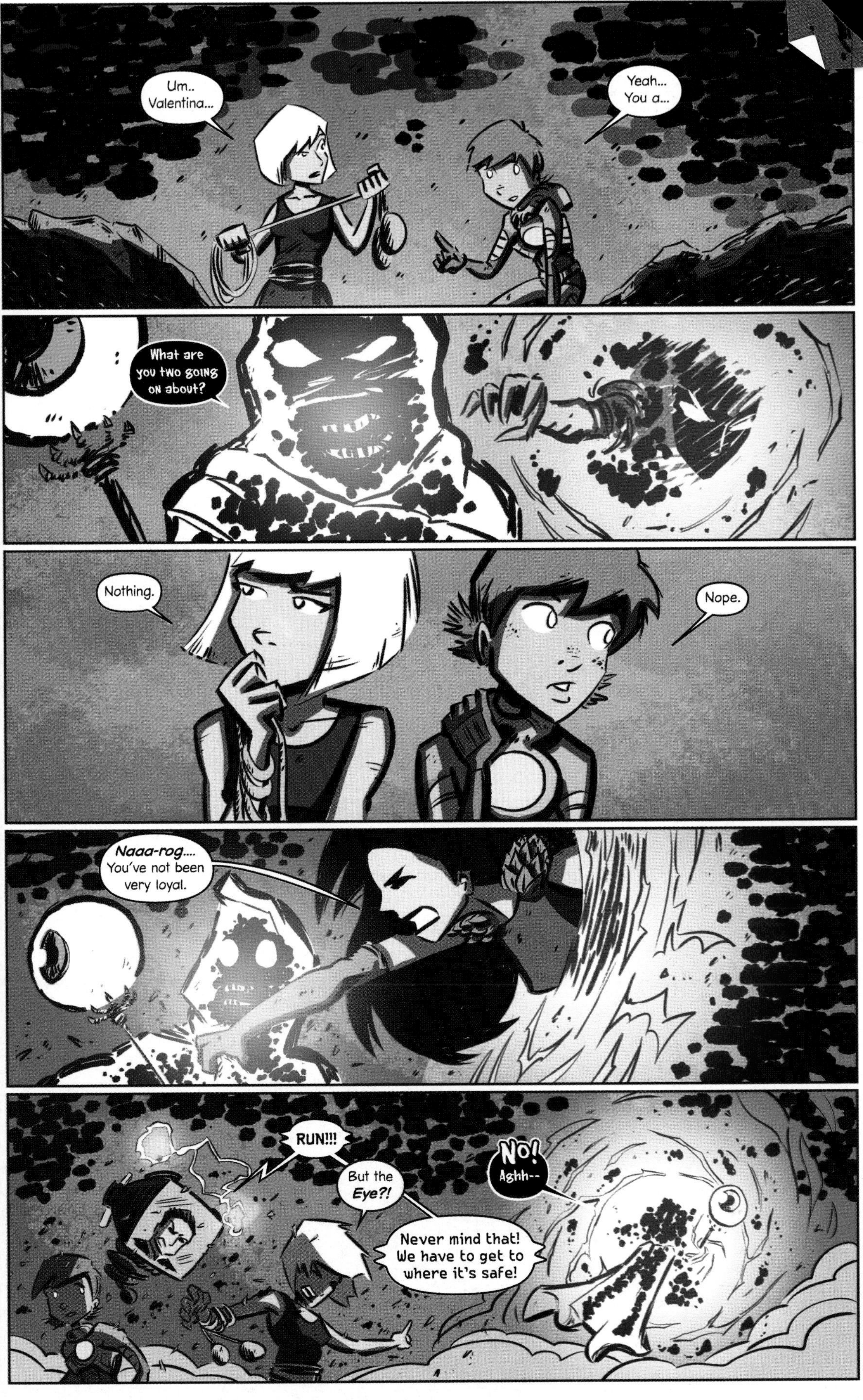
Um..
Valentina...
Yeah...
You a...
What are you two going on about?
Nothing.
Nope.
Naaa-rog....
You've not been very loyal.
RUN!!!
But the Eye?!
No!
Aghh--
Never mind that! We have to get to where it's safe!

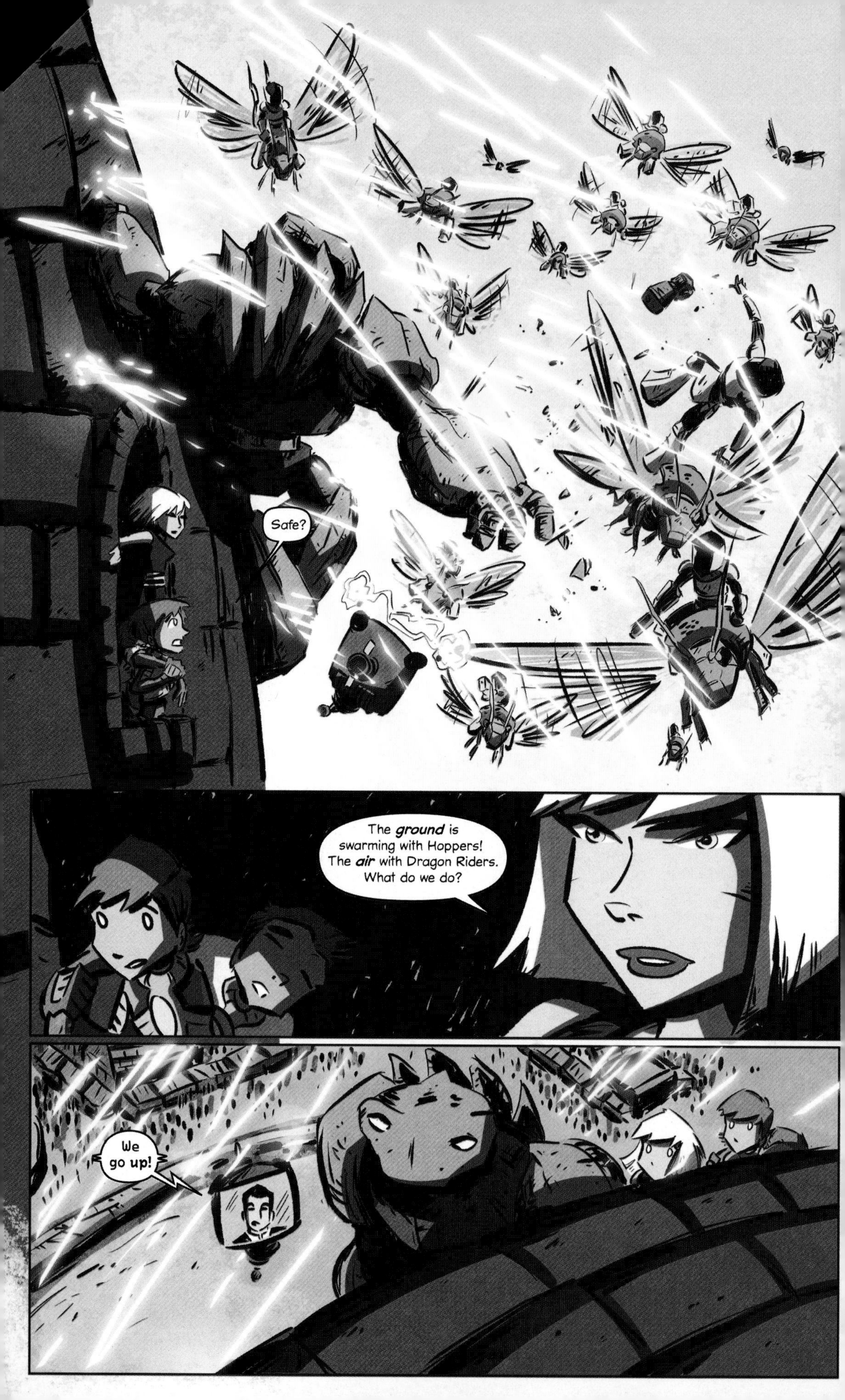
Safe?
The *ground* is swarming with Hoppers! The *air* with Dragon Riders. What do we do?
We go up!

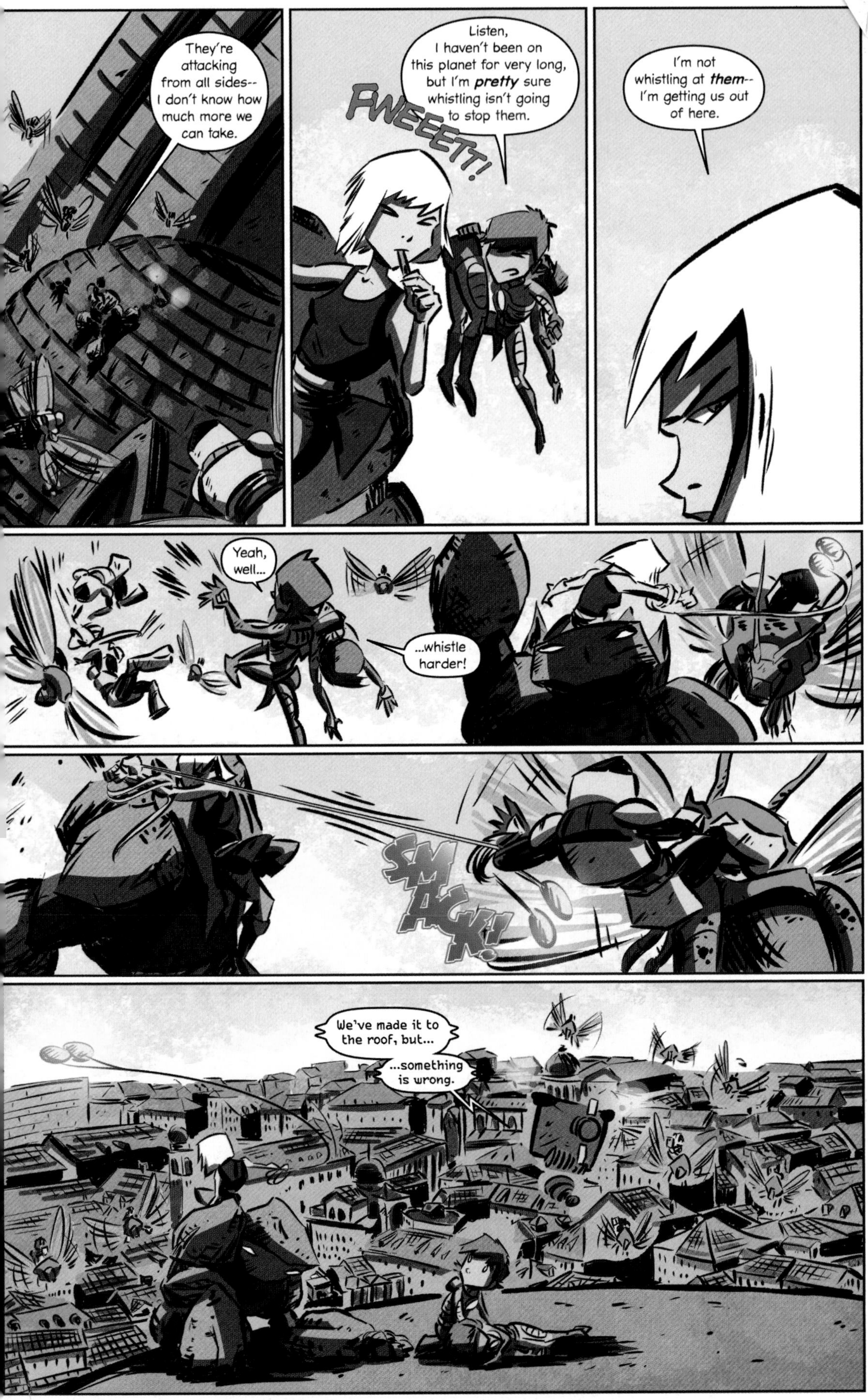
They're attacking from all sides-- I don't know how much more we can take.
Listen, I haven't been on this planet for very long, but I'm **pretty** sure whistling isn't going to stop them.
FWEEEETT!
I'm not whistling at **them**-- I'm getting us out of here.
Yeah, well...
...whistle harder!
SMACK!
We've made it to the roof, but...
...something is wrong.

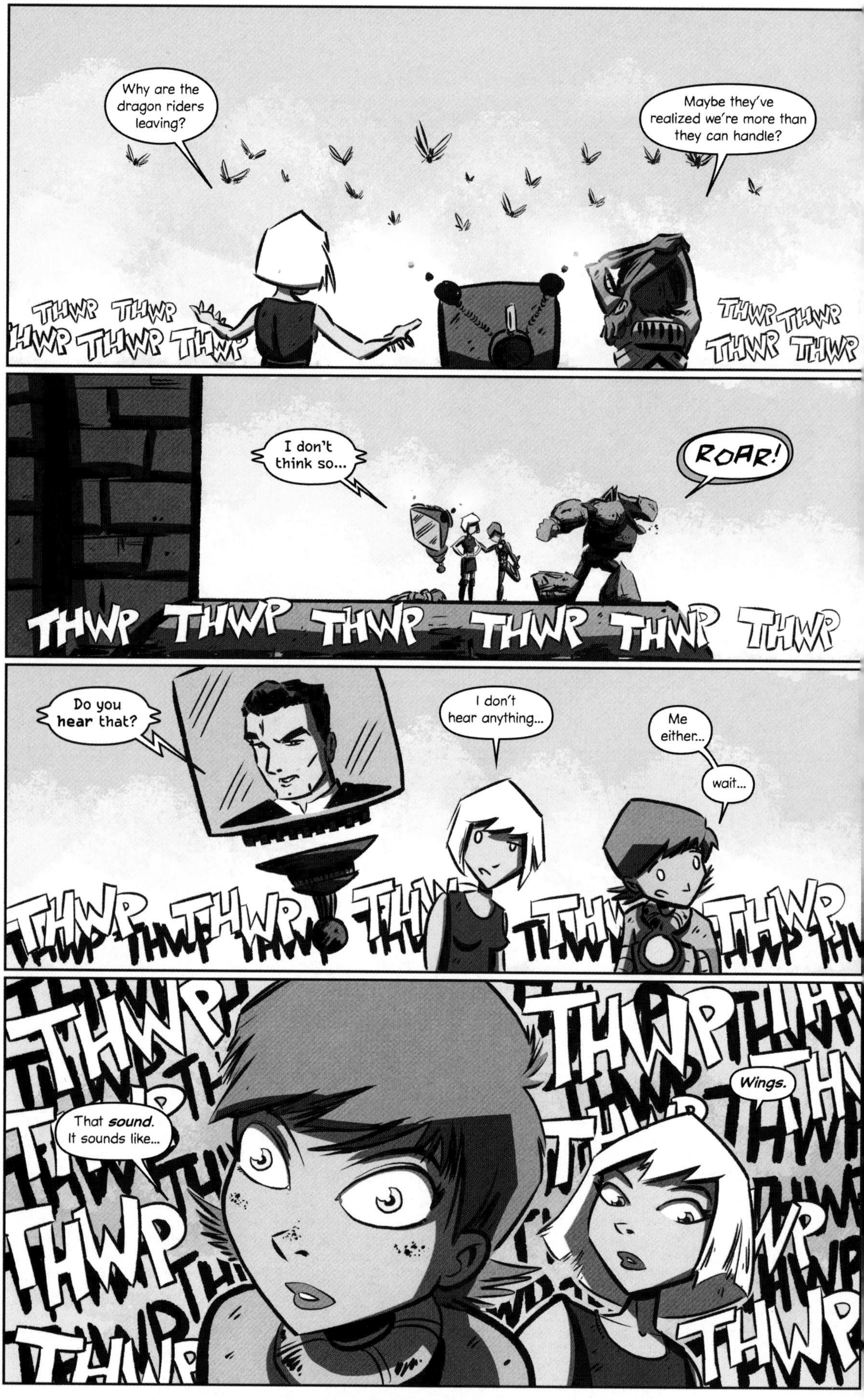
Why are the dragon riders leaving?
Maybe they've realized we're more than they can handle?
THWP THWP THWP THWP THWP
THWP THWP THWP THWP
I don't think so...
ROAR!
THWP THWP THWP THWP THWP THWP
Do you hear that?
I don't hear anything...
Me either...
wait...
THWP THWP THWP
That sound. It sounds like...
Wings.
THWP THWP THWP THWP

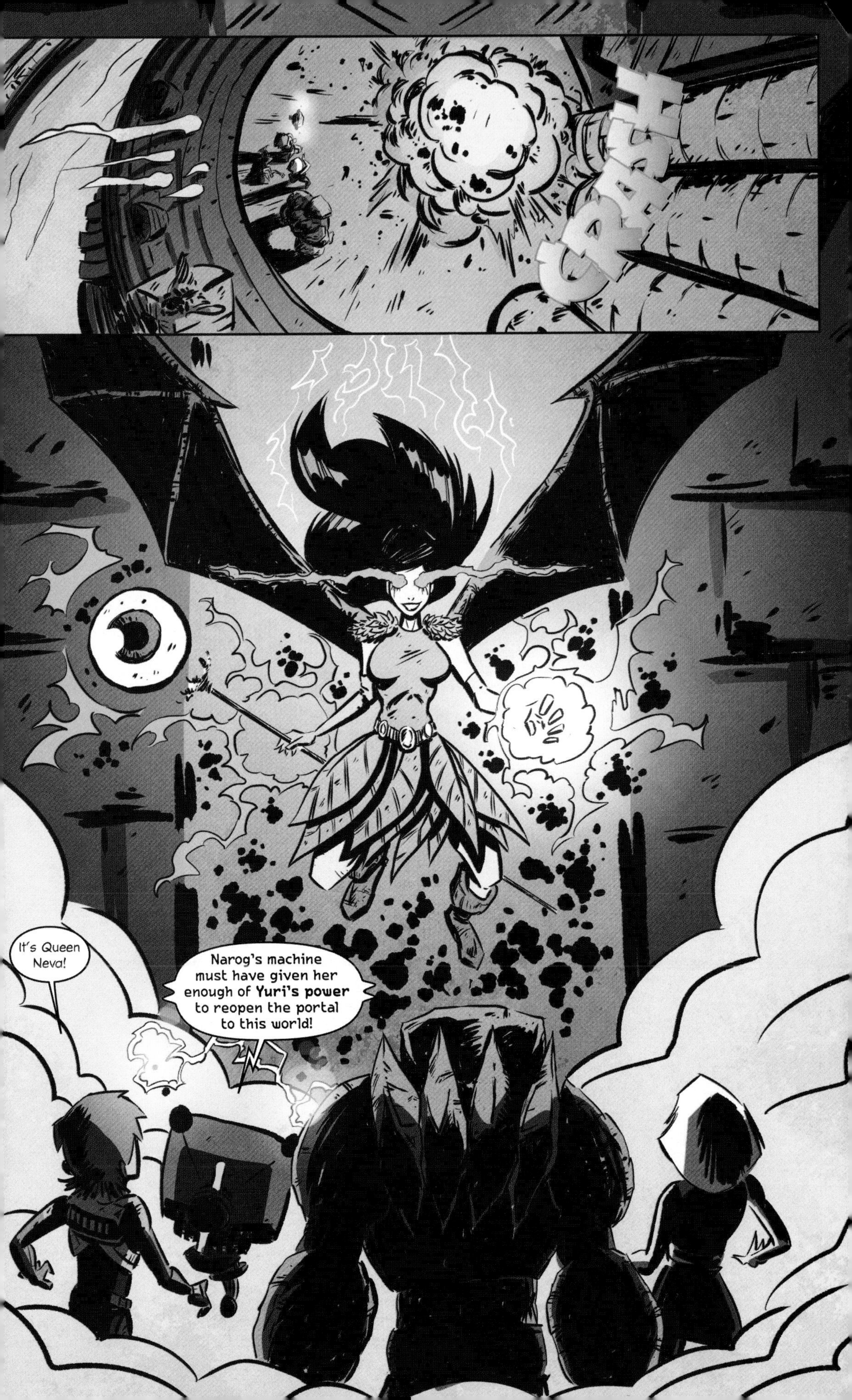
CRASH
It's Queen Neva!
Narog's machine must have given her enough of **Yuri's power** to reopen the portal to this world!

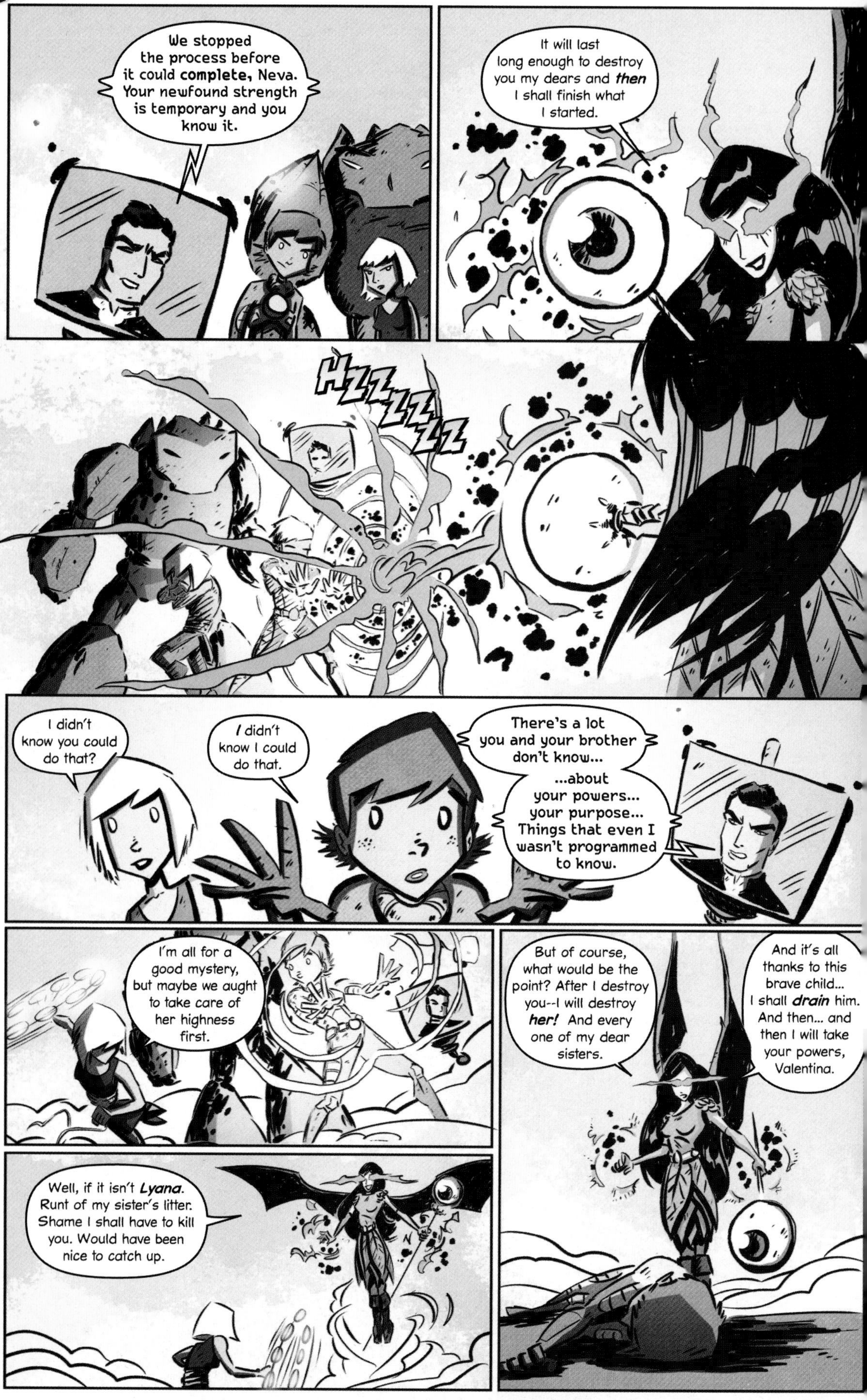
We stopped the process before it could **complete,** Neva. Your newfound strength is temporary and you know it.
It will last long enough to destroy you my dears and ***then*** I shall finish what I started.
HZZZZZZ
I didn't know you could do that?
I didn't know I could do that.
There's a lot you and your brother don't know...
...about your powers... your purpose... Things that even I wasn't programmed to know.
I'm all for a good mystery, but maybe we aught to take care of her highness first.
But of course, what would be the point? After I destroy you--I will destroy ***her!*** And every one of my dear sisters.
And it's all thanks to this brave child... I shall ***drain*** him. And then... and then I will take your powers, Valentina.
Well, if it isn't *Lyana*. Runt of my sister's litter. Shame I shall have to kill you. Would have been nice to catch up.

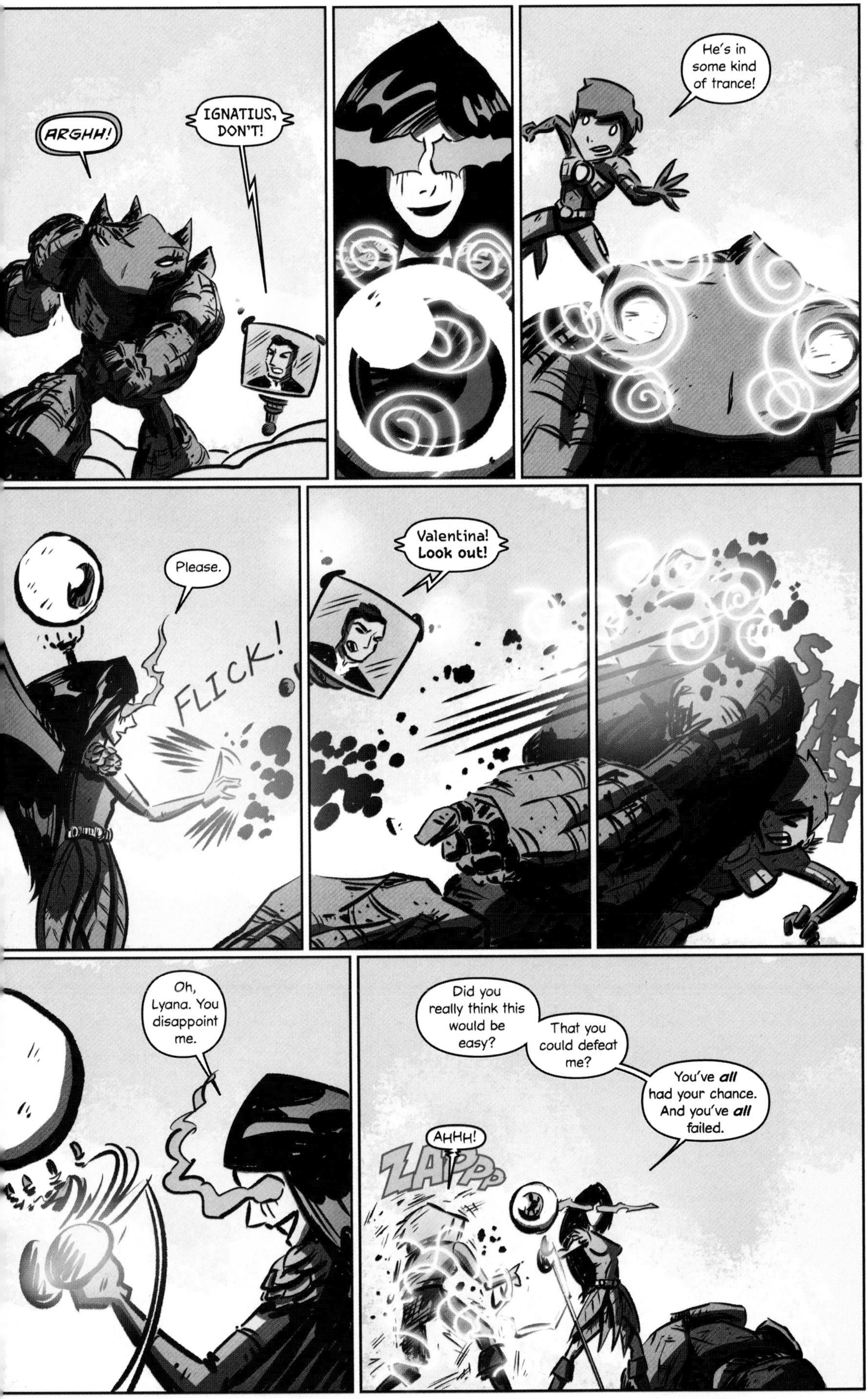
ARGHH!
IGNATIUS, DON'T!
He's in some kind of trance!
Please.
FLICK!
Valentina! Look out!
SMASH
Oh, Lyana. You disappoint me.
Did you really think this would be easy?
That you could defeat me?
You've all had your chance. And you've all failed.
AHHH!
ZAPPP

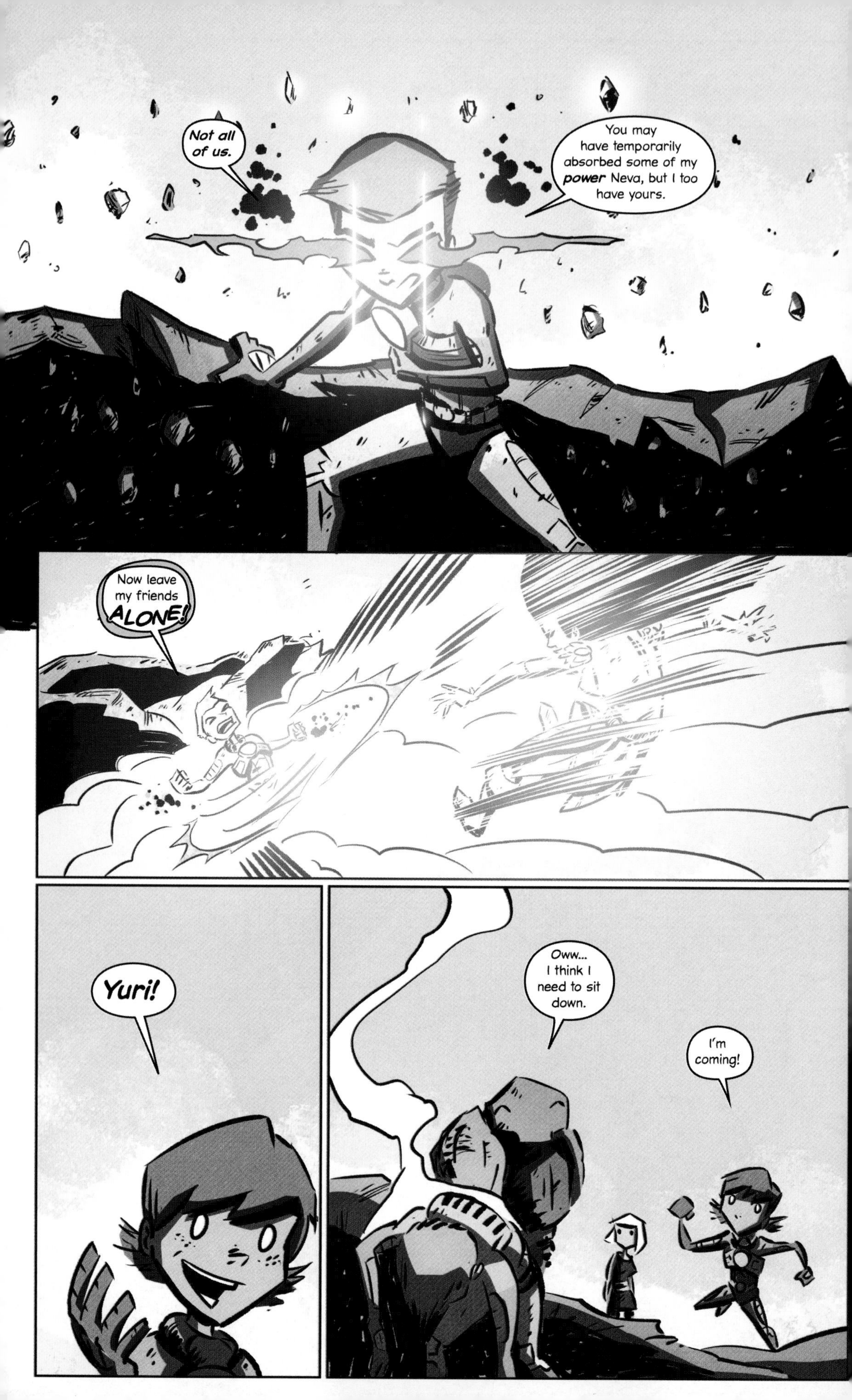
Not all of us.
You may have temporarily absorbed some of my **power** Neva, but I too have yours.
Now leave my friends ALONE!
Yuri!
Oww... I think I need to sit down.
I'm coming!

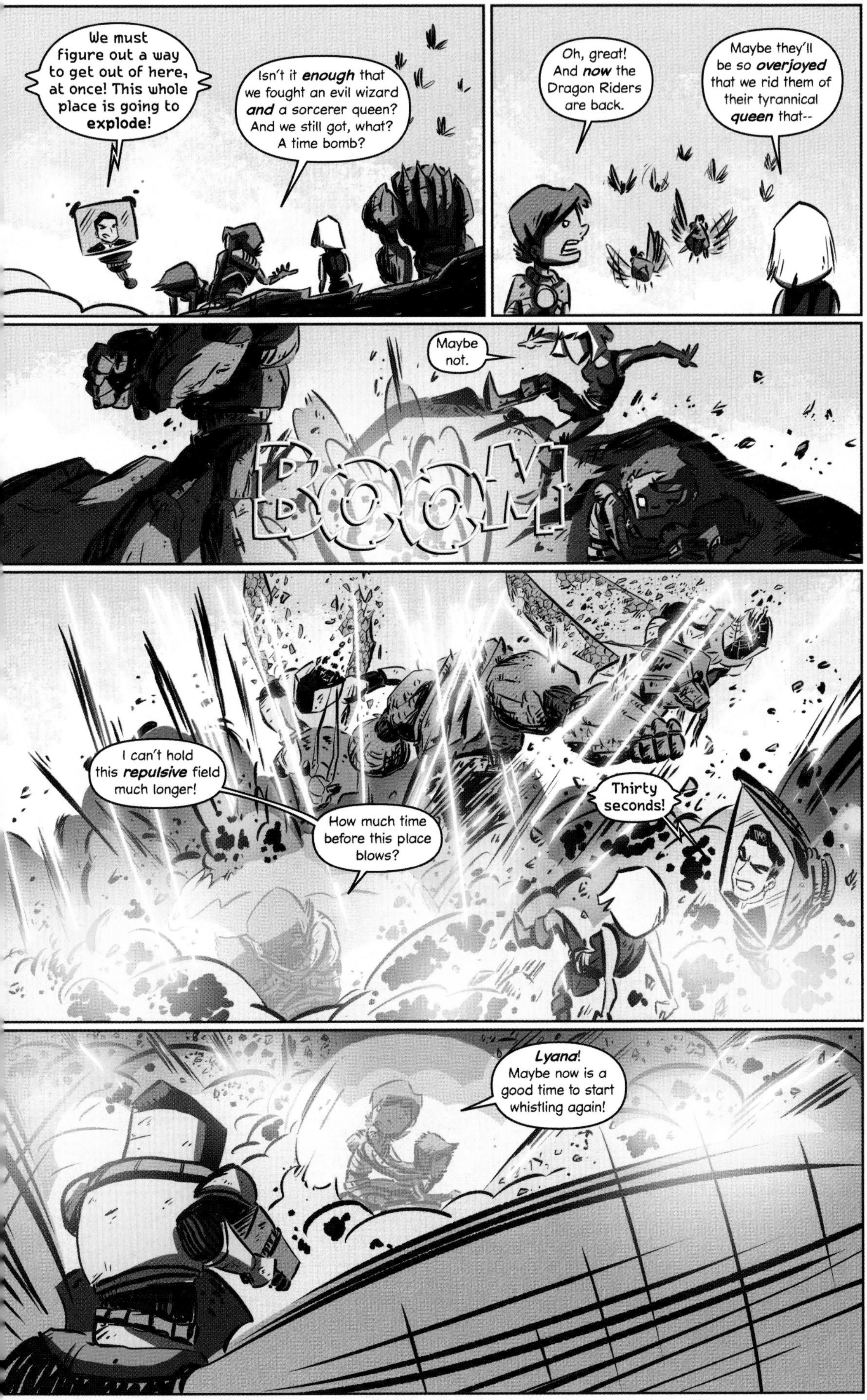

We must figure out a way to get out of here, at once! This whole place is going to **explode**!
Isn't it ***enough*** that we fought an evil wizard ***and*** a sorcerer queen? And we still got, what? A time bomb?
Oh, great! And ***now*** the Dragon Riders are back.
Maybe they'll be so ***overjoyed*** that we rid them of their tyrannical ***queen*** that--
Maybe not.
BOOM
I can't hold this ***repulsive*** field much longer!
How much time before this place blows?
Thirty seconds!
Lyana! Maybe now is a good time to start whistling again!

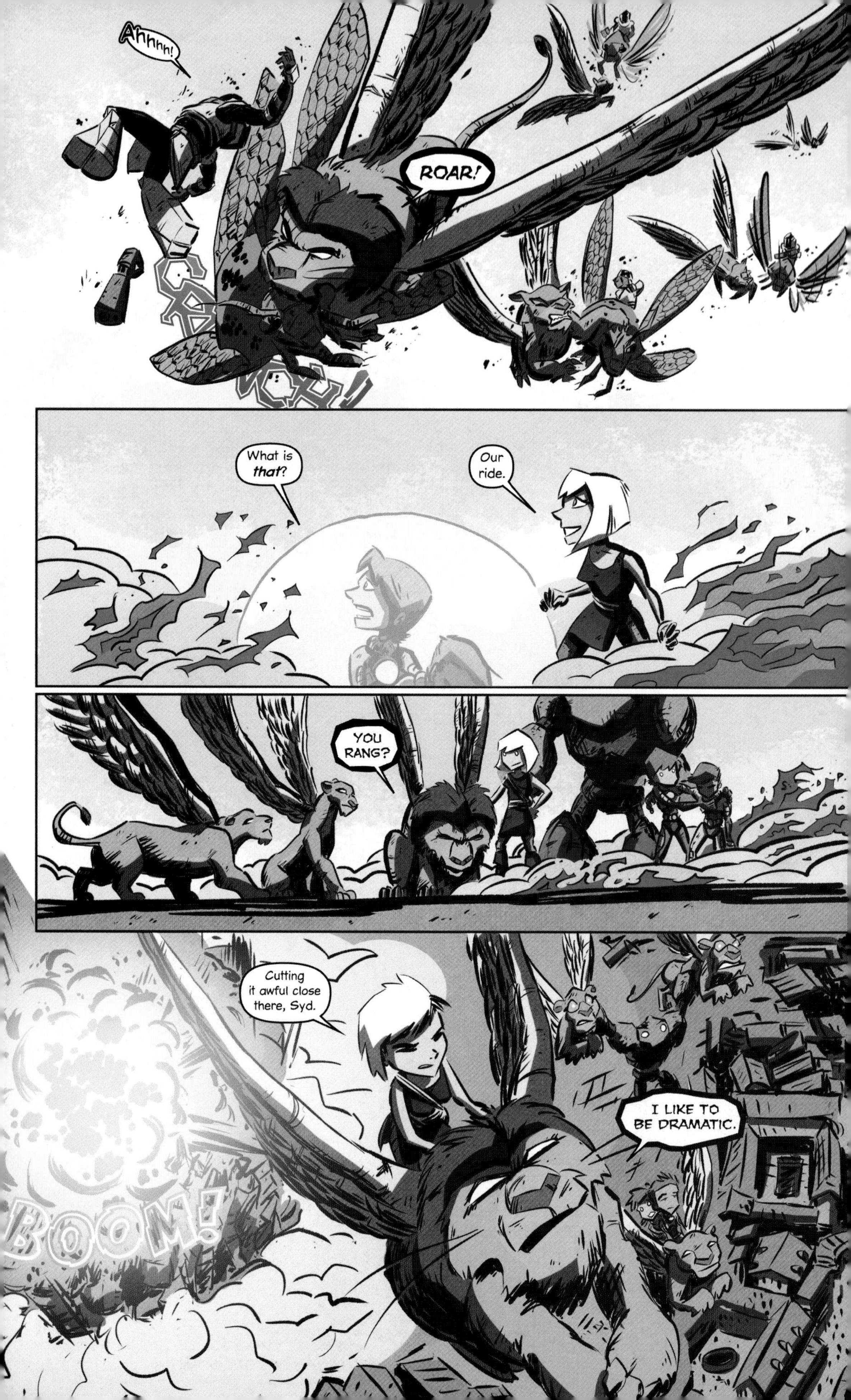
Ahhhh!
ROAR!
What is *that*?
Our ride.
YOU RANG?
Cutting it awful close there, Syd.
I LIKE TO BE DRAMATIC.
BOOM!

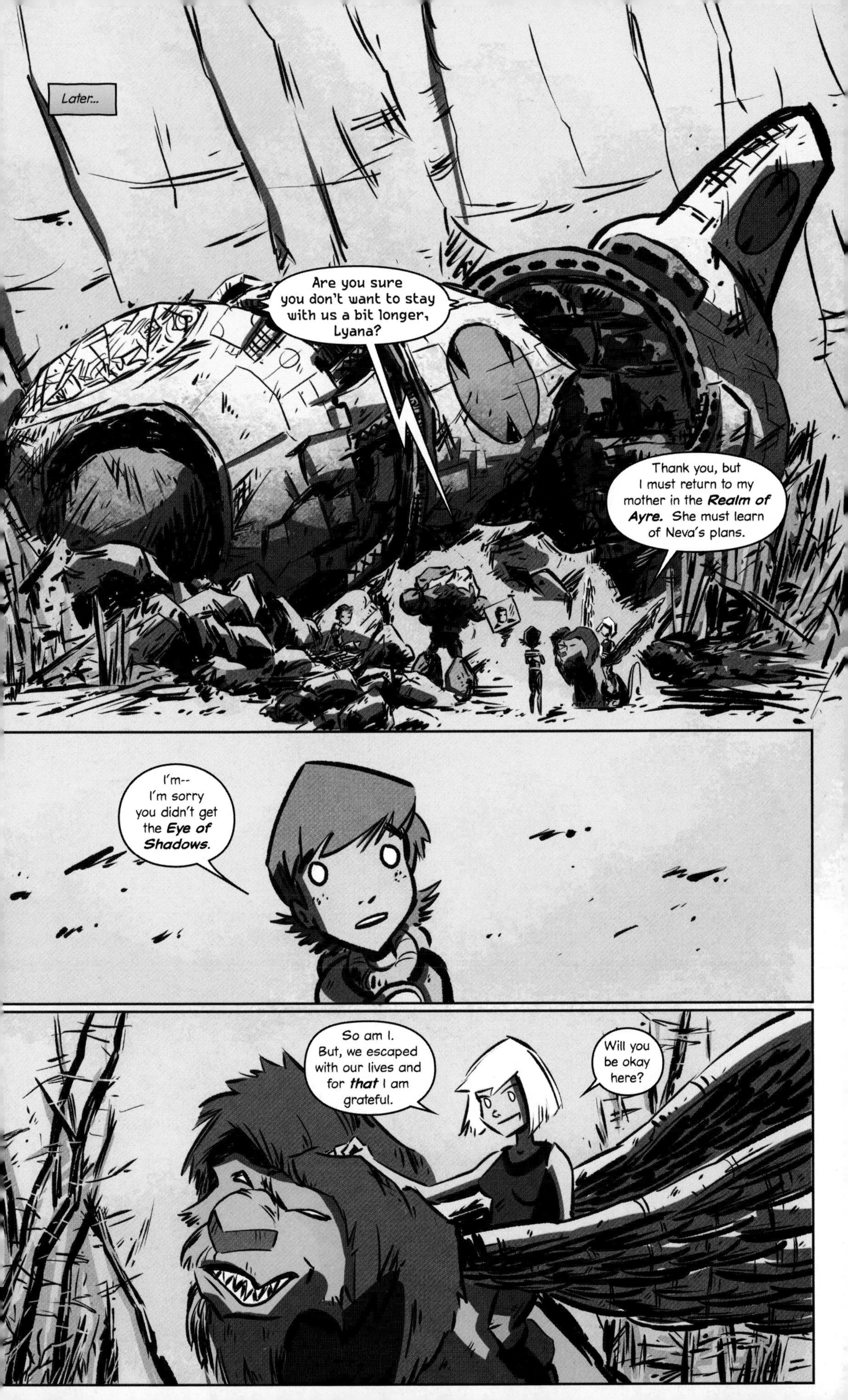
Later...
Are you sure you don't want to stay with us a bit longer, Lyana?
Thank you, but I must return to my mother in the **Realm of Ayre.** She must learn of Neva's plans.
I'm-- I'm sorry you didn't get the **Eye of Shadows**.
So am I. But, we escaped with our lives and for **that** I am grateful.
Will you be okay here?

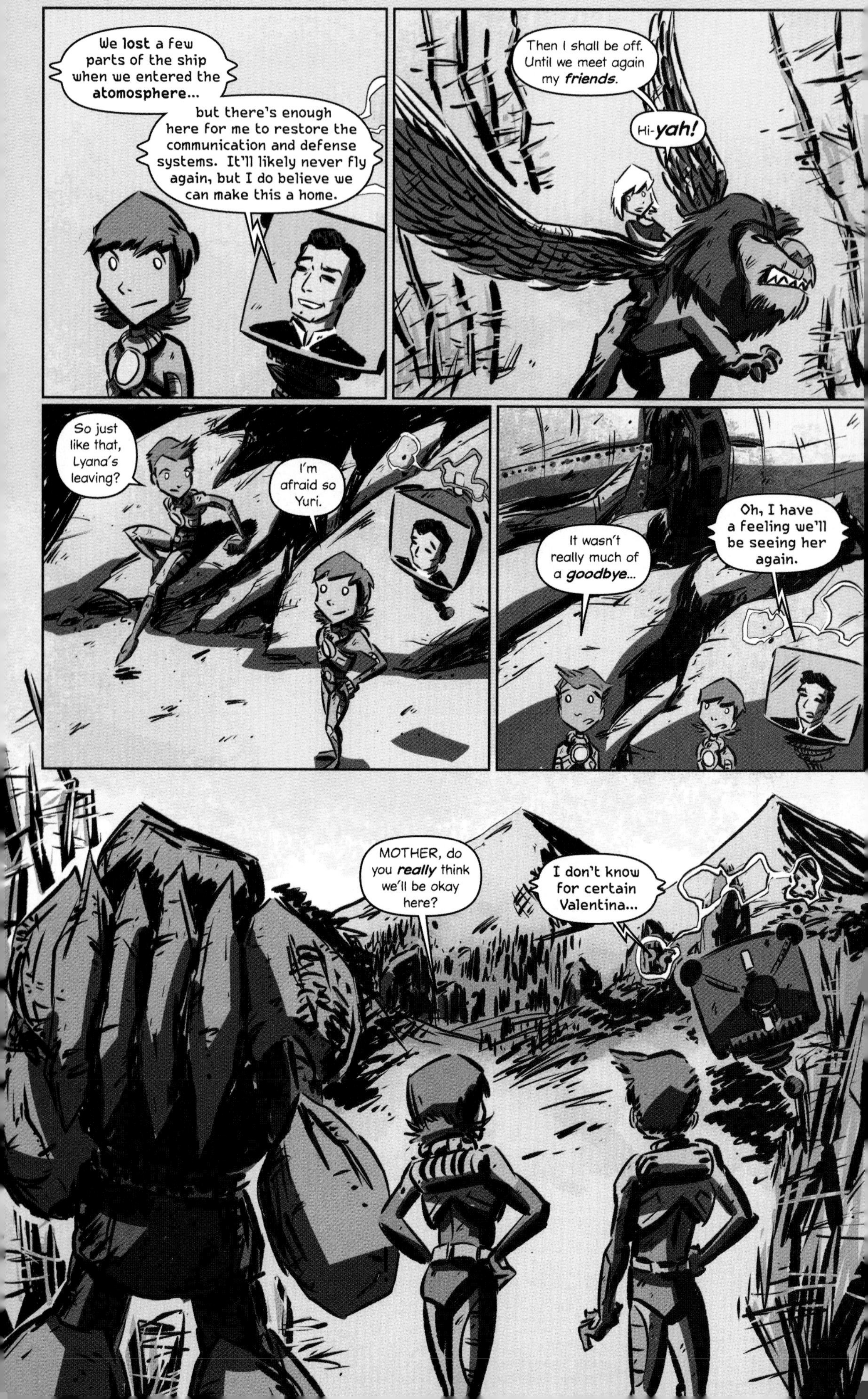
We lost a few parts of the ship when we entered the atomosphere...
but there's enough here for me to restore the communication and defense systems. It'll likely never fly again, but I do believe we can make this a home.
Then I shall be off. Until we meet again my friends.
Hi-yah!
So just like that, Lyana's leaving?
I'm afraid so Yuri.
It wasn't really much of a goodbye...
Oh, I have a feeling we'll be seeing her again.
MOTHER, do you really think we'll be okay here?
I don't know for certain Valentina...

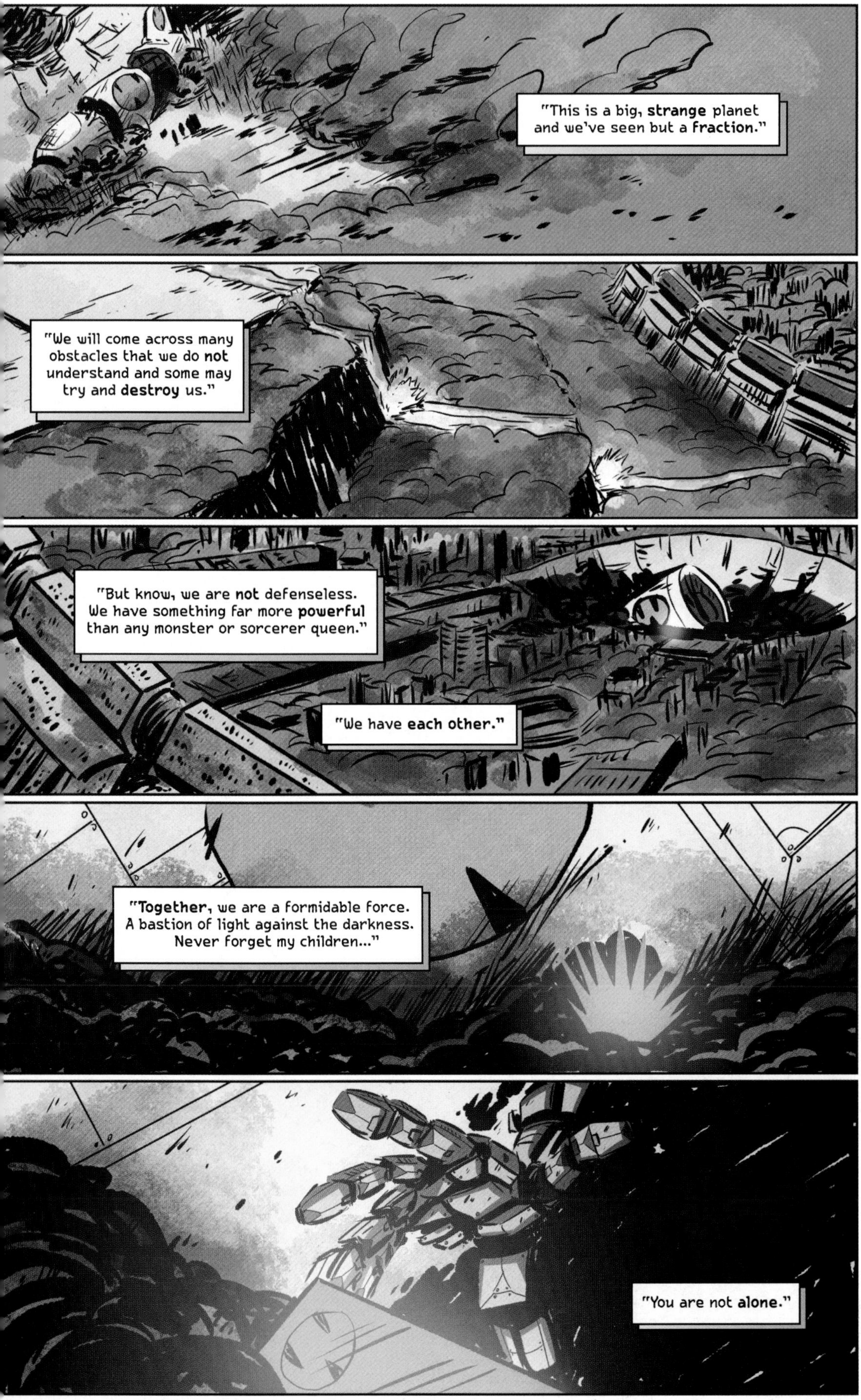
"This is a big, strange planet and we've seen but a fraction."
"We will come across many obstacles that we do not understand and some may try and destroy us."
"But know, we are not defenseless. We have something far more powerful than any monster or sorcerer queen."
"We have each other."
"Together, we are a formidable force. A bastion of light against the darkness. Never forget my children..."
"You are not alone."

APOCALYPSE NEVA

STORY BY ERIC GRISSOM / ART BY DAVID HALVORSON

THIS TALE MAY BE OVER BUT

PLANET GIGANTIC WILL RETURN!!

JOIN THE ASTRO-SPIES!

The Wunderkind Corporation is recruiting new members to its super secret experimental space program. *Do you have what it takes?*

Official Membership Kit Includes:
- Membership Card with Decoder!
- Letter from Dr. Alberta Reilly Herself!
- Planet Gigantic Stickers! (for scientific use only)

To join today, please get your parents permission and send $2 and a SASE to:

The Wunderkind Co.
Secret Astronaut Training Program
PO BOX 2131
Red Bank, NJ 07701-2131

sticker and membership card designs subject to change

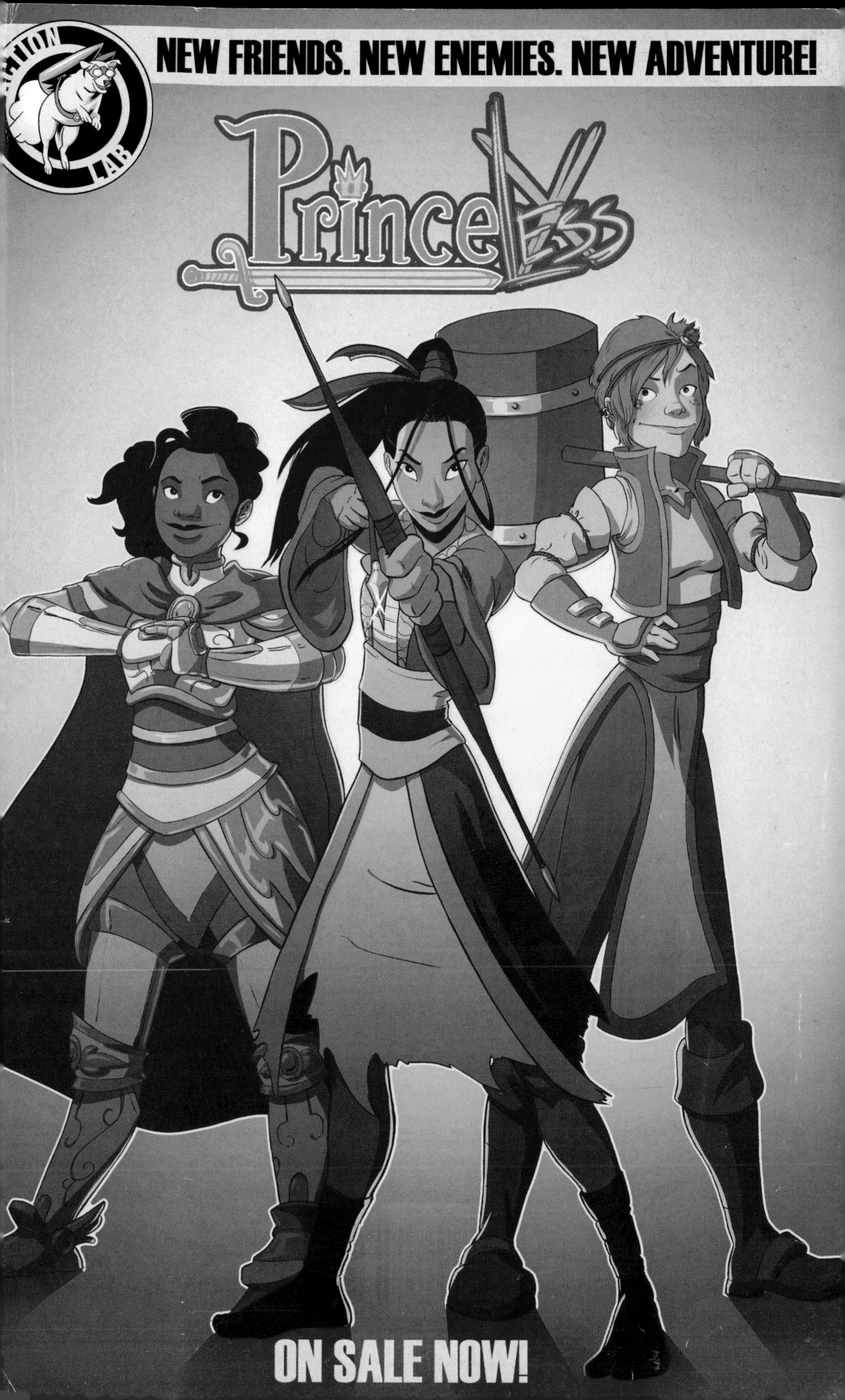
ACTION LAB
NEW FRIENDS. NEW ENEMIES. NEW ADVENTURE!
Princeless
ON SALE NOW!

READ MORE NOW

WITHDRAWN

For Every
Individual...

The
INDIANAPOLIS PUBLIC
Library

Renew by Phone
269-5222

Renew on the Web
www.indypl.org

For General Library Information
please call 275-4100